After a stop at St. Louis, the Frémont Third Expedition began its staging operations at Westport, Missouri (within present Kansas City). The party would be without the services of Thomas Fitzpatrick, who had joined Colonel Stephen Watts Kearny's scouting expedition and upon his return to Bent's Fort would join the detached party moving southward. But it included, in addition to Theodore Talbot, Lieutenant James W. Abert, son of the Colonel; Lieutenant William G. Peck; Joseph Reddeford Walker, who had joined Frémont's Second Expedition as it prepared to cross the Great Basin on its return east in 1844; Lucien Maxwell, Alexis Godey, and Basil Lajeunesse, all of whom, like Fitzpatrick of the Second Expedition, were highly experienced frontiersmen; and a Philadelphia artist, Edward M. Kern, whose duties would be those which Charles Preuss had performed for the first and second penetrations of the Far West.

From Westport, the expedition moved on June 20 towards Bent's Fort on the north bank of the Arkansas in present Colorado, where they were joined by Kit Carson and a number of Delaware Indian scouts. Few parties, in peace or in war, could have matched the cavalcade which moved out from the Bent and St. Vrain post on August 16 for the further ascent of the Arkansas to its headwaters and, fatefully, over the pass known today as Tennessee and later into the Great Basin.

The expedition performed its scientific chores in crossing the Basin, but almost immediately upon entrance into the Great Valley of California its directive as an official arm of the United States government became clear. Frémont conferred with those seeking independence, indirectly involved himself with the Bear Flag Revolt, and managed to be on the scene for the hostilities of the Mexican War. His scientific expedition was recommissioned as a fighting unit in the army and renamed the California Battalion of the Mounted Rifles, of which he became lieutenant-colonel. Talbot thus joined in the conquest of California. He was commissioned a sergeant major on July 23, 1846, and promoted to lieutenant adjutant on August 8, 1847.

Fighting Mexicans was only part of the problem of the conquest. Governing the new land was far more difficult. Commodore Robert Stockton and Major General Stephen Watts Kearny formed a triangle with Frémont which so complicated lines of command that Frémont found himself under arrest, recalled to Washington, and court-martialed. The expedition which had begun so jauntily limped home in the spring of 1847.

Despite this cloud, Frémont later wrote extensively, if inconclusively, of the Third Expedition (174 pages of the 655 in his *Memoirs of My Life* are devoted to this phase of his career). Talbot's letters, however, are unique in carefully describing the early months of this expedition so crucial to the story of American westward expansion. In this respect they possess values over and above those contained in Edward Kern's letters and journals of the same expedition, and offer the details and corroborations similarly found in another subordinate's memoirs of an earlier excursion into California, those of Zenas Leonard, who accompanied Joseph Reddeford Walker of Captain B. L. E. Bonneville's detached force of fur trappers in 1833–34. They have never before been published in their entirety.

Within a very few years, Talbot was again assigned to the Far West, returning to the Columbia River. Here the writings of the young officer on garrison duty underscored the successes and failures of the army in the development of the West. Robert M. Utley in his book, *Frontiersmen in Blue*, has tried to re-awaken Americans to the constructive role of the military in the West,[5] and W. W. Rostow has shown that the army plus other agencies of the federal government contributed heavily to the rapid amalgamation of the new regions into the national economy. Rostow has even suggested that techniques employed in the West might be used as

[5] New York, 1967.

ical points are scarcely worth the time and the expense which they occasion . . ."[3] The attraction of western expansion which Frémont had experienced almost from his first meeting with Senator Benton in 1841, now hardly cooled by his three-year-old marriage to the Senator's daughter Jessie, gave point to Colonel Abert's last-quoted instruction. Frémont had greatly exceeded his orders by "exploring" California and other parts of the Mexican domain during his Second Expedition.[4] What would he do this time?

Even before his orders were issued, Frémont had written to the botanist, John Torrey, at Princeton expressing his determination to return to California and to make up for the losses of botanical specimens during his Second Expedition. But by early April, 1845, the annexation of Texas caused Colonel Abert to alter his orders, so that Frémont might detach a party under a lieutenant on the arrival of the main expedition at Bent's Fort on the Arkansas, to explore southward. The situation for Frémont became a good deal more fluid than it had been in February. But a scientific venture as far as California seems never to have entered Abert's mind, only Frémont's.

In Washington, Frémont had been well briefed on the mounting border difficulties between Mexico and the United States. The new President James K. Polk had campaigned on an issue of fighting if necessary for expansion; with the admission of Texas in March, only two months earlier than staging time for the Frémont party, the acquisition of other Mexican lands in the Southwest seemed easily predictable.

[3] Abert to Frémont, February 12, 1845, Letters Sent, MSS, Corps of Topographical Engineers, Old Army Section, Record Group 77, National Archives.

[4] Whatever his responsibility or lack of it, Frémont's "scientific" ventures into foreign territory were not without precedents, notably Thomas Jefferson's five schemes of exploration in the Far West between 1783 and 1806, when Lewis and Clark finally achieved his goal, and Captain B. L. E. Bonneville's dispatch of one of his fur-trading parties under Joseph Reddeford Walker to California in 1833.

Westport, ascending the Platte through the South Pass to Fort Hall and the Columbia River. At the same time on the same road marched Marcus Whitman and Jesse Applegate, and with them went the destiny of the nation to wield power in two oceans.

They smelled the salt air at the mouth of the Columbia and then turned south, thereby exceeding Frémont's orders from Colonel Abert. In subsequent months they dined with John Sutter at his fort on the south bank of the American River near its confluence with the Sacramento, spent a short winter month in California, and crossed the Sierra Nevada and Great Basin to return to St. Louis in August, 1844. Talbot wrote to his sister in Washington that "a lady says that I am the blackest white man she ever saw, and a gent asked me 'when I expected to become civilized?' " He had "seen the elephant," beheld the mighty cleft of the Columbia, and admired the grassy banks of the Sacramento at their greenest in late winter and spring. For a decade (1843–53) California and Oregon would dominate his life, just as they would also color the politics of the entire nation, driven forward into western expansion by the designs of Senator Thomas Hart Benton of Missouri and Frémont, his son-in-law.

In 1845 Talbot was ready to go again. He had found that, whatever it might have done for his profession, the rough frontier life was beneficial to his health. Indeed, as with so many men of the outdoors, he suffered his first head cold only after he returned to civilization. His lungs were not strong, and his death would eventually come from tuberculosis. But the view west from St. Louis in 1845 was filled with health and hope.

Frémont's Third Expedition was well equipped for exploration, as indeed it should have been on a mission for the Corps of Topographical Engineers, committed by Colonel Abert's order of February 12, 1845, to "strike the Arkansas as soon as practicable, survey that river, and if practicable, survey the Red River within our boundary line . . . . Long journies to determine isolated geograph-

have been spent in the social arena. And his verbosity led him to expand and embroider his thoughts.

By the time Theodore was old enough to profit from social connections, the Talbots were on cordial terms with families bearing names like Adams, Abert, Kearny, and Frémont, and young Talbot undoubtedly heard in the upholstered salons of these people glowing talk of the unknown lands beyond the Mississippi and the predestined role of the Anglo-Saxon peoples to embrace North America from sea to sea. Politics for the young man was not as compelling an interest as for his father, but the powerful catalyst of expansion was only partly related to political alignments. Theodore would write with certainty that even Cuba, a non-continental area, would soon be ruled by the United States, and that on that island "our 'manifest destiny' bids fair for fulfillment." Likewise, he believed that Hawaii would be Americanized and "perhaps annexed to our already brilliant galaxy."

In 1843 Talbot joined John Charles Frémont's Second Expedition. He was not enlisted in the regular army nor did he have a special assignment on the payroll such as a botanist or a cartographer. Frémont explained that Talbot had come along at the recommendation of Colonel John James Abert, a family friend and commanding officer of the Corps of Topographical Engineers of the U.S. Army (as such, Frémont's superior), "with a view to advancement in his profession."[2] Because Theodore had once attended military school in Kentucky, the army was probably his intended vocation. And since during this period one of the prime obligations of the army was the exploration and mapping of the West, service with Frémont and the Topographical Corps could have been significant on his record. The Second Expedition took Talbot on a great circular route over the uncharted West, beginning with the Oregon Trail. In late May, 1843, the party left

[2] John Charles Frémont, *Memoirs of My Life*, hereinafter referred to as Frémont, *Memoirs*.

frankly write that she disliked them. Theodore once imagined a wedding for himself, but even in so doing he significantly shifted the responsibility for finding the wife to his mother—"I think that Mother should marry me to a rich heiress."

Talbot was born in Kentucky in 1825, just after another westerner, Andrew Jackson, had received a majority of the popular vote for the presidency, though not the office. Like Jackson, Theodore's father, Isham Talbot, was a western politician and had long championed the Jeffersonian cause of states' rights. All indications point toward a family background of wealth and social standing. Isham Talbot lived near Frankfort on an estate or plantation called Melrose. His first wife, Margaret Garrard, was the daughter of a governor. And his second wife, Theodore's domineering mother, Adelaide, was an heiress of English and West Indian society. Isham probably met Adelaide in Washington, where he served as senator from Kentucky from 1815 to 1819 and again from 1820 to 1825.

Isham's son, Theodore, showed signs of superior education and could readily use phrases in Latin or French and quote Horace and Shakespeare. He highly esteemed the "companionship of a good book" and cautioned his mother never to let her thriftiness curtail the purchase of books. He would take precious time during a short leave in New York to hear Anna Bishop at the opera. Peter Skene Ogden, the urbane bourgeois, once invited him to join a group of gentlemen. "Come here, Talbot, let's have a smoke and a glass of wine; you are one of us."

At times Theodore thought of himself as a shy man, uneasy with strangers and slow in making friendships. But on other occasions he described himself as talkative with a "gift of gab," and a rough, careless manner. The two characterizations contradict one another, but since human nature is inherently paradoxical both may nevertheless be true. Because he was reserved, his letters to his mother and sister were given time and attention which would otherwise

An old anecdote says that in the move west the Methodists and the Baptists came first, on foot or on horseback; the Presbyterians stayed home till the railroad was built; and the Episcopalians waited for the Pullman sleeper. Curiously, Roman Catholics do not even figure in the story. As far as the English-speaking frontier was concerned, Catholics were foreigners on the far-out fringes—the French Jesuit paddling a bateau or the Spanish Franciscan *Te Deums* beneath California oaks. Theodore Talbot was a Roman Catholic, yet he was clearly in the English frontier stream; he was not from Baltimore, the eastern center of Catholicism, New France, or New Spain, still he was an active Catholic interested in the affairs and doctrines of his church. Indeed, there were even some pronounced American aspects to his Catholicism, for he looked upon converts as inappropriate to the modern world. When one of his cousins entered a nunnery, he felt she had buried herself "in a living tomb." He seemed closer to his church when it was founding colleges than when it was saying catechisms.

Talbot was unmarried, and this fact might seem to qualify him for typicality in the masculine West. But his stated and restated belief that his bachelorhood was confirmed and unbreachable sets him once more apart. The traditional westerner would someday settle down and raise a family. His intentions were normal, if not his present social circumstances. Theodore, however, was different. While at a western post, he once gave three reasons for remaining single: he was too poor; there were no eligible women around; and most important in his mind, "I wouldn't if I could." The one girl he apparently ever courted chose someone else after years of patient waiting, while he himself waited for a robust state of health which never came.

The dominant woman in his life was his mother, to whom he expressed deepest devotion across the thousands of miles. In their relationship her personality was strong and confident enough that, after he went to considerable effort to find and send gifts, she could

# INTRODUCTION

*James Theodore Talbot* was a part of the central frontier thrust, but he did not conform to the standard image of the frontiersman. He was neither one of the "dauntless young braves" of Mark Twain[1] nor one of the neurotic escapists portrayed by modern skeptics. He partook of few of those qualities which most frontier images hold in common—he was not self-reliant and resourceful enough to quit the army and go his own way; his excess energy seemed restricted to the writing of lengthy letters home; his social standing was at least upper middle class, and in attitude he was distinctly aristocratic; his practicality and restlessness were tempered by the life of a junior officer on garrison duty; and his toughness never obscured his love of a soft bed. He represented aspects of the western experience in the 1840's and 1850's which are notably missing in our stereotypes but which are nevertheless significant to the frontier—education, culture, social standing, and rational analysis.

Certainly the intellectual was important in the westward push; think only of Meriwether Lewis, John Charles Frémont, John Russell Bartlett, Karl Bodmer, Francis Parkman, Sarah Royce, or John Wesley Powell. Talbot fits comfortably in this group. He was not a Teddy Roosevelt, a Wild Bill Hickok, or a Brigham Young. He could better understand a Clarence King, a John Muir, or a Junipero Serra.

---

[1] Mark Twain, *Roughing It*, 415.

*xi*

# ACKNOWLEDGMENTS

*Colonel Fred B. Rogers* and I became interested in the Talbot papers at almost the same time, and for a while, unknown to one another, we worked separately on the project. When our research trails crossed and we discovered the situation, Colonel Rogers, not wishing a joint editorship, kindly insisted on turning over his materials to me. Since that time we have kept in close touch, and my indebtedness to him is of mountainous proportions.

A number of assistants on the Riverside campus of the University of California have helped immensely—Robert Day, Terry Todd, Donald Barden, John Brumgardt, Timothy Crawford, Gary Caldwell, and Ronald Noricks. I am deeply grateful to each of them.

Jean Sharpless of the Hawaiian Historical Society and the staffs of the Huntington Library, the National Archives, and the Library of Congress must also be singled out for their particular co-operation.

At the University of Oklahoma the co-operation extended my collaborator, Savoie Lottinville, by Alice M. Timmons, of the Frank Phillips Collection in the University library, and by Opal Carr, librarian of the History Area, is gratefully acknowledged.

R. V. H.

*Riverside, California*
*January 12, 1972*

# SOLDIER IN THE WEST

UNIVERSITY OF OKLAHOMA PRESS  :  NORMAN

# SOLDIER IN THE WEST

*Letters of Theodore Talbot During His Services in California, Mexico, and Oregon, 1845-53*

## Edited by Robert V. Hine and Savoie Lottinville

By Robert V. Hine

*California's Utopian Colonies* (San Marino, 1953)
*Edward Kern and American Expansion* (New Haven, 1962)
(Editor, with Edwin R. Bingham) *The Frontier Experience: Readings in the Trans-Mississippi West* (Belmont, Calif.)
*Bartlett's West: Drawing the Mexican Boundary* (New Haven, 1968)

By Savoie Lottinville

(Editor, with George E. Hyde) *Life of George Bent Written from His Letters* (Norman, 1968)
(Editor, with Robert V. Hine) *Soldier in the West: Letters of Theodore Talbot During His Services in California, Mexico, and Oregon, 1845–53* (Norman, 1972)

International Standard Book Number: 0–8061–1002–3

Library of Congress Catalog Card Number: 74–177337

Copyright 1972 by the University of Oklahoma Press, Publishing Division of the University. Composed and printed at Norman, Oklahoma, U.S.A., by the University of Oklahoma Press. First edition.

*Soldier in the West: Letters of Theodore Talbot During His Services in California, Mexico, and Oregon, 1845–53* is Volume 61 in *The American Exploration and Travel Series.*

For **LOUIS B. WRIGHT**
and **E. M. HUGH-JONES**
**Guides to Trails of the Mind and Spirit**

models for federal action in underdeveloped countries throughout the modern world.[6] Inasmuch as Talbot was involved in that development, his long and perceptive letters home are most valuable. "In the Army you cannot tell one day where you will have to go the next," wrote Talbot as he sailed from Oregon in December, 1852. He was never again to see the Far West. In January, 1854, he served in Lancaster, Pennsylvania, as a recruiting officer, but after April of that year and until his death in 1862 he was on garrison duty at a series of installations along the eastern seaboard—Fort Monroe and Old Point Comfort, Virginia; Fort McHenry (which he liked because of its nearness to a cathedral and social events of baronial splendor); Forts Capron, Jupiter, and Brooke in Florida (which he called the land of insects); Fort Moultrie, South Carolina; and finally Fort Sumter during the seige of 1861. In this latter island fortress Talbot witnessed the birth of the Civil War, much as he had seen the conquest of California begin in 1846. And at Sumter, as at Santa Barbara, he was entrusted with secret dispatches and assumed high levels of responsibility.

Through all of his varied assignments after leaving Oregon he continued to write long letters home, letters which tell of monotony, frustrated ambition, discouragement over money, the character of his fellow officers, and the inefficiency and favoritism in the army. For a picture of army life on the Atlantic coast in the 1850's, these letters are excellent, but they are not included here because they add little to the particular focus of this book—the character of Talbot and his role with the army in the development of the Far West.

At Fort Sumter, Talbot had been promoted to captain on March 16, 1861, and thereafter was transferred to the Adjutant General's Office in Washington. Five months later, on August 3, he became a major. Ironically and tragically, moving from front-line danger to more comfortable housing in the Capital, Talbot suffered a

---

[6] Walt Whitman Rostow, *View from the Seventh Floor*, 128–29.

return of his old lung ailment, which this time proved fatal. Thus, on April 22, 1862, while Grant rested after Shiloh, another officer of western garrisons, Major James Theodore Talbot, died of tuberculosis at the age of thirty-seven. Like Ulysses Simpson Grant, he was not the kind of soldier who would hanker after death with sword drawn; more likely he was pleased that the end, when it came, found him in bed at home. He was buried from St. Aloysius Church.

If Talbot had not written his long letters and kept his journal, he would, like most men, have remained unknown to history. His short life affected his times very little, if at all; but his times affected him dramatically. He felt the intoxication of national expansion—at St. Louis, in California, in Vera Cruz, on the Columbia River—pushing him with some unclear purpose; but the goal was not of his own making. The President might point toward territorial destiny, and Talbot would assent and even echo the words. But, because he was not a great man, his deepest dreams were far more limited—his own promotion, a modest income, or a future fireside. He was a chip in the current, not the diversionary dam. Still, viewed differently, more history is made by men who react and respond than by those who believe they control. It was what Talbot's contemporary, Ralph Waldo Emerson, meant when he wrote, only shortly before Talbot first went West, "Civil and natural history of art and of literature, must be explained from individual history, or must remain words."[7]

[7] "History," *Essays,* 20.

# EDITORIAL NOTE

*In editing the letters* original spelling and punctuation have been retained throughout, except that ampersands have at times been replaced by "and." The use of *sic* has not been considered necessary. Editorial insertions or explanations, when not in footnote form, have been square bracketed. The omissions, all of which are marked by ellipses, are purely personal family references, usually repetitious expressions of respect and love.

The Talbot letters, preserved by the family, were given to the Library of Congress in 1920 and 1952. They now reside beside the manuscript journal kept by Talbot between April and October, 1843, and again between November, 1848, and December, 1852. The journal was edited by Judge Charles H. Carey and was published in Portland in 1931. Whenever important material contained in that work has not been covered in the letters, entries therefrom have been included in the footnotes.

# CONTENTS

Acknowledgments                                    *page ix*
Introduction                                            *xi*
Editorial Note                                         *xxi*
I.  Preparations for the Trail, 1845                      3
II.  The Conquest of California, 1846–47                 33
III.  To Vera Cruz in the Shadow of War, 1847–48         58
IV.  Toward the West by Sea, 1848–49                     81
V.  Oregon, 1849–52                                     118
Bibliography                                           183
Index                                                  191

# ILLUSTRATIONS

Theodore Talbot                          *following page* 134
Christopher (Kit) Carson and John Charles Frémont
Joseph Reddeford Walker
Bent's Fort on the Arkansas
A Frémont Camp
Astoria
H.M.S. *Beaver* Off Fort Vancouver, 1850
Colonel B.L.E. Bonneville

*Map*

John Charles Frémont's Third Expedition                    38

**SOLDIER IN THE WEST**

# I.

# PREPARATIONS FOR THE TRAIL, 1845

*S*t. *Louis in 1845* was as exciting, optimistic, and forward-looking a place as the Western World could offer. In Paris Saint-Simon smelled old class conflict still in the air. In London the factory system had produced repression which led to outbreaks like the Peterloo Massacre. In Washington thoughtful men worried that the Compromise of 1820 was too threadbare to last. But in St. Louis the spirit was fresh and vital like the prairie grass in May. The previous autumn the young Lochinvar, John Charles Frémont, had come out of the West for the second time and had spent the winter with his dynamic wife Jessie writing a stirring account of the wilderness. For one example of what he described: the Great Salt Lake was an "Inland Sea stretching in still and solitary grandeur far beyond the limit of our vision. . . . I am doubtful that the followers of Balboa felt more enthusiasm when, from the heights of the Andes, they saw for the first time the great Western ocean. . . . to travellers so long shut up among mountain ranges a sudden view over the expanse of silent waters had in it something sublime."[1] Now, in the spring of 1845, Frémont would lead another scientific expedition toward Chrysopylae, the Golden Gate which he had named.

Beneath the throb of romantic adventure the men of St. Louis sensed that they were soon to reap some overripe harvests. Talleyrand had predicted to Robert Livingston and James Monroe while signing the Louisiana Purchase, "You have made a noble bargain for yourselves and I presume you will make the most of it." The eventual

---

[1] John C. Frémont, *Report of the Exploring Expedition to the Rocky Mountains in the Year 1842, and to Oregon and North California in the Years 1843–'44*, 151.

consummation of that bargain could hardly be less than the owner-ship of Pacific shores. Toward them ran a true passage to India, not an ice-choked sea lane or a tropical Strait of Ánian, but a dusty road leading due west from St. Louis. England would hardly fight over Oregon, and if Mexico balked, how little it would take to frustrate a man like Santa Anna!

Thus Frémont, young Theodore Talbot with him, would move from St. Louis to the staging field at Westport (within modern Kansas City), and around him would cluster the hundreds of young bloods dying to join the adventure. Wherever he went "he would gather a little train around him," and there were genuine tears in the eyes of those refused. Colonel Stephen Watts Kearny and his Dragoons were nearby and moving in the same direction. And Frémont, the thirty-two-year-old captain, would contemplate once more dragging a how-itzer, as he had on his previous trip to California in 1843–44, for what scientific purpose it was hard to ascertain. But the ambiguities were realities. Frémont was also a scientist, a good one, and there were barometers and telescopes and transits to balance the spirit of the howitzer. Because of these scientific purposes, Frémont had been care-ful in his choice of men for the expedition and was delighted that the roster included so many "young gentlemen" like Talbot. Talbot appreciated his opportunity and was glad that he could be on such good terms with his commander and with the nation he served.

St. Louis. May 26, 1845

Dear Mother

At my last date I was at Louisville. Captain Fremont[2] with [Richard K.] Jacob and [Henry] King had stopped at

---

[2] In his letters Talbot uses various, confusing army ranks for his commander. Frémont's record: second lieutenant, Topographical Engineers, 1838; brevet captain, 1844; major, California Battalion, 1846; earlier that year in Wash-ington appointed lieutenant colonel in new unit, Mounted Rifles; resigned (fol-lowing court martial), 1848. Francis B. Heitman, *Historical Register and Dictionary of the United States Army*, hereinafter cited as Heitman, *Register U.S. Army*.

the Kentucky River intending to visit Col [Thomas H.] Benton at his farm:[3] this would have been a good opportunity for me to have seen the Frankfort people but Capt. F. [Frémont] was so urgent for me to go on immediately to St. Louis that I could say nothing. He even charged me to stop in Louisville no longer than was absolutely necessary, there was no need however of that for as you know I was lucky enough to See Mr [Hamilton] Smith.[4]

Our Steamboat was rather crowded as we had Two Hundred and thirty-four passengers. We Steamed along very pleasantly until we reached a place in the Ohio called Frenchs Island where there is a Sandbar. We found 4 Steamboats lying fast aground and feared lest we too should be anchored against our will. But our pilot profiting by the mishaps of his neighbors, took a better path and after sufficient delay to make us feel anxious we passed over triumphantly. We met with no other obstacle although the water was very low, reaching St Louis by Sunday. Having placed William [Chinook] who accompanied me, in good quarters I went to the Planters

[3] Many of Frémont's men in the Third Expedition would later become officers in the California Battalion, which helped conquer California. Richard K. Jacob served as captain in that unit. He should not be confused with Richard T. Jacob, who about the same time came overland to California with Edwin Bryant.

Henry King of Georgetown, like his friend and messmate, Talbot, early gained the confidence and respect of Frémont and, like Jacob, served in the California Battalion. King later joined Frémont's Fourth Expedition (1848) during which he met death by starvation. His brother, James, who also came to California in 1845, took for himself the name of James King of William. Fred B. Rogers, "Rosters of California Volunteers in the Service of the United States, 1846–47," *Annual Publication of the Society of California Pioneers* (San Francisco, 1950), 17–28.

[4] Hamilton Smith, a former Kentuckian, practiced law in St. Louis and appears to have been a friendly consultant to the Talbot family.

*5*

House.[5] There I found [James W.] Abert and [William G.] Peck.[6] Peck seems like most young officers and appears to be quite amiable. [Edward M.] Kern is so far a good humored and a very long legged fellow. Said to be a fine artist.[7]

I met Mr [Josiah] Dent or rather he called to see me. He is settled here with his mother. [Thomas] Fitzpatrick has gone out as guide with the dragoons.[8] Godare [Alexis Godey] and several others who are to go with us are here, and hundreds of applicants who would like to do so.[9] [Lucien] Maxwell of Kaskaskia who was with us a short time last year came up in the same boat with me from Cape Girardeau. He is just down from the Mts. (Bents Fort etc.) so I have all the news from that part of the world.[10] I saw Mr [Charles] Bent this morning.[11]

[5] Frémont brought the young Indian, Chinook, from the Columbia River on his Second Expedition. The boy had spent the following year in a Philadelphia school, and Frémont was now returning him to his people. Frémont, *Memoirs*, 424.

[6] Lieutenant James W. Abert, son of Colonel John James Abert, commanding officer of the Topographical Corps, and Lieutenant William G. Peck, two young West Point graduates, were assigned to Frémont's expedition in 1845, but were soon reassigned to explore and survey the Arkansas, Canadian, and Purgatory rivers. Frémont, *Memoirs*, 426.

[7] Edward Meyer Kern (1823–1863), a Philadelphia artist and scientist, was a replacement on this expedition for Charles Preuss, the artist and topographer of Frémont's Second Expedition. Kern became sufficiently trusted by Frémont to be made responsible for much of the surveying. Frémont named the Kern River in California for him. Robert V. Hine, *Edward Kern and American Expansion*, 2–46.

[8] Thomas Fitzpatrick (c. 1799–1854), trapper, scout, and Indian agent, was one of half a dozen most respected mountain men. On various occasions he worked with Frémont, Kearny, William Ashley, and Jedediah Smith. He entered the fur trade in 1822 under Ashley and Andrew Henry of St. Louis. By the Indians he was called Broken Hand.

[9] Alexis Godey was described by Frémont as "insensible to danger, of perfect coolness and stubborn resolution." Frémont included him with Kit Carson and Richard Owens in a triumvirate of top frontier scouts. Frémont, *Memoirs*, 427.

I am up to my eyes in business running here and there buying the thousand things required for our expedition. By this means Capt F. will be saved much delay and great loss of time which is becoming of consequence as this is a fine travelling Season. I meet with very great assistance from Mr Robt Campbell who is a sort of agent to Capt F. in these expeditions.[12] I have had no time to myself I have so many engagements to fulfill and even now write in a great hurry expecting to be called off every moment. In a few days however I hope to have more leisure. I am going to run down to the post office now in expectation of finding a letter from you. Dearest Mother we must both cheer up, our separation may be long, let us then make it as little painful as possible, and putting faith in all wise providence look forward to a brighter and

[10] Lucien Maxwell (1818–75), long-time close friend of Kit Carson, had come west on Frémont's First Expedition in 1842. Later he became owner and manager of what was then the largest single ranch in the United States, the Maxwell Land Grant of New Mexico. Jim Berry Pearson, *The Maxwell Land Grant, ad fin.*

[11] Charles Bent was in St. Louis on May 9, according to the *Missouri Republican* of May 12; whether his younger brother William, also a leading figure in the firm of Bent, St. Vrain and Company, owners of Bent's Fort on the upper Arkansas, was there at the time cannot be ascertained. But both men apparently were in and out of the city on freight-hauling expeditions to and including July, 1845.

[12] Robert Campbell (1804–79), an Ulsterman, had responded to a notice in the *Missouri Republican* of March 20, 1822, calling for one hundred young men to go up the Missouri as fur trappers for William H. Ashley and Andrew Henry of St. Louis. Other men later notable in the fur trade who joined were Jedediah S. Smith, David E. Jackson, Campbell's partner-to-be William M. Sublette, Étienne Provost, Jim Bridger, and Thomas Fitzpatrick. Ten years later, after extensive experience as trappers and traders, Campbell and Sublette formed a partnership, dated December 20, 1832. Their ensuing success made both of them wealthy men, widely active in, and as suppliers of, the fur trade. Sublette died in July, 1845. Paul Chrisler Phillips, *The Fur Trade*, II, 396–97, 524, 537; John E. Sunder, *The Fur Trade on the Upper Missouri, 1840–1865*, 92ff.; Sunder, *Bill Sublette, Mountain Man*, 151–73.

happier future. Give my love to Sister. Remember me to Mrs T. to all our kind friends The Larneds Kearneys Adams etc.[13] I do feel anxious to know what arrangements you are going to make but any rate I feel much happier to know that you cannot want for money until I return. Pray dearest Mother for your affectionate son whose whole object, aim and hopes of happiness in this life are centered in you his dearest friend, his Mother.[14] Some one has come to interrupt me as I anticipated but I shall not budge until I have fairly finished So Adieu,

Your Affectionate Son.

THEO. TALBOT

PLANTERS HOUSE May 30th [1845]

DEAREST MOTHER,

As I wrote you, I have been much occupied in ordering and superintending the making of things for the Company. You may well imagine how many are required; one article procured, it suggests the purchase of another and so on until the list appears almost interminable. As regards myself, thanks to your kind forethought and judicious preparations I shall be relieved of the most troublesome part of my outfit. The few things which I have yet to obtain being of a

---

[13] Here and elsewhere Talbot's references to friends suggest the rather high social climate from which he sprang. We do not know which Larneds or which Adamses he here refers to, but the Kearnys were undoubtedly the army family, which included Stephen Watts Kearny and Philip Kearny, both of whom were to become generals before they were through.

[14] This section of extended reference to Talbot's family, especially his mother, is here retained as a sample. Almost all of the letters hereafter contain such passages, which, however psychologically revealing, have been deleted as repetitious and historically unimportant. Omitted sections are full of such phrases as "If ever there was love on earth I love you above all, my whole happiness in this world is with you . . . my dearest, my *more* than dearest Mother."

nature that I am better able to judge of: I shall go out this time infinitely better prepared than I was last year and of course I shall have a proportianate degree of comfort. The young gentlemen are occupied in obtaining their outfits. I think that I shall get along very well with them. Abert I suppose is reconciled to going by this time, and Peck says it has been his desire to make a trip of this kind ever since he entered West Point. St Louis is not very lively at present as the spring trade is just concluded. There are a few Santa Fé Traders still here: a day or two ago a party of sixty men came down from the Yellowstone R. in the Fur Company's Steamboat "Frolic."[15] Most of them, French men and presenting the usual wild appearance which a prolonged residence in the wilderness begets. There is now lying in port a mammoth Steamboat called the Missouri, she is just built and is upwards of 300 feet in length.[16] Her cabins are fitted up very handsomely with marble tables, rich carpets, mirrors etc. Mr Peck and myself rode out as far as "bide [vide] poche" a little village about six miles distant from St. Louis, the other evening. The weather has been very pleasant and not too warm. Capt Frémont intends publishing his 3 reports, the two previous and the coming one in one large and handsomely illustrated standard volume. I have been waiting day after day for a letter from home, I constantly go to the Post Office, but as often come away disappointed; I cannot account for it, for the time when I should have received tidings from you

[15] The *Frolic*, a 126-ton steamer owned by the Union Fur Company of St. Louis, had spent the winter of 1844–45 frozen in at Fort George, on the Missouri twenty miles below Fort Pierre. It reached St. Louis on May 27. *St. Louis American*, May 28, 1845.

[16] The *Missouri* was an 886-ton sidewheeler constructed in Cincinnati, Ohio, in 1845; home port, St. Louis. She was lost in 1851.

has long since elapsed, perhaps your letters have been lost— but I will try and be patient - - - - - -

Capt. Frémont has just arrived today he was not so lucky as I was, for his Steamboat stuck twice on Sandbars. He had scarcely arrived here today and was not even landed when he was assailed by people anxious to accompany him. wherever he goes he gathers a little train. To morrow I shall have my hands full: he has yet to engage nearly all of his men. Basil Lajeunesse, Alexis Godare [Godey], [Auguste] Archambeau, [Raphael] Proue and one or two others who were with him before will probably go this time.[17] [Christopher] Carson we will find at Bents on the Arkansas.[18] You will find a very correct genl skech of our intended route in the [Washington, D.C.] "Union" quoted from the preface of Capt F's report of last year. Our surveys being somewhat south of last year's lines as it is at present contemp. circumstances however may induce him to modify his present plan. Remember me to all our friends. . . .

THEODORE TALBOT

[17] The three French Canadian trappers, Basil Lajeunesse, Auguste Archambeau, and Raphael Proue, were all, like Godey, long associates of Frémont. Lajeunesse would be killed by the Indian attack as Frémont's party moved grudgingly out of California in April, 1846. Archambeau served under Frémont all during the conquest of California. Proue helped Frémont on each of his expeditions until he died of exposure on the tragic Fourth in 1849. Frémont, *Memoirs, passim.*; Alpheus H. Favour, *Old Bill Williams, Mountain Man,* 190-95.

[18] Christopher Carson, one of the best known of western scouts, came into the Far West from Missouri in August, 1826. It was not, however, until he met Frémont on a steamboat on the Missouri in May, 1842, as the latter began his First Expedition, that he began to win national notice. Carson had finished a stint as hunter for Bent, St. Vrain and Company at Bent's Fort, having previously spent fourteen years in the fur trade in the Far West. He guided Frémont's Second and Third expeditions, down to the California conquest, in which he also played an important role. Christopher Carson, *Kit Carson's Own*

PLANTERS HOUSE June 1st [1845]

MY DEAR MOTHER

. . . . Mr King I perceive is still incorrigible. Jacob has this moment come into the room, as he goes out he is making enquiries as to when I intend "coming down" Capt F. has hid himself in some French house down the City, but it wont do, they are beginning to find out his whereabouts One of the Clerks of this house told me that he was going to have a sign painted and placed over the main entrance stating that Captain Fremont did not stay here. . . .

[Signature and part of letter clipped.]

PLANTERS HOUSE June 4th 1845

MY DEAR SISTER

I have not been able to sit down and write you a letter in a satisfactory manner until this evening. If you could see how much I am occupied I am sure you would pardon me for not having sooner answered your exceedingly agreable letter, as I promised to do, through Mother. But I have had to buy, order and superintend a part of the things bought here, which is no trifling duty I assure you. and in addition to that for the last few days I have had to examine and take lists of the applicants, to advance money to those engaged, give orders for goods, drafts etc. Just think of it!!

You ought to have witnessed the scene which we had here on Monday. Capt Fremont it seems gave notice to those who wished to accompany him, through the papers, saying that if they collected at the Planters Warehouse (one of the

*Story of His Life*, ed. by Blanche C. Grant (Taos, n.p., 1926); Edwin L. Sabin, *Kit Carson Days, 1809–1868* (N.Y., Press of the Pioneers, 1935); Frémont, *Memoirs*, 73–74.

largest houses in the City of that kind) that he would explain the objects, duties, pay, etc. of the Expedition. Long before the appointed hour the house was filled and Capt Frémont found it necessary to adjourn to an open square. I walked round to the place of meeting about this time with Mr Bent to see what was going on. The whole street and the open space was crowded. We could easily trace the Captain's motions by the denser nucleus which moved hither and thither. They broke the fences down and the Captain finally used a wagon as his rostrum but it was impossible for him to make himself heard. Each one being unwilling to allow his neighbor the advantage of having a word with or even being seen by Frémont, so it was a grand tustle. Frémont at last took refuge in a hotel. His house is absolutely besieged they rush into his bedroom and all Jacobs strength and vigilance has been inadequate to keep them out. The captains last expedient is to have himself locked up and the key taken off, this plan has been highly successful though rather inconvenient for Jacob has once or twice left him in duresse rather longer than he desired. This morning those selected some Fifty-five were apprised of it, and he takes no more here, though he will probably engage 6 or 7 men at Westport. He has many very fine men, old mountaineers; several however who will not render him much service have been thrust upon him in spite of him through the influence of their friends. I think it probable that he will leave some of these last named employées on the Arkansas at Bents or the Pueblo,[19] supplying their places with good men. We will find Kit Carson there. Clément Lambert

[19] The name given the small plaza at the site of present Pueblo, Colorado, described in picturesque terms in Alexander Barclay's unpublished papers in the Bancroft Library, University of California at Berkeley.

and Bogard who were with him on his first trip are to go on this.[20] Proue, Basil Lajeunesse, Archambeau, Godare [Godey]; and [Joseph Reddeford] Walker if we can meet with him, of the last one.[21] In my anxiety to write, you see I have not stopped at a blot If it is in any manner legible I know you will excuse this letter. I spent the evening very pleasantly at Robt. Campbell's with Cap Fremont etc. a few nights since. Capt Frémont starts off to morrow morning if it is possible. I think that I shall remain until the end of the week. We will leave the frontier before the 20th or 25th of June As far as I have heard we will winter in California if that is the case may I not hope to hear from you? Mrs Frémont will know something about this, and in case she writes you can do so also

[20] In his *Memoirs* (p. 75) Frémont says he hired Clément Lambert in St. Louis for his First Expedition. There is no mention of Bogard on the list, although possibly François Badeau was the same. Badeau was also mentioned in close proximity with Talbot at the beginning of the Second Expedition (*Memoirs*, 169).

[21] Joseph Reddeford Walker (1798–1876), a trapper since 1819, had led Captain B. L. E. Bonneville's detached party of trappers into California in 1833–34 during the latter's fur-trapping ventures in the Far West which began in 1832. Walker Pass in the Sierra Nevada was discovered during Walker's conduct of the Bonneville party. Walker subsequently met Sir William Drummond Stewart's hunting expedition in 1837 at the Green River Rendezvous and was captured both in portrait and in action by Alfred Jacob Miller, Stewart's artist on the expedition. During its return from California, Frémont's Second Expedition encountered Walker in the Great Basin and profited from his knowledge of this interior desert and the route to Bent's Fort on the Arkansas, where Walker left them in August, 1844. A reticent man, though a natural leader, old "Bourgeois" must be seen through the descriptions of others, notably Miller (Marvin C. Ross, ed., *The West of Alfred Jacob Miller* [*1837*]); Zenas Leonard, who accompanied him in 1833–34 (John C. Ewers, ed., *Adventures of Zenas Leonard, Fur Trader*); and Daniel Ellis Conner, who accompanied him from Colorado into Arizona as the Civil War drew on (Donald J. Berthrong and Odessa Davenport, eds., *Joseph Reddeford Walker and the Arizona Adventure*). Like that of his contemporaries, Jim Bridger, Old Bill Williams, and Kit Carson, his geographical knowledge of the West was very extensive.

under cover to Captain Frémont.[22] I am afraid from what you say in your letter that I may hear again from you here if I do not I hope for several at Westport. I have so much to write that I become confused and as you see write nothing at all. Remember me kindly to all the family and expect to have another hieroglyhic manuscript before long: until then, Adieu —Your Affect Brother

THEO TALBOT

PLANTERS HOUSE. ST. LOUIS
June 6th 1845

DEAREST MOTHER

... Fremont treats me very kindly and I feel in a very different situation to that of last year. I hope to get along smoothly with the others who certainly appear entirely amiable in civilized life. pray for me that I do well in all things. Frémont was harassed until the last moment by applicants and it became even painful to witness the unbidden tear which welled up in many a stout hearted man's eye as he turned away disappointed after months of eager longing and mayhap after a journey of several thousand miles, (as many did). The most of the men chosen are fine looking fellows and still more of them superb riflemen. A large party of them went off yesterday evening. I rode over to St Charles with Capt F. who joined the same Steamboat at that place. Abert, Peck etc. have all gone up. I did not return from St. Charles which is 20

22 In view of the frequent historical puzzlement over Frémont's lack of regard for orders, it is interesting to note that even a civilian member of his Third Expedition knew so far in advance that the ultimate destination of the topographical exploration was, in fact, California, for the second time. An interesting point of conjecture is whether young Lieutenant J. W. Abert, the son of Frémont's commanding officer in Washington, also knew, as seems entirely likely.

miles distant from St. Louis, until this morning. You may rely upon it I have had plenty left on my hands to do and to have done. This evening I sent off another batch of our recruits and any quantity of our Camp equipage We have engaged about 60 men here and we shall take 10 or 15 from the 200 who are awaiting the Captain's arrival there (at Westport). I think I shall leave this place on Monday. The whole party are to leave the frontier about the 15th or [word torn out] I say 25th June. It is pleasant to know that it can be cool anywhere about this time, for it is most unconsciably hot about St Louis. But *I* dont mind it at all, for I am quite well and in good spirits. Remember me kindly to all who enquire for me. . . .

Theo. Talbot

St. Louis. June 9th 1845

My dear Sister,

On Friday last I wrote a letter to Mother announcing Capt. Frémonts departure, and this I believe will have to tell you of my own as I expect to start to morrow having got through with nearly all my business. Last evening I sent off the third detachment of our recruits, only one or two remain who will go with *me*. One of the city papers speaking of the embarkation of the first party, "Says it was amusing to see two West Point Cadets among the crowd; staring about and wondering at the tactics of the "Mountain boys," an apt illustration of theory versus practice etc." Our howitzer has not yet arrived from Memphis so it will probably be under my escort. It is so exceedingly warm in St Louis that it makes me long after the fresh, pure air of the prairie. If it were not for the hope I have of hearing from you a few times more I wouldn't care how soon I were launched forth into the ocean prairie. But as long as I can hear of, and be heard from, by you, I imagine myself in a manner near, but when this second separation takes place and I enter upon my blank existence, I cannot but feel as the bleeding victim whose gaping wounds are yet again torn open by some rude and cruel hand—but I must not repine—the ways of Providence are just. We will look only on the brighter side and most assuredly we have that to contemplate. When I recall all those sad faces—The hundreds who were more bent on going than I was and yet were doomed to disappointment, when I think what mortification we should all have felt had I been left out, and how easily they might have dropped me, the gloomy prospect which I could not but anticipate had they done so, I am content, nay more I shall be as *happy* as I can be when separated from you. The time may pass more rapidly when we are employed. We may all of us be together again in 15 or 18 months. You must still continue house-keeping, if we are rich enough we will buy a handsome one and have a fine garden, you must get books and papers for they are *cheap* enough (though you musnt believe all the apochyrphal news they will certainly give you of our Expedition) I am delighted that you are going to make such a proficient in mantua making, by that means you will of course increase your pocket money; take care however that you have not been bragging too early, for you know I am disposed to be highly critical in such matters. I have already written Mother, that I thought *you* (I meant to have written *I*) would winter in California. pray excuse that slip of the pen and change [word torn out] those little pronouns, for someone who lives overhead has been whipping a child all the morning, and it raised such a yell together with its cries of "murder" that for a time I have been completely distracted and it is a wonder that I did not write that "I hoped you would *not* winter in the vicinity of such squalling brats." I think one line of our travel will be along Mary's [Humboldt] River it will not be down on Frémonts map but I will give you its course, —It heads near Fort Hall and runs in a Southwest course, emptying into a lake near the *point* or pass of the California Mountains through which we came *out* of California on our return. Another, may be on the Col[orado] taking it from its mouth and exploring its tributaries—you notice that we have *already* crossed it twice nearer towards its source.) This however is all guess, but it may please you to have even a guess if it be a rational one which I am inclined to think it is. I am sorry that Frémonts report is so very succinct, but I have no doubt that when you have read it, you will have a better knowledge of that country, its characters and its inhabitants that [than] nine tenths of the people who pretend to know all about the whole country West of the Mississippi.

I have seen Mr Dent several times since I have been here; his Mother lives with him and he intends to make this place his permanent residence. There is an immense deal of every Kind of business going on here though I do not know he has any share in it as yet. I am going out this afternoon to Col W.[illiam] Sublett's place a few miles in the country.[23] He has the domesticated buffalo and other wild game. He has also Swans, brants etc. . . .

THEODORE TALBOT

[23] William Lewis Sublette (1799–1845), one of a numerous breed of mountain men centered in Missouri, enjoyed an exciting career in the fur trade of the Far West. In 1835 he built a house on an idyllic farm of 779 acres at Sulphur Springs, six miles from St. Louis. At the time of Talbot's visit, Sublette was a

CAMP NEAR WESTPORT MO.
June 15th 1845

MY DEAR MOTHER

I started the day on which I wrote to Sister that I thought it probable that I would leave St Louis. The Missouri had been very low, but a day or two before I embarked the annual June rise commenced, so the "White Cloud" met with no obstruction in her progress landing us safely at the Kanzas. I found that Capt Frémont had encamped out in the prairie six or seven miles west of Westport. Passing through the latter place I met with Lieuts Abert and Peck who had not as yet joined the camp, both were quite well and in excellent spirits. Going out to the Camp I found the Captain superintending the making of tents, distribution of stoves etc. All of us told, we amount to seventy men and we most certainly present a very formidable appearance and one calculated to strike awe into the bosoms of any evil disposed marauders we may chance to encounter. We are all well equipped and provisioned and we will have an opportunity of amply recruiting them should we think proper, from Government supplies which are stored at Bents Fort on the Arkansas. Doctor [James] McDowell, [Charles] Taplin and others whom you know are here, all well.[24] The camp has not yet been organized.

---

colonel in the Missouri Militia. A short time later, Sublette left for the East, where he died of tuberculosis on July 23. Cf. John E. Sunder, *Bill Sublette, Mountain Man.*

[24] Probably the son of Governor James McDowell of Virginia, a close relative of the Thomas Hart Bentons and cousin to Frémont's wife. Young James McDowell would travel briefly with Frémont on the Fourth Expedition. Charles Van Linneus Taplin came west with Frémont on the Second, Third, and Fourth expeditions, dying shortly after the last, presumably as a result of its hardships. Hine, *Edward Kern and American Expansion*, 12.

Last night, my first of prairie life, Campaign No 2, we had a tremendous storm with an accompanying little hurricane. The whole Camp were drenched out and out. But as I have often told you such trifles cannot phase me now. I rose up this morning just as well and more supple than If I had been reposing in a feather bed instead of being enveloped in a wet blanket. Things are in great confusion at present so it will take us at least four or five days to reduce our chaos to anything resembling order. We will then start out making no further delays than are absolutely necessary for the observations etc. Most of the Camp details I have already given you: many of our men are of very respectable families more than two thirds of them are Americans the remainder French.[25] I can only say that all looks fair and affords the happiest promise. . . .

THEODORE TALBOT

CAMP NEAR WESTPORT<br>June 18th 1845

DEAREST MOTHER,

Since I wrote you last the weather has still continued as unpleasant as ever, raining and storming almost without any intermission both day and night. We have been able to do little or nothing in camp But the Captain has become so tired of lying by doing nothing that he has determined on

---

[25] In the years after 1763, when the French empire in North America was extinguished (and only briefly re-established prior to Napoleon's sale of Louisiana Territory to the United States in 1803), the hardy, restless class of French-speaking *coureurs de bois* appears increasingly in the employ of U.S. and Spanish expeditions. Individuals of the class have remained all but nameless, save where, as in Frémont's reports and *Memoirs*, they have been signalized, or where in infrequent instances they have left their own journals or recollections, as in the cases of Antoine Tabeau (*Tabeau's Narrative of Loisel's Expedition to the Upper Missouri*) and Gabriel Franchère (*Adventure at Astoria, 1810–1814*).

moving camp to morrow or the day after. I rode about 25 miles through the rain yesterday but I have an India Rubber coat and we went at a pretty rapid rate. I passed through Westport and saw Abert, Peck and Kern all well they stay there. Things not being arranged as yet in the camp. The Captain is I believe going to have a very small mess this year. The most of the gentlemen with myself will constitute another mess. I am quite at home in camp now, and with the exception of Doctor McDowall none is more at ease. The others are afraid of the Captain. There are two artists who have been at camp repeatedly and are exceedingly desirous to join us.[26] Frémont is half inclined to take them. We have round Marquee tents and there being ten messes we have quite a handsome camp.

June 20th. I have not had any chance to send my letter to the Post Office as the weather was so bad, so I did not finish it. We start to morrow I believe. Talking with the Captain he told me privately (and you of course will mention it to no one) that he intends dividing the parties at Bents Fort on the Arkansas sending one party home (by the way of Red River I believe, or some Southern Route) He will keep on to Salt Lake and the country West of that, California etc. He will take me with him I *think* and I may have a chance of assisting him in his operations in astronomical observations etc. Things work exceedingly well as far as I am concerned, more, much more agreably than I had ever anticipated. The gentlemen all appear likely to agree with each other and with me. If I am placed to assist the Captain as he has partly promised

[26] Alfred S. Waugh and John B. Tisdale, two footloose artists so desperate to join the expedition, were shortly hereafter turned down by Frémont. Alfred S. Waugh, *Travels in Search of the Elephant*, ed. by John Francis McDermott.

I will soon become sufficiently au fait with their proper mode of assisting, as to render him some service and my position will be more important as it were in the camp. Every one in the camp will find occupation as the Captain intends to do much work and keep steady at it until he has accomplished all his objects. If I can only get to take down and note time etc. for the Captain in his observations I shall have one of the best berths about the camp.

I have not received a line from you since I left St Louis but I still hope to do so. There has been quite a rise in the Missouri from the incessant rain of the last few days. We are to move Six Miles into the prairie to morrow. So the whole camp are fully occupied and I am so much occupied that writing to any one but you would be an absolute impossibility. If I should not have a chance of writing or rather of sending a letter I must bid you good bye until we reach Bents. . . .

Your Most Affectionate Son
THEO TALBOT

NEAR WESTPORT 2D CAMP
June 25th [1845]

MY DEAR MOTHER

Since I last wrote you we have moved camp four or five miles farther from Westport the bad weather has prevented us from travelling at all. Last Sunday Capt Fremont ordered me to go to Fort Leavenworth[27] and endeavor to

---

[27] In continuous operation since 1827, when it was established to help protect caravans engaged in the Santa Fe trade, Fort Leavenworth is one of the oldest forts in the U.S. Army system. From the Fort Captain Bennet Riley had led the first military escort of caravans over the Santa Fe Trail in 1829; Colonel Henry Dodge's Dragoon Expedition of 1835 had returned from the Rocky Mountains by way of the Fort; and from here in 1845 Colonel Stephen Watts Kearny led

procure some articles which were absolutely necessary for our command. So I went to Westport the same day and starting from there the next day endeavored to cross the Kansas River with a light carriage but when I got there the river was booming, the late rains having caused it to overflow its bottom for miles to the high bluffs on either side, so a crossing was impracticable, the ferry boat not being able to traverse the bottoms on account of the timber. I then went round to the Missouri River and waited till the afternoon for a Steamboat, when one passed by and took me up to the Fort about 40 miles; the River was so powerful in its current that that the Steamboat could scarcely battle against it and the Kansas where it entered the Missouri ran over to opposite side blocking up the Missouri and making it still-water like a mill pond  I reached the Fort about ten oclock that night but one of the officers happened to be at the landing and hospitably took charge of me carrying me to his quarters and fixing me comfortably for the night: next morning I saw Maj [Clifton] Wharton the Comdr and transacted my business with him.[28] Two Companies of 1st Infantry and a very few dragoons are there. I was most hospitably received by all the officers. I took two dragoons with the things I had purchased and reached the Kansas River (25 miles) by ev[enin]g having left the Fort after dinner. I slept at "Delaware Town" and I was so fortu-

a Dragoon expedition to South Pass and the Rockies. Talbot's final route from Westport here described took him approximately thirty-eight miles to the Fort on the west bank of the Missouri, north of Westport. National Park Service, U.S. Department of the Interior, *Soldier and Brave: Military and Indian Affairs in the Trans-Mississippi West* . . . , 125–28.

[28] Clifton Wharton, a Pennsylvanian and captain in the Dragoons since 1833, would be promoted to lieutenant colonel in 1846 and die two years later. Heitman, *Register U.S. Army*.

nate as to arrive in time for a grand dance which took place there that night and was kept up until daylight the next morning. With some difficulty we crossed the Kansas and instead having to travel a day or two to overtake the command as I had expected to have to do I found the Captain camped within 6 miles of where I had left him. He had a letter for me dated June 9th the only one I have had since I left St Louis. I am very glad it was directed to Robt Campbell as by that means it reached me sooner than if it had been directed to Westport. The regular mail coming by land and being excessively slow. Whereas Campbell sent it up the Missouri River by a steamboat, saving at least ten days. If you have a chance to write to Monterey or elsewhere to me you had better direct under cover to the Captain. Your letter makes me feel very happy to think that you are in good hopes and spirits. I myself feel entirely so as I wrote you before the Captain is very kind to me. I shall be with him in making time and notes etc. for his observations I hope. So I will be much in contact and I think be able to make myself useful. Capt F and Dr. McDowell with Alexis Godare [Godey] constitute his mess Abert, Peck, Kerne and King from Washn. who is a sort of superdt. of Camp and guard duty etc. etc. etc. and myself form another. Also William [Chinook], a Negro and our cook. I do not know whether it is that I am accustomed to this sort of life and things appear easier, but at any rate I enjoy myself very much. I have now something to keep me always occupied and I think that is one great reason, I am more independent too and able to do for myself. Capt F also is very much kinder    The weather still prevents us from moving: constant rains

I have just now a chance of sending in a letter so I seal

up without being able to write more—We moved 5 miles farther today    I shall have a chance of writing again farther out
by some who will return    Love to Sister
                              Your Most affectionate Son
                                   THEODORE TALBOT

                         July 3d 1845
            CAMP, ABOUT 110 MILES FROM WESTPORT
DEAREST MOTHER
        I had day before yesterday the unhoped for delight
of a letter from you dated June 13th. The two Artists who I
wrote you wished to accompany us came out thus far in hopes
that some letters which they had obtained would influence
Capt. Frémont in their favor. They failed however. With
them came my letter, the latest date wh. has been received
in Camp. I cannot thank you too much for writing to me so
kindly on such an uncertain contingency. Abert was of course
delighted to hear that his family were well. Capt F. the same.
The camp is organised but we have been compelled to move
slowly for the roads are very bad and we have 4 heavy laden
wagons and a dearborn for the instruments besides 3 ox
wagons wh. have been carrying along part of our Camp equipage until were brought into proper train. These will return
back probably in the morning and by them I now write. I
have already told you as you desired how we were all fixed,
but as you may not have Received my last I will venture to
recapitulate. Fremont, Doctor McD. & Alexis form one
Mess. Myself, Abert, Peck & Kern and King another, with
Silas (a Negro)—Belanger a frenchman to saddle our horses
etc. A German named Schriber is our cook and William Chenook is also with us. The camp is divided into ten messes We

                              24

have somewhere about 70. We have two Delaware Indians
and expect to obtain several more Capt. F. having written to
procure them. Abert & Peck Sketch the route for their duty
Capt. F. permits me to sketch for my private improvement
whenever I have time or inclination. I have barometrical and
other meteorological observations to attend to. I am to be his
assistant in Astron. Observns. noting time etc. etc. The Doctor
has not begun his operations in Nat. History yet. I shall assist
him I suppose King collects botanical specimens & Kern paints
them. I am so far on the best of terms with all of them. The
Doctor, Abert, Peck etc. Peck turns out to be a very fine fellow so far. he has of course much talent. Abert has a turn for
sketching, music etc. and is amiable and agreable but somewhat eccentric Alexis Godare [Godey] an old and kind friend
of mine has charge of camp under Frémont attending to the
packing, giving orders for time of starting etc. Lambert, who
wd have had this place returned home on account of a law-
suit pending in St Louis. I have two very good riding animals
a very fine Mule and horse. Altogether I am very well off.
We have had no rains lately so the road improves every day
and we expect to reach Bents Fort early in August. To day we
met Bents Convoy of wagons 14 in number coming into the
States laden with Robes and Furs. None of the gentlemen
were then [with them], having come in advance from Pawnee.[29] You mention the rumor of our three years absence. I
think that there is no truth whatever in the report. Frémont
says as low as 14. months, let us say 18. The party who leave
him at Bents will reach the United States some months earlier
than his own, so much he told me. Whether he takes me or

[29] Pawnee Rock, on the Santa Fe Trail just west of the Arkansas River on
its Great Bend.

not I cannot say   I think that I will make the trip with him however. By the Salt Lake Mary's River Green River and Upper California. There are many Santa Fe wagons travelling along the Road and more of them at "Council Grove"[30] a short distance ahead that being the Rendesvous. . . . I shall write a letter at Bents Fort which I hope will be brought down by Kearney's Command who will probably pass that way in October.

Farewell Dearest Mother and Sister<br>Your Affectionate Son<br>THEODORE TALBOT

BENT'S FORT. Aug 10th<br>1845

MY DEAREST MOTHER

Since I wrote to you (4th July) our trip has still continued as pleasant as it at first promised. We left the Santa Fe trace at the Pawnee Fork of the Arkansas River, taking up that stream which trends from the N.W. to S.E. We past several companies on the trace to Santa Fe going out and small parties of Kickapoos, Kansas & other Indians on their return from buffalo. The first day that we travelled up the Pawnee Fork we saw buffalo in great numbers and for the first time. We camped early that afternoon and Abert, Peck, Kerne, with Alick Godare [Godey], Archambeau Basil Lajeunesse & myself started out all mounted on fine horses, for a grand buffalo chase. It was a most exciting scene to witness the pell mell Confusion which our onset created among the frightened buffalo. We galloped slowly to give the buf-

---

[30] Council Grove, another stopping place on the Santa Fe Trail, in present Morris County, Kansas.

26

falo a chance to herd up & then charged in lines the flying bands. Alick & myself entered a band together. We had hardly come up to it when a bull missing his footing fell prostrate before us, it was too late to check the wild career of our horses & almost to think, so we gave rein to our animals & both sprang gallantly over before the Bull had time to rise. Choosing our cows we separated them from the band, and soon each of us was hidden from the other by the fastly intervening rolls of the prairie. My horse was fast and kept near the cow but was somewhat difficult to manage, being spirited and never having been trained to run buffalo I could scarcely turn him quick enough to avoid the desperate lunges the cow made when hard pressed. We rushed at mad speed over hill & dale, leaped up and down steep banks & over Ravines after an animating chase of more than a mile I succeeded in giving her the Coup de Grace. I tied my horse to the horns of my well earned prey & proceeded to butcher it in true hunters style. Tying the choice pieces to my saddle and being bespattered with the proper quantum of blood over clothes face and hands, I mounted my horse & rode back to camp. One by one the others came back to camp some having met with the usual incidents of a buffalo chase, having lost sight of the buffalo they were chasing, being thrown etc.

From the head of the Pawnee Fork we struck over to the Smoky hill Fork of Kansas River, down wh we travelled last year. We met along here a war party of Arapahoes with some Comanches who travelled with us a day or two. I went out buffalo hunting with them. Higher up the River we found a Sheyenne village with the great men of which we smoked. Our road was rough and our wagons delayed us much  We struck the Arkansas River 25 miles below the Fort and the next evening we reached it. (1st Aug.), exchanging salutes we encamped in our camp of last year   Col Kearney's command had passed the fort three days since. We sent an express (by which I did not write for Capt Fremont told none of us until the express had gone) for Fitzpatrick who is their pilot & whom the Captain wanted to act as guide to a party of 35 under command of Lieut Abert who goes south & by whom I forward this letter   Lieut Peck goes south also.

We found a party of Delaware at the Fort awaiting us. Capt Frémont had engaged them at Westport to follow us & they had taken the shortest road to Bents. Since we have been here a Sheyenne village has come to the Fort & are camping near us for the purpose of holding council with the Delawares & making peace.[31] There has also been a Caravan of 27 wagons belonging to Santa Fe traders camped at the Fort and another still larger company of Santa Fe Traders is daily expected from "below" as they call United States. The Sheyennes have had great rejoicing over a Pawnee scalp just brought in by one of their most promising warriors. The men danced, and the women gave a *grand* scalp dance.[32] We have

[31] The Delaware-Cheyenne peace council and the events immediately preceding it are related in parallel accounts contained in George Bent, *Life of George Bent Written from his Letters by George E. Hyde*, ed. by Savoie Lottinville (90–93), and George Bird Grinnell, *The Fighting Cheyennes* (75–78), both having been taken from Cheyenne informants. The year of the Cheyenne-Sioux fight with Delaware trappers at the forks of the Republican in western Kansas was 1844. The peace talks between Cheyennes and Delawares took place at Bent's Fort on August 9, 1845. Frémont, *Narrative of the Exploring Expedition to the Rocky Mountains*, 288; Lieutenant J. W. Abert, *Report*, 29 Cong. 1 sess., *Senate Document 438*, 4.

[32] The long drawn-out enmity between the Cheyennes of the Algonquian family and the Pawnees of the Caddoan group dated from the loss of the Sacred Arrows, talismans of the Southern Cheyennes, to the Pawnees in "the Year the Stars Fell," according to Cheyenne oral tradition. This year may be set at 1833,

also had a dance in our honor. Capt. F. has been much occupied with his transit Insmt. at which Mr King assists him, & in other astronomical & meteorological obsnvs. in which I assist him. He has also been preparing for the division of parties We are waiting here now for a moon culmination to determine the longitude of this place with the Transit Instrument. I have been kept pretty busy about camp attending to one thing and another. My health and spirits are [and] have been excellent. I have no bleeding from the nose or other unpleasant symptoms, although the weather has been very hot. I hope that it has been pleasant with you and that you are as comfortable as I wish you to be. Love to all Friends. Dr McDowell leaves us here & I will write by him again as he takes the 1st opportunity to the States. . . .

Your Affet Son THEODORE

BENT'S FORT. ARKANSAW RIVER<br>August 16th 1845

MY DEAREST MOTHER

Doctor McDowall having become tired of prairie life and intending to return home from this place as soon as possible I have availed myself of the chance to write to you. We left the Santa Fe Road from whence I wrote to you last, at the Pawnee Fork of the Arkansaw River and followed up this fork to its head from thence we struck over to the "Smoky hill fork" of the Kansas River and keeping our general route of last summer reached this post on the 1st August We had much delay in finding a road for our wagons having to make many detours on their account but we had abundance of fat

when a Leonid Shower occurred. The event was a turning point in Cheyenne history. Bent, *Life of George Bent* . . . , 48–54.

buffalo in exchange for the mosquitoes which had annoyed us much on the Arkansaw River   We met a war party of Arapahoes with some Comanches but they were entirely friendly and travelled with us for a day or two. We met also a Sheyenne village, and traded meat, Ropes etc. When we arrived here we were welcomed by Mr StVrain one of the elder partrners of the company & Mr Geo. Bent who we saw last year with several others that we had met before.[33] We found that Col Karney's command of Dragoons had passed two or three days down the River. Capt. Fremont immediately sent an express for Fitzpatrick who was their guide as he wished to obtain him to guide the party which goes south under Abert. ( I would have written but I was not aware

[33] Céran de Hault de Lassus de St. Vrain was born at Spanish Lake near St. Louis in 1802 and in the 1820's became engaged in the fur trade, basing his operations at Taos, New Mexico. Around 1830 he formed a partnership with Charles Bent (b. 1799 at Charleston, West Virginia) and William Bent (b. 1809 at St. Louis). Their outpost was first in the form of a picket post on the Upper Arkansas at the confluence of Fountain Creek with that river, and in 1834 in the more imposing establishment known as Bent's Fort lower on the Arkansas, at a point on its north bank between present La Junta and Las Animas, Colorado. Here Colonel Henry Dodge's Dragoon Expedition of 1835 saw Bent, St. Vrain and Company in full operation. The best depictions of the fort are those of young Lieutenant J. W. Abert, of Frémont's Third Expedition in 1845–46, to whom we owe an accurate drawing of its floor plan as well as a perspective of its massive adobe construction. As "junior partners" in the fort, St. Vrain and the two elder Bent brothers had the two other Bents, George (b. 1814), not to be confused with William's half-blood Cheyenne son, George, and Robert (b. 1816). Much of Charles Bent's time was spent in pursuit of the company's business at Taos and Santa Fe, though he was not an infrequent traveler with company caravans to St. Louis. William Bent normally managed affairs at Bent's Fort with Céran St. Vrain, the two of them also traveling separately with wagon trains of furs and hides to St. Louis and returning with trade goods and supplies required at the fort. In the location of Bent's Fort, Yellow Wolf of the Cheyennes was decisive. Young Abert did his portrait during his stay with the Bents and St. Vrain in 1845. Bent, *Life of George Bent* . . . , 58–59, 88–89; Donald J. Berthrong, *Southern Cheyennes*, 77, 90, 102; J. W. Abert, *Western America in 1846–1847*, ed. by John Galvin, illustration, Yellow Wolf.

he was going to send an express until it was gone) There are several lodges of Kiawah Indians about the Fort: they live to the South and associate much with the Comanches, over whom, it is said, they have much influence.[34] We found here 7 Delawares whom the Captain had engaged at Westport and who were to follow us. they took the main road and so missed us. Six of them are picked men sent by the Council of the Delawares all distinguished for their bravery, the seventh a small boy, a sort of page or equerry, has also been a great traveller. We have besides two more Delawares who joined us at the start as soon as we arrived expresses went to the Sheyennes to gather them in to a Council. One of our Delawares, Jim Swanick is son of Swanick late great chief of the Delawares, who with 15 others was killed last summer by the Sheyennes.[35] The Delawares having been aggressors in the first instance offered the pipe of peace with strings of wampum. After many ceremonies, much speaking and smoking, peace was concluded. The pipe which was used was one that has been in the Pottawattomies, from almost time immemorial, tradition says that it came to them from far Northern Nations & it had been

[34] The Kiowa Indians, of a distinct linguistic stock, had moved on to the Southern Great Plains because of pressures from their neighbors, the Cheyennes, Arapahos, and Sioux as far north as Montana. J. W. Abert (*Journal of Lieutenant James W. Abert, from Bent's Fort to St. Louis in 1845*. 29 Cong., 1 sess., *Senate Executive Document 438* [1846], 42) observed the influence exercised by the Kiowas over their Southern Plains neighbors, the Comanches of the Shoshonean linguistic group, with whom they were first in conflict then at peace as they moved south of the Platte in the nineteenth century.

[35] The other Delaware with Swanok was Sagundai, also a chief. Frémont was not the only figure who admired and employed Delawares as scouts. Colonel Henry Dodge had done so during his Dragoon Expedition of 1835, as had also succeeding military and civilian expeditions. The Delawares were of Algonquian stock, long associated with whites from their original homeland in Pennsylvania and New England to the Southwest. F. W. Hodge, *Handbook of American Indians* . . . , I, 385.

used some years since in a council of 27 Nations as the Calumet of peace & friendship. The indians keep up great dancing and rejoicing. We had all the time parties of Santa Fe traders, Mexicans and In[dian]s to enliven us. Capt Fremont has put [up his] Transit Instrument and has been waiting for a moon culmination to determine the longitude of this place. In the meantime he has been arranging for the party which goes South under command of Lieut Abert, with Lieut Peck asst and Fitzpatrick as guide With 34 men and 4 wagons. They started to day. When we first started it was his intention to send me with the Southern party but he has since changed his mind. Although less independent I prefer to accompany him, it being more agreable in every way. The Southern party by their orders must be in by December so their trip will be short. They explore the Red River.[36] We start from here to morrow. We have a very fine body of men in our camp this year. All well armed and equipped Kit Carson, [John] Scott, Alick Godare [Godey] etc. go with us.[37] We shall also have Jos. Walker, the best man in the Country. We wont have any wagons to delay us & will reach California long before winter & so avoid the Cold. I do not know exactly what duty I shall have now as the camp is not yet organized But whatever it may be I shall always do my best. . . .

For Your Ever Affectionate Son

THEODORE TALBOT

[36] Actually the Canadian. Cf. Lieutenant James W. Abert, *Through the Country of the Comanche Indians in the Fall of the Year 1845* . . . . ed. by John Galvin, 1, and map facing 68.

[37] John Scott was born in England. Bancroft and others have thought that he may have been in California before Frémont arrived, a possibility dispelled by the Talbot letter. Scott, after serving in the conquest of California, joined the Frémont Fourth Expedition in 1848. Hubert Howe Bancroft, *California Pioneer Register and Index.*

# II.

# THE CONQUEST OF CALIFORNIA, 1846-47

*After Talbot's letter* from Bent's Fort in present Colorado nearly a year elapsed before his next message, written from Monterey California, in July, 1846. From the fort in August, 1845, the expedition had marched up the Arkansas River to its source high in the Rockies. They crossed the Continental Divide at an elevation of over ten thousand feet and shortly thereafter drank from a small stream, the fountainhead of the Colorado River of the West. They traced some of the Colorado's tributaries, like the Green, and pushed on to the Great Salt Lake. In November they broke through the rough ridges of the Great Basin and followed the dreary river which Frémont named after the German scientist Alexander von Humboldt. From Walker's Lake at the base of the Sierra Nevada, Frémont passed directly over the mountains into California, while Talbot led the main party southward by a less precipitous route. Talbot with his men celebrated Christmas in the San Joaquin Valley.

The trip had gone smoothly. At Bent's Fort Frémont had hired Joseph Reddeford Walker, one of the best of Western scouts, whose skills were a happy complement to Frémont's efficiency. The Captain had been given further opportunity to observe young Talbot in the field, was impressed with Theodore's "sense of responsibility," and was hence willing to assign him positions of command. A reciprocal respect was implied when Talbot wrote that "I am like Mr. Frémont in manner, mode of expression and even (heaven save the mark!) in face." By the time the party reached California, after six months in the wilderness, they may all have looked alike. Talbot said he arrived with nothing but "his riding equipage, a mosquito bar, and a dirty shirt."

The six months between Talbot's arrival in January and his letter

33

of July witnessed a rapid series of exciting events (Talbot called them "the present stirring times") which make understandable his delay in writing home. Alta California, as a frontier Mexican province, suffered unusually from the ills of political confusion during the Age of Santa Anna. States' rights movements sought greater decentralization within Mexico, and a small handful of Mexicans with a group of newly arrived Anglo-Americans looked forward to independence and possible annexation to the United States. Thomas Larkin, the United States consul at Monterey, was a potential leader of independence, and John Sutter at Sacramento was ready to join should events so indicate. He was like many others, playing his cards close and waiting for men of action like Frémont to lead.

At another level within the province, personal hostilities played an important role. General José Castro, the military governor, issued orders from Monterey which often antagonized Pio Pico, the civilian governor presiding in Los Angeles. It was the Monterey commander, General Castro, with whom Frémont and his men tangled first. Castro became suspicious. Frémont's purposes seemed other than scientific, and the Americans were ordered to leave. They resisted, raised an American flag, thought better of their rashness, and begrudgingly moved north. Talbot in his letters reflected irritation over "peremptory orders to quit." They retreated by the longest route possible, through the Sacramento Valley, where the majority of the settlers from the United States had been taking up farms. Frémont's party moved slowly enough to be recalled when news of imminent hostilities with Mexico arrived. Thus, returning to the environs of Sacramento and Sonoma, they were on hand to witness and participate in the first events of the war in California in June, 1846, known as the Bear Flag Revolt. There still was no news that the nation had declared war—it did not arrive until early July. But even before the Bear Flag Revolt, Talbot's words reflected a warlike atmosphere, with talk of "spies" and of "subduing Foreigners."

Descriptions of the war in California always smack of the *opera bouffe*. Talbot's letters, too, can be read that way—fandangos between battles, the capture of a handful of horses or mules, the wounding of a few soldiers. But the stakes were high, including California and

34

ultimately an entire corner of the continent. The U.S. Navy rushed Commodore Robert Stockton to the scene to replace the less vigorous Commodore John Drake Sloat; and the army ordered Major General Stephen Watts Kearny to California, even though its initial intelligence had reported complete military success under Stockton and Frémont.

Following the first military victories, Talbot was placed in charge of the town of Santa Barbara ("a pretty place," he called it). He commanded nine American soldiers and "the statliest Dons and prettiest Señoras in all California." But the early elation was premature, and while in Santa Barbara Talbot heard news of the insurrection in Los Angeles. As the rebellion spread northward, there followed for Talbot a melodrama of motto seals hidden in cigarillos, midnight retreats, and guerrilla engagements in the hills. Talbot and his men withdrew across rugged terrain toward Monterey, despite "starvation, cold, nakedness, and every sort of privation." It was the hardest trek of his life, and "I have had some rough ones," he wrote.

Stockton hurried north from San Diego to join with Kearny; Frémont moved south from Monterey; and the rebellion in Los Angeles was subdued. The local capitulation was signed, shooting in the area ceased, and only a peace treaty remained to ratify the conquest. Talbot's march from St. Louis to Santa Barbara had indeed paralleled the expanded sovereignty of his country.

MONTEREY, ALTA CALIFORNIA
July 24th 1846

MY DEAREST MOTHER,

Since I wrote in August last from Bent's Fort until the present time I have not had the slightest chance of writing until the present time. When we left Bent's we proceeded up the Arkansas tracing that River to its source high in the Rocky Mountains, traversing the Bahia Salada and pase.[1]

---

[1] The details of the route of the Frémont Third Expedition between Bent's Fort and Salt Lake are in most sources obscure. Talbot's information here is helpful. The party followed the Arkansas River to its headwaters near the

Crossing one of the main forks of the Rio Grande we fell on
White River all this time travelling in a handsome Mountain Country abounding in game, buffalo elk deer and mountain sheep.[2] White R. possesses but little interest to the
voyageur but much to the Geologist from its curious shell for-
mations. On White R. we met sevl villages of Youtas from
whom we purchased horses to recruit our own weary stock.[3]
We also fell in with Jos Walker who joined us as our guide.
White R. empties itself into the Colorada of the West[4] nearly
opposite to the mouth of the Vinté River which as you remember we explored last season. We took up the Duchene
Fork of the Vinté reaching the Lesser Youta Lake by way
of the Timpanoga River. We then went north camping on
the southern side of the Great Salt Lake into which the
Youta Lake empties itself: this was early in October.[5] After

Continental Divide above present Leadville, Colorado. Beyond present Tennessee
Pass they picked up the Piney River and then traversed several ridges to examine
points on various tributaries (the White, Uinta, and Timpanogos rivers) of the
Grand and the Green. The expedition spent at least twelve days on and around
Salt Lake before entering the Great Basin. From Crane's Branch and the Mary's
River they moved along the larger stream which Frémont named the Humboldt
(Talbot called it Mary's River). This they followed to Walker's Lake named
for Joseph Reddeford Walker (Talbot mentions the lake of the Salmon Trout
River) on the skirts of the Sierra Nevada. Here the party separated and Talbot's
group moved south to Walker's Pass, through which they entered the San
Joaquin Valley.

[2] Talbot here probably mistook the Colorado for the Rio Grande, one of the
"main forks" having been the Eagle River, although Piney Creek is indicated on
Lieutenant G. K. Warren's "General Map to Illustrate the Reports of Surveys for
Railroad Routes from the Mississippi River to the Pacific Ocean," in *Pacific
Railroad Reports*.

[3] Youtas were the Utes, an important division of the Shoshonean group, whose
historic home was in much of central and western Colorado and eastern Utah.

[4] Rather, Green River.

[5] Utah Lake is a fresh-water body, which in his encounter with it during his
Second Expedition in 1843-44 (even with Joseph Reddeford Walker present

remaining a few days exploring the islands etc. etc. we struck westward and after a few days the Company was divided the Captain taking with him 15 or 20 men and travelling directly westward, while I in charge of the rest of the party with Walker for guide struck over to Mary's River which we followed in its devious course to where it empties into Mary's Lake. Then bearing South we reached the lake of Salmon Trout River at the foot of the California Mountains, our appointed Rendezvous in the end of November. From here the Captain went into the mountains intending to cross and from Sutters to return with supplies to another rendezvous on a stream running from the mountains into the valley of the San Joaquin River. I remained nine days at S Trout Lake to recruit the animals leaving it about the 8th of December I believe (for I have not got my note book with me or in fact anything beside my riding equipage, a mosquito bar, and a dirty shirt). Most of the men were afoot our food horse meat and the country sublimely desolate affording no game and inhabited by hostile indians. We spent a rather gloomy Christmas and on the 27th of December reached our appointed rendezvous. In accordance with my orders I lay three weeks at this place but the deer on which we had been living at this place failing and a single snow of two feet having fallen on a little mountain which lay between us and the valley, I deemed it advisable to hurry into a better Climate. We soon reached the valley of the Joaquin coming in abreast of the large Tulare Lake. There I could learn nothing of Frémont from the nu-

and ready to correct him) Frémont made a part of Great Salt Lake, as shown in the map contained in his *Report* of 1845. Warren's map of the Trans-Mississippi West of 1857 shows the lake emptying into the Jordan River, which feeds (with the Bear and the Weber) Great Salt Lake.

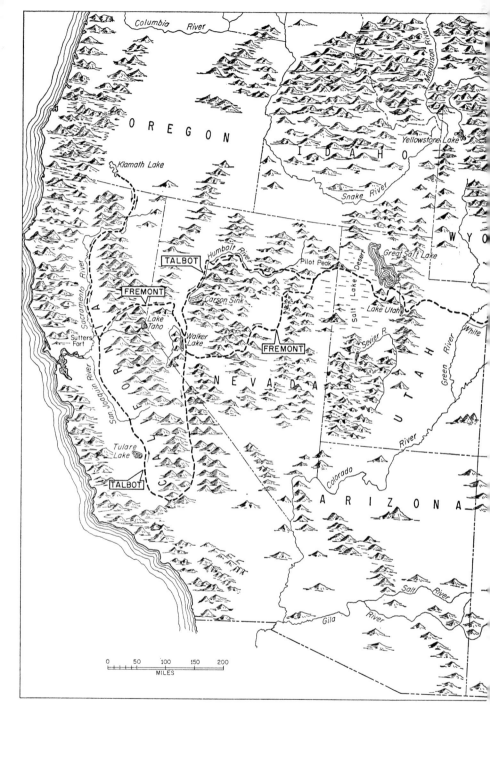

Routes of John Charles Frémont's Third Expedition to California.
Based upon the Frémont (Charles Preuss) Map of 1848 in *House
Misc. Doc. 5, 30 Cong., 2 sess., Serial 544: Geographical Memoir
upon Upper California, 1849.*

merous rancherias of indians which line every stream. Concluding some accident had occured I took up the line of march for Sutter's Fort, moving as fast as the state of our animals and men would allow: we had abundance of game Wild Horses, Elk, deer bear etc. etc. When I reached the Calaveros I met a man [Le Gros Fallon] from Sutters Fort who told me the Captain had come in to Sutters and started with Cattle and provision to meet us but owing to a misunderstanding with Walker as to the place of rendezvous had gone into the Mts on a different stream to the one we were laying on[6] and losing his Cattle and horses had returned to Sutters and was now in a town South of the Bay of San Francisco [San Jose] preparing to search for us again. I sent Walker ahead to the Captain and we turned our march that direction. The Captain sent out fresh horses and in 4 or 5 days we joined camps at the Pueblo de San José a Spanish town   The Captain having received permission to pass through the country and buy stores and recruit generally. I have much tell you of the settlements the Californians their manners the Missions and a thousand other things which I could not even name in a hurried letter. But all this I must reserve to bore you with when I return to our own dear hearth, O how I long to be there and how sorrowful it makes me to think about home but God knows I should not. For I am well, treated kindly and perhaps better satisfied than if I was at home idle but still there is nothing in all the world like being petted by a Mother and an affectionate Sister. But I must stop my digressions for I could

---

[6] The misunderstanding was occasioned by the assumption that only one river, instead of two, ran into the Tulare basin. Frémont subsequently corrected the error by naming the Kern River for Edward M. Kern, thus distinguishing it from the Kings River.

never get tired of telling you how much I love you though perhaps you might. So I will try to talk about something more interesting.

After the Camp was once more reunited we travelled slowly through the settlements and farms or rather Cattle Ranches for they raise little else but cattle and horses taking our ease. We visited Santa Cruz a little town immediately on the ocean and lay there several days. We then went on towards Monterey, and had got within a few days travel of that place when we received peremptory orders to quit the Country from Genl. [José] Castro on account of orders from Mexican Govt and some rows our men had got into.[7] But the true reason was he wanted to make a move against Pio Pico the actual Governor who he wishes to throw out.[8] Captain said that he wd leave the country, but wd not be driven out. So we took position in La Natividad Mt. and Castro marched out 200 men to St Johns a fortified place, taking no steps against us though within 4 miles; we left on the third day for Sutters Fort which we reached March 23d. I was sent down the Sacramento and across the Bay of San Francisco to Yerba Buena to buy supplies. While I was there Taplin my old friend left the Capt to go with Walker (who had also left us) to the United States. The Captain wrote home by him, so I hope

[7] José Castro (ca. 1810–60) was raised in Alta California and engaged in various revolutionary activities, such as support of Alvarado in 1836. After leading the revolt against Micheltorena in 1844–45, Castro became commander general and military governor of the province. Thomas O. Larkin, *The Larkin Papers*, ed. by George P. Hammond (10 vols.), V, vi–vii; hereinafter cited as *Larkin Papers*.

[8] Pio Pico (1810–94), like Castro, was a native Californian who participated in the various local revolutions. After the overthrow of Micheltorena he became constitutional governor of the province in 1846. *Larkin Papers*, V, vi; Pico to Larkin, June 29, 1846, *Larkin Papers*.

that you will hear that I was well, also the reason why I did not write, having no knowledge of Taplin's intention. About 25th of April we started for Oregon but had only reached the Klamet Lake when Lt [Archibald H.] Gillespie of the US Marines overtook us with orders directly from the United States for us to return to California.[9] he also brought me letters from you my dearest Mother. One which you say will be the last dated October. Need I tell you the pleasure they gave me and how happy I was to hear you were so comfortable We lost here 3 men killed by indians. One of them Basil Lajeunesse [also Crane and Denny]. We returned to California soon after we got in a party of the Am. Settlers started from Sutter's [?] Neighborhood and brought Genl [Mariano G.] Valejo and his brothers with a Mexican Col. prisoners back to Sutters.[10] They left 25 men in possession of the Sonoma Mission. As soon as the news reached Castro he prepared to come and attack sonoma. We went to the rescue, before we got there however, one of Castro's best Capt's [La Torré] had crossed with 70 men[11] he had attacked a little party of scouts [under H. Ford] consisting of 15 Americans from Sonoma the garrison having been reinforced by new settlers.[12] The 15 killed 2 of the 70 recovered 2 prisoners and

[9] Lieutenant Archibald H. Gillespie (ca. 1813–73), the United States Marine whom Werner Marti has called the "messenger of destiny," brought secret dispatches from the War Department. He remained in California and fought during the conquest. Marti, *Messenger of Destiny, passim*; *Larkin Papers*, V, v. ff.

[10] The Californians captured in the Bear Flag Revolt, June 14, 1846, were Mariano Vallejo (ironically enough, an advocate of Californian independence from Mexico), his brother Salvador, Colonel Victor Prudon, and Jacob P. Leese. *Larkin Papers*, V, 81.

[11] Joaquin de la Torré was the young captain sent by Castro to control the Bear Flag outbreak. *Larkin Papers*, V, 95.

[12] Henry L. Ford (ca. 1823–56), a New Englander, was one of the early settlers of the Sacramento Valley and subsequently active in the conquest.

Pico out of power and Castro himself usurping it. Soon after taking these horses the same party went to Sonoma surprised Genl. Valejo the head of that department, took him and his brothers and some other officers prisoners back to Sutter's Fort leaving a party in possession of the Sonoma Mission which is a place fortified with cannon. A boat from the US Ship Portsmouth brought us supplies to Sutter's but the Comman[der] [John B.] Montgomery could not interfere in the impending struggle until news came of war from US or Mexico.[16] In a few days we heard that Castro was sending an army for the purpose of retaking Sonoma and exterminating the Americans. We immediately started post haste for Sonoma 80 miles distant and arrived the day after a party of scouts only 15 in number had had a skirmish with La Torré one of Castro's bravos and best captains and killed 2 recovering two prisoners. They However killed two Americans going express to rouse the settlers to arms. They butchered them very cruelly cutting them to pieces limb by limb. We started immediately for San Rafael where we heard the Californians were 40 miles from Sonoma. We charged in about noon but we found that they had run off the day before. We took the Alcalde and several other prisoners; in the evg. our men shot 3 couriers who had just landed from San Pablo a point of land on the other side of the bay opposite to the Mission of San Rafael. There lay another detachment of Castro's troops under Carillo[17] who wished to cross and effect a junction with

[16] John Berrien Montgomery (1794–1873), commanded the *Portsmouth*, which was guarding San Francisco Bay. *Ibid.*, 538.

[17] José Antonio Carrillo (1796–1862), had been banished by Pico, but during the Bear Flag revolution in 1846 he returned to act as one of Castro's chief lieutenants. He signed the Treaty of Cahuenga as Mexican Commissioner in January, 1847.

La Torré. The Capt. started after La Torré leaving me with a little party to hold San Rafael and to watch their movements at San Pablo etc. etc. La Torré escaped precipitately seizing some boats at Sausalita and crossing the bay. We all went back to Sonoma. I spending the 4th of July there and the Captain arriving the same night. We had a fandango there We then returned to Sutters Fort and had hardly got there when an Am. Flag and orders from Comm Sloat arrived, for the Captain to join him as soon as possible at Monterey. Our own old party we have about 55 or 60 men. The Californians have organized into 3 companies with their own Captains. All told there are about 250 men all under Capt Fremont's immediate orders. Friend Kern is in command of Sutters. We started for Monterey and arrived five days since. We found there Commd Stockton in the Congress who takes the place of Sloat in command of the squadron and is sent specially for this taking of California. Capt [Samuel F.] Dupont[18] brought me a letter from Mother dated July he is in the Congress. The Cayenne [Cyane] Savannah Levant and Congress with the Portsmouth which has taken Yerba Buena etc. We stayed at Monterey 2 or 3 days and the whole time our camp was filled with Am and English officers who admired much the fine rifle shooting and the rough hardy mountaineers who handled them. Nearly all the officers were on shore the evening we arrived. We frightened the Spanish ladies terribly such a half wild looking set we are. Bye-the-bye there are a great many very handsome ladies in Monterey

---

[18] Commander Samuel Francis Du Pont (1803–65), grandson of the munitions-maker for the American Revolution, had been appointed to the U.S. Navy at Jefferson's intercession. He now captained Commodore Stockton's flagship, the *Congress. DAB.*

but they are rather shy of attentions from Americans just now. I met sevl Washingtonians on ships Lieut [Edward F.] Beall,[19] [William A.T.] Maddox,[20] [William P.] Speiden,[21] Forrest, and Capt Frémont has recd Commission of Major with command of California Battalion. This Morning I recd the following orders

"US. Frigate Congress
Bay of Monterey

"Sir

You are hereby appointed a Sergeant Major
"in the California Battalion of United States troops
"and will report to Major Frémont for duty.

| To Sergeant Major | Faithfully |
|---|---|
| Theodore Talbot | Your Obt Servt. |
| California Battalion | BF. Stockton |
| | Commander in Chief etc." |

I act as Sergt Major of the whole Battalion: In our Com-. pany Carson [Richard] Owens[22] Maxwell are lieutenants. Mr Gillespie I believe has been made Captain in our old Company. Dr. [Edward] Gilchrist is first surgeon[23]--purser

[19] Edward Fitzgerald Beale (1822–93) came to California with Stockton and Du Pont in the *Congress*, with the rank of master in the navy. He fought in California during the conquest and as a courier made six trips from ocean to ocean, 1847–49; from 1852 to 1856 he was Indian agent for California and Nevada. *DAB*.

[20] William A. T. Maddox was appointed by Stockton to command the central section of California during the conquest.

[21] William O. Speiden, was purser on the *Congress*.

[22] Richard Owens, with Kit Carson and Godey, was one of Frémont's triumvirate of the greatest Western scouts. Frémont, *Memoirs*, 427.

[23] Edward Gilchrist, surgeon for the *Congress* and the *Cyane*, served in the same capacity for the California Battalion.

47

[Daingerfield] Fauntleroy is in command of a party at St Johns Mission.[24] I have to take some orders papers to town directly and our letters to Commodore Sloat so I must stop writing and obey orders as we are now US Troops. Though much against my will I am inclined to think that we are fixtures here in California for the next six months. The thought makes me homesick but fate wills it and we must be resigned. Captain does not think he can write if not assure his amiable wife of his good health. remembrances to all my friends

and unceasing love for Mother and yourself.

Your Affect Brother

THEODORE TALBOT

(Castro has gone South to join Pico and we are going after them. I will try and write again if it be possible J.T.T.)

CIUDAD DE LOS ANGELES—
UPPER CALIFORNIA
Aug 29th 1846

MY DEAR MOTHER,

We sailed from Monterey the 26th of July in the US Ship Cyane Capt. Dupont. We had a passage of 3 days to San Diego the lowest port of Upper California in Lat. 32° + min. We took peaceable possession of the little town of San Diego. Castro being 150 miles north near the Ciudad de los Angeles the seat of Government of California, having effected a junction for the country's welfare with his enemy Gov. Pio Pico.

We lay at San Diego till the 8th of Aug. being unable to proceed for want of horses We at length succeeded in

---

[24] Daingerfield Fauntleroy (1799–1853), purser on the *Savannah*, was engaged in commanding Dragoons at Monterey in 1846.

mounting our own company of 80 men and part of Captains [Henry L.] Ford and [Granville P.] Swift's[25] Companies having about 120 men, leaving 50 men under Capt. Gillespie to garrison San Diego. We pushed hard towards Angeles but before we arrived there discovered that Castro had fled to the south to Sonora a Dep. of Mexico with a very few men. Pico lay concealed and the whole force of 500 men disbanded. Com Stockton had made a landing at San Pedro 25 miles from Angeles and was marching up with cannon. We camped two miles from Angeles: the same day Stockton came up with his force of Marines and sailors and we all marched into the town.

This is one of the principal towns of California, they cultivate the grape here to a considerable extent and the place is surrounded by fine vinyards. We stayed here two days and then Cal Battn. marched South. I stopped at the Mission of San Luiz Rey which is govt. property, when I have an opportunity I have much to tell you of interest regarding these splended Missions. [Ezekial] Merritt[26] with 20 men finally ascertained that Castro was gone to Sonora and Pico will give himself up shortly, so the war is over. Major F. went to San Diego 35 miles from San Luiz in a few days however we all reunited in the vicinity of Angeles. We will next move North to Sutter's Fort 700 miles and upwards. Frémont has been appointed Governor of California for one year and Gillespie Lieut. Govr. The new Government will be organized shortly. The present military force of California is to be kept up and

[25] Granville P. Swift was an early settler in the Sacramento Valley and, after the conquest, first treasurer of Colusa County.
[26] Ezekial Merritt, rough Kentuckian, pre-conquest settler in California, was a leader of the Bear Flag Revolt.

increased. Our old *party proper* are compelled to remain here this winter and return home next Spring if they wish. Fremont has as yet done nothing for me; the appointment I now hold of Sarge Major being one of no consequence to me. Whether he will or not I can't pretend to say. He treats me kindly however and my health is excellent and also what I esteem much I have the good will of our men. I have found many agreable associates among the naval officers. We have just heard of the declaration of war.[27] I suppose there has been a great turmoil in the states. I have been overwhelmed with work last few days overhauling the public archives which I found in a house in town concealed. An Express is on the eve of starting to the United States under Carson and Maxwell. It has been kept perfectly secret and it said they will be allowed to take no letters. they leave this evg. I have had barely time to scribble these hasty lines. I hope to slip them along. If they reach you they will assure you of the unceasing love of a devoted brother and son Kind remembrances to every Friend. I hope you will see Carson or Maxwell in Washington that they may tell you how hardy and well I am. Treat them well. I like Maxwell much.

Ever your Affect Son
THEO. TALBOT

ANGELES. Jan 15th 1847

DEAR MOTHER

I have this day received the first intelligence from you for 17 long months. Capt. [William H.] Emory[28] tells

[27] Congress declared war on Mexico on May 13, 1846. It is hard to believe that Talbot did not know of the declaration before August 29, the date of this letter, since word had come to Frémont and the men near Sacramento on July 10 or 11.

me that he was requested by Col Abert to inform me, in case
he should meet with me, that you were quite well; this was
in June last and is the only news from home that I have heard
since your letters handed me by Capt Dupont USN dated
July in 1845. Think Dearest Mother what are my anxieties
and how sad my heart ever involuntarily yearning towards
you. But why burden you with *my* gloomy thoughts when I
know dear Mother that you too have pined so long for your
own, own Son! Let me rather induce you to bear with tranquil
resignation that fate divine which rules our mortal destiny.
I trust ere this that you have been cheered by my letter of
last Sept, which would assure that I was well and as contented
as a man may be away from his life, his happiness. O how
justly but too late have I learned to value the priceless purity
of your love as I look with introverted eyes on those brief
months spent so happily, when I was first taught to faintly
estimate a Mother's love, and I wake with a chill shudder to
the cold selfishness of the world around me. Since last I wrote
you I have led an active life; Col Frémont left the Pueblo
de Las Angeles in Sept, under command of Capt. A. H. Gillespie with 30 odd riflemen, the Commodore [Stockton] having entirely withdrawn his forces and proceded with his
squadron to San Francisco. We moved to the north, the Col
having with him only some 40 men (his old party) the rest
of the force having in part preceded us, and part been disbanded, with the exception of two small parties stationed
South of Angeles. I was left as Military Commandant of the

[28] William Hemsley Emory (1811–87), West Pointer who distinguished
himself chiefly in surveying the West, especially the Northeastern boundary,
1844–46, and the Mexican Boundary, 1848–57. William H. Goetzmann, *Army
Exploration in the American West, 1803–1863,* 158–201.

town and jurisdiction of Santa Barbara a pretty place lying on the ocean 100 miles North of Angeles: and the principal town between Angeles and Monterey. There were only nine men left with me, it being the Colonel's intention to recruit at the North and return immediately. The Prefect, the principal civil authority of the Southern Dept. resided there and I was left for the purpose of supporting him. My position was a very pleasant one, Santa Barbara being the residence of some of the statliest Dons and prettiest Señoras in all California.[29] I had been here however but a few days. when I received a Correo post haste from Capt Gillespie, bringing news of a rebellion in the South. The Pueblo being surrounded by 500 of the Californians under arms. The courier had barely escaped with his life and brought me only Gillespie's Motto Seal concealed in a cigarita, to vouch for the truth of what he told. Having warned me he hurried to the North to give the news to the Colonel and Commodore. I spent several anxious days every moment expecting to be attacked in my barracks. Hearing news only through the women who noble and disinterested always in the hour of need would give me such little information as they could obtain with regard to the motions of the insurgents. Here let me remark that nothing has surprised me so much in my little intercourse with the Mexicans as the humanity and charity of the women as compared with the almost brutal ferocity of the men. You will recollect that Kendall sustains the same opinion with reference to the Santa Fe Expedition.[30] Although my position was

[29] Talbot was probably housed with Thomas Robbins, local businessman and rancher, judging from a letter in the New York *Weekly Tribune*, April 10, 1847, which says Talbot was quartered in "Robin's house."
[30] George Wilkins Kendall, *Narrative of the Texan Santa Fé Expedition* (2 vols., New York, 1844).

very precarious I kept a firm *upper lip* in order to keep *down* the people of Santa Barbara which has some 70 fighting men and several resident Mexican Officers, until aid could be received from the North. I succeeded in this until the Pueblo was taken and Gillespie forced to Capitulate. Manuel Garfias the commander then marched with 200 men on Santa Barbara.[31] They surrounded the town and sent in a letter demanding my surrender and guaranteeing our lives etc. etc. They gave us two hours to deliberate. We had all determined not to surrender our arms and finding the place we then occupied untenable with so small a force, we determined to push for the hills, (our best ground for fighting) or die in the attempt. I accordingly marshalled my little force and marched out of the town without opposition, those who lay on the road retreating to the main force which was on the lower side of the town. The few foreigners living in the town dared not assist me and the Californians all of course took arms against us. Having so unexpectedly been allowed to pass their force I camped in the hills overlooking the town and determined to remain there a few days and cooperate with any force which might be landed at Santa Barbara I remained here eight days when the Californians having discovered my whereabouts,

[31] Manuel Garfias came into Alta California with Micheltorena's army in 1843 and stayed after Micheltorena was ejected by the Californios. Garfias acquired the San Pasqual Ranch (modern Pasadena) soon after his arrival.

In a footnote, Bancroft points to the Talbot letter of January 14, 1847, as having been used by Thomas C. Lancey in preparing his diary for the San Jose *Pioneer*, February 1, 1879–September 10, 1881. This fact suggests that Mrs. Talbot let others read Theodore's letters at the time. Theodore Hittell, *History of California* (San Francisco, 1897), II, 603, adds that Talbot himself raised the flag over Santa Barbara when the town was retaken by Frémont on December 27, 1846. Since Talbot was with Frémont at the time, the story is quite likely true.

finally determined to rout us out. Not knowing my exact position they had divided into 2 or 3 parties and one of them consisting of some 40 men happened to strike upon the very spot where I was. I was aware of their coming, and had given my men orders not to fire until they were in among us. But my men were so eager to get a shot, that two of them who were posted in the arroyo or ravine nearest the enemy, forgetting my instructions fired just as they came marching in on us. They had fired too far for their own shots even to be effective. Killing only the horse of one and wounding the horse and grazing the hip of another of the enemy. But the Californians fled nor would they again come within reach of our rifles, pouring a fire from their long carbines, from the neighboring hills. They sent a foreigner to me, offering to allow me to retain my arms and freedom giving my parole of honor not to interfere farther in the war about to be waged. I sent the man back with word that I preferred to fight. Finding I would not give up, they put fire in all round me and succeeded in burning me out. I eluded them however and after lingering another day in hopes that a force would arrive, I determined to push for Monterey I came down on a Ranch called San Marco where we got something to eat, for we had been starving for several days. We were also so fortunate as to find an old soldier of Genl [Manuel] Micheltorena[32] who was naturally inimical to the Californians. He piloted us across the Coast Mt. which is here 90 miles wide and very rugged, into the head of the Tulare Valley to the lake of Buenavista. Here I was familiar with the country and after a months travel coming some 500 miles, mostly afoot, enduring much hardship and suffering

[32] Manuel Micheltorena was appointed governor of Alta California in 1842 but was deposed in a provincial rebellion led by Pico and Castro in 1845.

we at length effected a junction with Col Fremont at Monterey. They were all very glad to see us for they certainly thought we were all killed, in fact the Californians had circulated that report. You must excuse me for dwelling on my little adventure, for the fact is I suffered more from downright starvation, cold, nakedness and every sort of privation than in any trip I have yet had to make, and I have had some rough ones. Col Fremont had started from San Francisco for the lower country in the ship Sterling but after being out 20 days and much bad weather he was compelled to put in to Monterey. I found him recruiting more men from the new Emigrants and preparing to go by land to the South  A day or two after I arrived, a part of 2 companies under Command of Captains [Charles D.] Burrows [Burrass] and [Bluford K.] Thompson were attacked by the Californians 80 in number the Americans having 57, they fought, 4 Amns. were killed and 3 Californians.[33] Capt Burrows was among the killed. We marched to their assistance to the Mission of St Johns from which place th[ey] were afraid to move as they had a Cavalcade 400 head of horses. We left St John's for the south the 26th of November and arrived at San Fernando the 10th of Jany. This place is 25 miles from the Pueblo which we heard the Commodore and Genl Kearney with 700 men was in possesion of. The Commander of the Californians Don Andres Pico[34] finding it impolitic to wage the war farther sent a deputation of his officers offering to surrender to Col Fre-

[33] Charles D. Burrass had brought south from the Sacramento some thirty-four men to join Frémont at Monterey and was killed in his first engagement. Bluford K. Thompson ("Red-headed or Hell Roaring Thompson") was a captain in the battalion, itching for a fight. Frémont, *Memoirs*, 594–96.

[34] Andrés Pico (1810–76), Pio's brother, had broken his parole to fight in the insurgence and lead the Mexicans at San Pasqual.

mont. Their surrender was accepted and we marched into their Pueblo the 14th of Jany. The volunteer force will be soon disbanded and I will have a chance of returning home I hope. I have written a long letter and said but little except the intention. Love to all friends

THEO. TALBOT

PUEBLO DE LAS ANGELES<br>January 16th 1847

MY DEAR SISTER,

The Commodore's express for the States by the way of Panama still being delayed I hope to slip two instead of one into the letter bag. When last I wrote you we thought the war was over and the Colonel was going to the North to be installed Govenor of Upper California. But no sooner had we withdrawn the force than the people rose, killing some capturing others and in short playing the very de[v]il with us. Carson who was going to the States Express was met this side of Santa Fe by Genl. Kearney with a force intended for this country. He told him the war was over and so Genl. Kearney came on with only a hundred with Carson for pilot. He arrived in the midst of the rebellion, from the Colorada, and was attacked by 150 men of the Californians. They killed Capt B[enjamin D.] Moore Capt [Abraham R.] Johns[t]on Lieut Hammond of Dragoons and wounded Gillespie.[35] 20 were killed of the Dragoons You will see an official report of this disastrous affair There have been several skirmishes in the vicinity of San Diego for the last two months.

[35] Benjamin D. Moore before he came to California served as a midshipman. Abraham R. Johnston, a West Pointer from Ohio, was made captain just before his death at San Pasqual. Thomas C. Hammond, West Pointer from Pennsylvania, was a second lieutenant when killed in the same engagement.

Capt [William] Mervin[e][36] in the commencement of the war landed with 300 and was assisted by Capt Gillespie who had retired to San Pedro the port of the Pueblo de Las Angeles. Capt Mervin[e] was defeated with the loss of 5 or 6 men by 120 Californians the naval forces then took possesion of San Diego which they fortified and about which they have kept their principal force until 14 days since when they commenced their march for this place by land. The Commodore [Stockton] had 700 men including 80 Dragoons and Genl Kearney, they fought twice on the road on the 8th and 9th. Both sides behaved well, 500 Californians were in the fight of the 1st day and two hundred in that of the 2d day who charged on the whole force of the Commodore. There were 3 or 4 killed and several wounded on each side. The Californians drew off their forces and allowed the Commodore to enter the Pueblo without molestation.

Fremont at this time was about 30 miles from the Pueblo with his whole force 400 men and 4 pieces of Artillery. I was made Adjutant of the regiment with rank of 1st Lieut. when I joined at Monterey. We had been forced to move very slowly having to travel in the rainy season with all its impediments. It was the intention of the Californians to have attacked Fremont and they were waiting for that purpose, but when the Commodore came so close they could not resist the temptation to give him a brush. But they had not their former success with the naval forces. Genl Kearney directing their formation . . . . [page torn]

THEODORE

---

[36] William Mervine was captain of the *Cyane* and later the *Savannah*.

# III.

# TO VERA CRUZ
# IN THE SHADOW OF WAR, 1847-48

*After California,* Talbot found himself in a tent (he called it a "rag house") on Governor's Island in New York Harbor. All was crowded and confusing, like any embarkation depot during wartime. "One set of officers come and another go," he wrote. Mess hall conversation, when not on the war, was sparked with rumors regarding the coming court-martial of Captain Frémont. He had been charged by General Kearny with insubordination and conduct in California unbecoming an officer. Talbot was strong in defense of his former commander, wrote at least one newspaper letter to that effect, and narrowly escaped being called to Washington as a witness. When Frémont was found guilty, Talbot was convinced that a conspiracy of West Pointers was involved. More philosophically, he rationalized, "As long as a man remains below a certain mediocrity all is well, he is promising, gallant, this, that and the other; but the moment he rises beyond that point, a host of enemies crowd round, their fawning turned to envious snarles."

In these months Talbot was worried over his own promotion, perhaps sensing that he bore the Frémont stigma, especially to the West Pointers in the army. He dolefully told of one young officer who had stood at the head of the line for twelve years before receiving promotion.

The most engrossing topic on Talbot's mind, however, was the war. It was not a popular war, and the embarkation of the New Jersey Battalion was anything but stirringly patriotic. The men were drunk and obstinately refused to obey orders to board ship, and one officer, attempting to create a semblance of discipline, "got his finger bitten by a private."

On October 12 Talbot embarked for Vera Cruz. It was already too late to see much fighting, and the tardiness was aggravated by shipwreck in the Bahamas and delay in Charleston awaiting transshipment. The battalion did not reach Vera Cruz until March, 1848. By then, Talbot wrote, "the talk is all for peace."

Vera Cruz was the natural approach by sea to the capital. In March, 1847, General Winfield Scott, after establishing a beachhead, besieged and occupied Vera Cruz. The weak Mexican defense at the fortress of San Juan de Ulúa ("the Gibraltar of America" to Talbot) partly accounted for Theodore's feeling that the vanity of the Mexicans was "in inverse ratio to their courage." By the time Talbot arrived, however, even the cause for Mexican vanity had weakened, for Scott had defeated the Mexican Army at Cerro Gordo, and in spite of his army's exhaustion and the bloody battles at Churubusco and Chapultepec, he had entered the capital city.

Any serious Mexican patriotism must also have been undermined by the internal political squabbles which raged between Santa Anna and a host of challengers. Chief of these, General Mariano Paredes, in a coup of December, 1845, had assumed the presidency of Mexico and through his hostility to the United States had been partly responsible for the declaration of war. General Scott, in a proclamation of May, 1847, labeled Paredes an unpatriotic usurper who had caused the United States to take up arms to assist the Mexican people in preserving their republican institutions. Paredes had been everthrown by Santa Anna in August, 1846, been banished for awhile, but was back in Mexico by the time Talbot arrived. He and various others continued to oppose Santa Anna, sometimes leading small military detachments in open revolt.

From March to August, 1848, Talbot sat in Vera Cruz. The treaty which ended hostilities and ceded California and New Mexico had been completed on February 2. In less than a month the United States Senate had approved, but the Mexicans were understandably less prompt. The final exchange of ratifications took place May 30, over two months after Talbot had arrived in Vera Cruz. On June 12 United States troops began to evacuate Mexico City, and by the end of July the last of them shipped out of Vera Cruz. Talbot overheard a cynical, "half-witted" Mexican say that the problem facing the Americans now was no longer "nibbling the cheese, but how to get out of the trap." Theodore found the town a dull place, with no cordiality in its people. Could he possibly have thought that a conquering army would find it otherwise? The constant heat robbed him of energy. He watched the troops pouring back from the interior, gamblers and camp followers at their heels. He described the pink walls of the town and the domes of the churches, but only because he could think of nothing else to write about. There seemed to be no songs in the streets of Vera Cruz as the American troops returned from their first invasion of foreign soil.

"FOWL CAY, ABACO REEFS, BAHAMAS"

Oct 24th 1847

[Without salutation.]

"I know that you will be surprised at the dating place of my letter, so hoping that no ill news may anticipate this mission, I will at once proceed to the Explanation.

"We left Sandy Hook the 12th inst and with few exceptions had favorable winds, and were sailing rapidly to our destination. Both officers and soldiers had entirely recovered from the depression produced by the sea sickness of the first two days. I was, happily, exempt from this evil.

"All things, in fact, promised a pleasant voyage when about midnight of the 17th we were roused from our slumbers by a violent shock, followed by a succession of others, still more severe, together with the gush and gurgling of water, as it forced a passage, telling but too plainly that our noble ship had stranded on the rocks. It was pitchy dark on deck with a slight storm of wind and rain, which soon abated. This proved our salvation, for we had struck on a coral reef, and had the storm increased the ship would probably have been dashed to pieces.

60

"As soon as we struck, sentinels were immediately placed over the main hatch, who prevented any of the soldiers from coming on deck, or interfering with the management of the ship. Our position was very critical for the six hours which intervened from the striking of the ship until daylight revealed our true situation. I need not describe to you (who have felt all the horrors of shipwreck) the anxious suspense of those long hours, when we did not know but that at the next instant we would be engulphed in the raging billows which again and again spent their fury on our shattered hull, making every timber crack and yield in the unequal contest. During this long interval of time I have seldom or never seen more cool courage than was exhibited by the whole command, as they calmly awaited that fate, which apparently promised *but destruction*. The dawn of day however, disclosed, to the westward, and about a mile distant, a low chain of reefy islands, and still farther west, the wooded shores of the Island of Abaco, proving that we were more than fifty miles out of our reckoning, a strange and fatal error! As it became more light we discovered a large ship some miles to the East which was just escaping from the same danger that had overtaken us; while, from the shores of Abaco, we could see the light sail of the wreckers pushing boldly forth to sea. Soon a little fleet of the eggshell craft in which the wreckers tempt the waves, hovered round about our dismantled vessel, like wolves over the carcass of a buffalo.

"Many of them boarded us, and, contrary to the opinion, generally received of this class of men, exhibited much willingness in lending assistance. With their aid, in less than three hours the whole command with most of the personal baggage was safely landed on Fowl Cay. Though saved from the perils of the deep, we found ourselves on a ragged mass of coral rock without water or food and entirely dependent for provision on what might be saved from the ship; for the near Island of Abaco is inhabited only by these poor wreckers, who live on fish and a few of the tropical fruits. In a few days we managed however to collect a good supply of provisions and except in the particular of water, which was scant, lived very well on our newly populated Island.

"Lt Hill was in the meantime despatched to Nassau, 120 miles distant, the capital of the Island of New Providence.[1] There reside the English Governor and the Amer Consul; it is also the principal depot of the British West India Troops. Lt. Hill engaged transports there to carry us to Charleston So. Ca. where we will refit."

I will send this letter by the earliest opportunity. You may expect to hear of me from Charleston to which place write a receipt of this. With much love I am,

Your Affect Son,
(signed)     THEODORE TALBOT

OFF CHARLESTON HARBOR
Sat Nov 7th 1847

DEAR MOTHER

I wrote the accompanying letter expecting an opportunity of sending it to U States before I should sail myself but none occuring I acted as bearer. We embarked on the 27th from Fowl Cay in the following order. Lieut [William] Read[2] with 120 men in a Baltimore clipper, and myself with

[1] Bennett Hoskin Hill (     –1886), District of Columbia West Pointer, became a captain in 1848; rising to brigadier general by the close of the Civil War. Talbot would serve with Hill in Oregon as well as on the Vera Cruz expedition. Heitman, *Register U.S. Army*; ensuing identifications, unless otherwise designated, are from Heitman.

my Company on a Yankee Schooner, the Tulma, bound for Charleston So. Cara. while Capt Van Ness with the rest of the command went in some very small vessels to Nassau where they will get a Brig to carry them to Charleston.[3]

We parted company with our consort bound to North, the same evening that we sailed and after a very long passage have just now taken our pilot off Charleston Harbor. We lay too seven days in a NE gale. The pilot tells us that Lieut Read only arrived yesterday noon detained of course by the same adverse winds. We disembark at Fort Moultrie on Sullivan's Island in the Harbor six miles below the city of Charleston, where we shall remain until refitted. We will probably be here some weeks so you must write often. I will write as soon as I get on terra firma again. This little Episode in our campaign has been rather unexpected and very much more worst than agreable but "C'est la varieté etc" Give my kind remembrances to *all* Friends. My Love to Larned's and Mrs Thornton. Send me a copy of the Last Register issued the middle of the year

Much health and happiness to you Dearest Mother and Sister.

Your Affectionate
THEODORE

FORT MOULTRIE
Jan 2nd 1848

DEAR SISTER,

. . . I have strange to say received no orders yet, but they take their own time about these matters at Washington:

---

[2] William Reed (     –1884), from Delaware, a West Pointer, left the army while still a lieutenant in 1850.

[3] David Van Ness (     –1849), a New Yorker, was advanced to captain, 1842; major, 1848.

in the meantime I find it very dull, having no duty, nor much amusement . . . .

Your Affectionate<br>THEODORE

FORT MOULTRIE<br>So. CA. Jan 31st 1848

[Without salutation.]

. . . We were all made glad a few days ago in seeing the safe arrival of the ship Republic at Vera Cruz. For we had almost begun to fear that she too, had struck up an acquaintance with some coral reef. We have since had the pleasure of receiving letters from several of the officers, in which they say that they have had an exceedingly pleasant passage and are now safely quartered, some in barracks in the city, the others in the Castle of San Juan d'Ullua. Col Bankhead proposes getting up an expedition against Orizaba and some have his promise to be allowed to accompany it. The 1st Artillery are to be the permanent garrison of Vera Cruz. Maj [Justin] Dimmick is Governor of the city,[4] Capt. [George] Nauman of the Castle.[5]

We had some rain last week but the weather is generally most delightful. I have given up expecting orders and have been to a tailor to get a suit of citizen's clothes. They will take me by surprise some fine morning I suppose, but

[4] Justin Dimick (      –1871), a New Englander from West Point, was made a captain in 1835; major in 1850; and colonel in 1861; he retired in 1863. He had been decorated at Contreras, Churubusco, and Chapultepec.

[5] George Nauman (      –1863), a Pennsylvanian who had graduated from West Point eighth in his class, became captain in 1837, major in 1853, and colonel just before his death in 1863. He had fought gallantly at Cerro Gordo and Churubusco.

dans la même temps I shall make myself comfortable. I wish that you would work me another pair of slippers, talking about comfort, for I miss exceedingly the last pair which you made for me.

Capt Van Ness discovering that our larder was in a rather dilapidated state, cleared out for Charleston and if I do not follow his example and take t[he] next boat, I shall be minus my dinner. With much love to Mother and yourself.

I am, Your Affect. Brother

THEODORE

Sun 19th 1848. March
HEROIC CITY OF VERA CRUZ
MEXICO

DEAR SISTER,

The ship New Orleans arrived yesterday, by her, I received a letter from Mother addressed to me at Charleston which had been forwarded. Lt Col Emory, came out passenger and is going into the interior: with him go Dr. Ringold, who is from Washington, he is a relation of Dr. Thomas'.

Genl [Joseph] Lane with his staff also arrived in advance of the train from the City of Mexico, yesterday morning.[6] With him came Lt. Hays of the 8th Infy of whom you may have heard me speak, when I first went to Fort Columbus.[7] He says that they have had some very exciting skirmishes

[6] Joseph Lane (1801–81), had been made a brigadier general of Volunteers from Indiana at the beginning of the Mexican War. Prior to that he had served in the United States Senate. In late 1848 he was appointed territorial governor of Oregon, which subsequently elected him its United States Senator. *DAB*.

[7] Alexander Hays (1819–64), Pennsylvanian and West Pointer, served courageously at Palo Alto and Resaca de la Palma. He resigned after the Mexican War but returned to the service during the Civil War. He was breveted colonel at Gettysburg and died in the Battle of the Wilderness.

with the guerillas. Now the cry is all for peace—peace. He has had some difficulty with Genl. [William O.] Butler and resigned his commission in consequence.[8] He has a rich wife whom he married in Pittsburgh so that he can afford to resign with more ease than most subalterns can. I am sorry however that he should leave the Army. Mrs Capt. Chase, I just hear, has come over with her husband in the New Orleans. She will remain only a few days returning in the same vessel.

Col Tenobia sent in word to Genl [David E.] Twiggs, that he intended to comply with the terms of the armistice and asked permission to enter this city with his troops: he offers to cooperate in putting down the guerilla warfare.[9] Genl T. thanked him for his offer but at the same time intimated that he considered the Colonel not much better than his fellows. Some of these troops came in this morning. Our own train is also coming in to day. Many officers on their way home to the United States, are accompanying it down. Genl. Twiggs will go home in a few days, Col [Henry] Wilson relieving him in the command of the department.[10]

Last Thursday afternoon, four Companies of our Regt. had to perform the melancholy part of funeral escort to the remains of Lt Co. [George W.] Allen of the 2nd Infy, who

[8] William Orlando Butler (1791–1880) had fought with Andrew Jackson at New Orleans and with Zachary Taylor at Monterrey, succeeding Winfield Scott as commander shortly before the treaty of peace. After the war he entered politics.

[9] Probably Cenobia Jarauta, sometimes referred to as Col. Zenobia. See fn. 26 below. David Emanuel Twiggs (1790–1862), fought in the War of 1812. Just before the Mexican War he became a colonel and served with Taylor. His controversy with Worth caused considerable trouble in Taylor's command. He was military governor of Vera Cruz between December, 1847, and March, 1848.

[10] Henry Wilson ( –1872), Pennsylvanian, had begun his service in the War of 1812 and had worked his way up to lieutenant colonel in 1842. He was decorated for bravery during the Mexican War and resigned the army in 1861.

died the day previous of Pneumonia and fever.[11] I had the command of Capt [John H.] Winder's Company:[12] the whole escort, commanded by Maj. [Joseph H.] Lamotte.[13] He was buried at the "Campo Santo," ½ a mile from the City. The funeral Service was read by an officer of his Regiment. Firing three vollies over his grave, we filed from the grave yard gates, when our band struck up a lively air and we marched in quick time, back again to the City. But the gayest air and step will not serve to banish from our minds the thought that we too are mortal and that many who returned keeping pace with that gay music would yet be borne back accompanied by its most solemn dirges. There is a Chapel in the middle of the "Campo Santo," but being on the line of the American invest-ment it is much injured by the missiles of the Mexicans.

In writing to me I wish that you would number your letters in regular series, in order that I may know whether I am receiving them consecutively. I heard from Orisaba yes-terday. All the officers who were in the "Republic" not of our Regiment, went in that expedition. They are much pleased with that portion of the country. Col Bankhead remained in command there.

Remember me to Mrs Thornton Larneds etc.

Your Affectionate Brother

THEODORE

---

[11] George Washington Allen (    –1848), from Massachusetts, had become a major in 1846. He had fought against the Florida Indians and during the Mexican War had been breveted lieutenant colonel.

[12] John Henry Winder (1800–65), West Pointer from Maryland, was bre-veted lieutenant colonel for conduct in the Mexican War. During the Civil War he was in charge of prison camps for the Confederacy.

[13] Joseph Hatch La Motte (     –1888), West Pointer from North Carolina, was breveted major at Monterrey.

VERA CRUZ. Monday April 10th 1848.

Sister, Your affectionate letter has given me great pleasure, except that you inform me that you have not yet got rid of your cold, which appears to cling to you with all the tenacity becoming that class of unwelcome visitors. But the return of mild weather, will, I hope, soon set you free.

It actually appears strange to think that any one can be suffering of cold. We could spare you two-thirds of our heat to ameliorate your winter and then easily realise the fervor usualy ascribed to the dog days. We had a Review yesterday on the plain outside the walls of the city. The armistice required that the U.S. Troops in Vera Cruz should be marched to the walls, while the Mexican elections were taking place, so Genl. K. availed himself of the opportunity to take a look at us. the General was accompanied by a large Staff, which consisted of the Louisiana Battalion of Infy. and our own, we (as you know) acting as Infy. It was an imposing sight as all Reviews should be and are when well conducted. The General first inspected the troops and then they marched past him to the music of their bands, he chapeau in hand returning their successive salutes. I had command of the Company at the head of the column—that being the post of Capt Winder. Genl. K. has ordered Nauman to take command of the Regt. he being the senior officer present, so he will probably have to leave the Castle of San Juan, which he prefers . . . .

Your Affect. Brother!

THEO. TALBOT

VERA CRUZ. MEXICO
April 20th 1848

DEAR SISTER,

We are living in statu    quo, patiently awaiting the

68

result of the negotiations pending between our commissioners
of peace and the Mexican Congress. In this dull town, we are
left completely to our own resources and very much to our
own Society; our officers do not associate at all with the Mexican and but very little with the foreign Society; there is no
cordiality of feeling existing towards us, for which this place
stands peculiar, as the American Officers have been well received in almost every town in Mexico. We are forbidden to
absent ourselves from the garrison limits, so that when there
is no news arrival, we have nothing to talk or to write about.
Such is our condition now. After looking up and down the
streets, in hope that some subject for my pen would make its
appearance, I have given up in despair, for all is dull and quiet
in this part of town and during this time of the day. I have
nothing left me unless indeed you would like to have a dis-
quisition upon the houses—perchance you would? Here goes.
The houses here, are built of coral rock imbedded in cement
and are constructed in a very solid, massive style, if not intended, at any rate *capable*, of making vigorous defence. The
entrances are always on the ground floor, through a large
gateway, into a paved court yard in the centre of the building
and thence by a broad stone staircase to the second floor. The
lower stories are only used for shops, offices and stables. The
other stories, the houses have generally but two stories however, are occupied by families. The rooms are paved with
either tiles or marble, with lofty ceilings and doors instead
of windows opening to the street from roofed balconies, protected by heavy iron or wooden balustrades. The houses are
painted on the exterior, either white or some light color and
the balconies green, edged sometimes with red. this style has
a gay, pleasing effect: if all the houses were kept in order in-

stead of being suffered to become black and dingy through neglect, as most of them are, the town would have quite a handsome appearance  None of the houses have yards or gardens attached to them and I do not think that there is a vacant lot in the whole city.

The house in which we live at present is in a somewhat elevated position and from its roof we have a good view of the city and adjacent country. The roofs in this part of the world are flat with a parapet wall running round their edges. The Mexican inhabitants commonly resort to these "azoteas," as they call them, at the decline of the day, in quest of the light pleasant seabreezes, which are unable to find their cooling way through the narrow and intricate streets beneath. Here, I also sometimes clamber up, to enjoy the purer air. Looking over the City it appears like one vast paved plain, the breaks made by the narrow streets being hidden from view; this uniformity being occasionally broken by some vast dome, or more towering spire. You can easily pass from house to house, in the same square, by the roofs. Speaking of domes, that of the Cathedral or "Parochia" is quite a conspicuous and handsome object. it is of a dark lead color relieved with white stucco ornaments in the arabesque or Moorish style. The church itself is a very large edifice containing many splendid Chapels and richly decorated altars. There is one Chapel in it, not yet completed, the altar, statues and ornaments, of which are all of pure white marble. Another prominent object, is the Convent and Church of the Franciscans, at present used as the "General Hospital" and now containing 1200 of our sick and wounded soldiers. Then there is the Church of San Carlos—but here comes an orderly with two letters for me, from home. they are postmarked Mar 28 and April 3d. So

I will conclude my letter, (very glad to make the exchange), and send it off to the post office by m[y] orderly. I have received also a register and papers.

With much love, I am,

Your Affect. Brother

THEO. TALBOT

VERA CRUZ, MEXICO

May 8th 1848

DEAR SISTER,

The arrival of the mail is ever a source of pleasant anticipation and we wait impatiently for a distribution of its contents. Thanks to your kind offices I seldom fail to receive home's pleasing tidings. The steamer Eudora, which came in on Saturday brought me your letter (no 8) and Mother's (no 9). I see that you are fully possessed of the laws which govern promotion in the "Line" and of *my* particular chances for the same. I hope that I shall have better fortune than an officer of one of our Infantry Regiments, who is said to have stood at the head of a subaltern grade, for no less a period than *twelve years.*

Among the officers who passed through this city the other day, accompanying the Generals, was my quondam compagnon de voyage, Chas Taplin, now a Captain in the 12th Regt. of Infy. Genl. [Nathan] Towson[14] and the other members of the court of Enquiry and Genl [Gideon J.] Pillow likewise,[15] following Genl Scott's example, went on board the

[14] Nathan Towson (    –1854), Marylander, had been promoted to colonel as early as 1821 and major general in 1848 shortly after Talbot's reference.

[15] Gideon Johnson Pillow (1806–78), from Tennessee, the law partner of James K. Polk and continued confidant of the President, was brigadier general of Volunteers in 1846, made major general in 1847, and fought in most of the

71

steamer which transported them to New Orleans, at the earliest practicable moment after their arrival here. Col Childs passed through with them.[16] he has a leave of absence for two months. I was "Officer of the Guard" the day they arrived and did not see any of them. It is rumored here that more than two hundred brevets have been bestowed on the distinguished officers in the late conflicts: if such be the case, Col. Childs will be made a General. The House of Reps. appear unwilling to take action on the new 11 Regt. Bill, they probably are awaiting the fate of the "Peace of Mexico treaty." I was amused the other evening at a forcible illustration of Mr Polk's policy with regard to the Mexican War, given in a remark made by a half witted Mexican fellow who overheard a party discussing the future policy of the American Government. "Ah Senores," said he, "the question with them now, is not about nibbling the cheese, but how to get out of the trap" having delivered himself of which sage remark he started in pursuit of some unfortunate might of a boy who had presumed to insult him by returning his grimaces.

The Mexicans have a place of resort just outside the "Gate of Mercy" or southern gate of the City; it is called the "Paseo" and consists of a long straight walk paved with stone flagging with stone benches on either side and a few straggling streets. I cannot say much for the good taste of the Vera Cruzians in their selection of a site for a promenade. Chaparral filling the prospect on the one side and the City wall looming up on the other. Nevertheless hundreds find

---

major battles leading to Mexico City but was involved in bitter feuds with General Scott.

[16] Thomas Childs (1796–1853), from Massachusetts, was breveted colonel at Palo Alto and Resaca de Palma; and a brigadier general at Puebla. He died of yellow fever in Florida after the war.

their way out here of an afternoon, come out to enjoy the breeses wafted from the city. Just within the gate of Mercy stand the Cavalry Barracks the largest set of buildings and among the handsomest of the city. they were last regularly occupied, I believe, by the "Muy Valiente Onze," about the time of Santa Anna's return to Mexico:[17] they then marched off to the Frontier to "strike a fatal blow at the North Americans." But whether they accomplished their object this deponent sayeth not.

I have no doubt that you will be fully qualified to instruct me in Spanish instead of my teaching you. I have no Mexican acquaintances and have not studied at all. This climate has completely taken away our energies the heat is so constant that it is impossible to resist its prostration. From the fact of not having much to do I ascribed the feeling to sheer laziness, with myself, but I believe that it may in truth be attributed to the influence of the climate.

My friend Morris' younger brother arrived here a day or two ago; he has come out as clerk to a newly appointed paymaster.[18] We have no news from Queretaro: it is daily expected. Opinions are nicely balanced, but slightly preponderate in favor of Peace. With the love of an affectionate Brother, I say Adios!

THEODORE

VERA CRUZ. MEXICO<br>June 11th 1848

MY DEAR SISTER,

You say in your last letter that 'summer has come

---

[17] The "most valiant ounce" derogates the strength of Santa Anna's men in the defense of Mexico.

[18] The younger brother of Lt. Lewis O. Morris. See fn. 28 below.

upon us suddenly and I feel like a new creature,' I can reverse the seasons and say the same thing. During the last few days we have had refreshing showers, with cooling winds from the North, which have changed the atmosphere entirely, purefying the air and driving away the golden mist which so generally hangs over and oppresses us, like some huge incubus or nightmare, depressing our energies and robbing us of every spark of vitality.

This pleasant change comes opportunely for the troops arriving from the interior, who have already begun to crowd our Mole, eager to embark for the home and longing to embrace the friends, from whom many of them have been long separated. Col Bankhead with a portion of his command from Orizaba has already embarked. Yesterday our seige Train arrived, bringing with them as trophies some forty pieces of Artillery, all captured on the battle field and many of them after most bloody encounters, to which the pieces themselves testify, bearing sundry dints and rude blows on their hard surfaces. One Mexn. piece was struck directly in the muzzle by an Amn. Cannon ball, which passing down the bore lodged in the chamber or bottom of the bore. In so doing it is said to have increased the diameter of the bore a quarter of an inch. I noticed also a beautifully finished field piece, cast at Chapultepec in May 1847. It was quickly destined to fall into the hands of "los Yankees." Others of these pieces were made in England and some in the United States.

Our own heavy guns attract much attention likewise. Capt [John F.] Roland's battery of the 2d arty and a foot company of arty. also arrived yesterday and embark today.[19]

19 John Frederick Roland (    –1852), a West Pointer from Pennsylvania, had been breveted major for gallantry at Monterrey.

Genl. [Robert] Patterson's Division is at a place called Encero merely waiting for transportation.[20] The other divisions are close behind. Officers from the City of Mexico think that there will be a pronunciamento there in a very short time, against the present government. The Vera Cruzians are going to raise a "Guard Mobile," shut their gates and declare themselves independent and the "ever heroic" City of Vera Cruz to be a "Free City." As we are to be the last troops who leave the country we may become witnesses of some their performances and perchance participants, if some growing Santa Anna ambitious of fame, should desire to have a leg shot off by our retreating companies.

It is thought we will leave here on or about the 15th of July, going to New Orleans; of our ultimate destination nothing is yet known, though the chances are in favor of our being stationed on the Gulf of Mexico. These are the least eligible of the Artillery Stations. Colonel Ban[k]head says his Regt. (the 2d) will be about New York. Major [William H.] Polk is here on his way home.[21]

Today is Sunday and as I am going to Church, I will bid you Adieu. Give my love to Mother, reserving a part for yourself. Your Affectionate Brother.

THEODORE TALBOT

[20] Robert Patterson (1792–1881), an Irish immigrant who had fought in the War of 1812 and had commanded a division at Cerro Gordo. Although he served again during the Civil War, his chief occupation was in the field of business—especially sugar, cotton, and railroading.

[21] William Hawkins Polk (1815–62), a Tennessean and brother of President James K. Polk, served in the Mexican War as a major. Before the war he had been a diplomatic minister to Naples and after the war he was elected to Congress, 1851–53.

VERA CRUZ. MEXICO
July 2d 1848

MY DEAR SISTER,

Vera Cruz has been full of noise and bustle during the last two weeks from the embarkation of the troops. All of the volunteers have finally embarked, including the Louisiana Regiment who have constituted (in conjunction with ourselves) the Garrison of the place. We 2d Lieutenants are very glad of this, for the paucity of senior officers renders it necessary that we should be promoted to the more exalted position of "Officer of the Day," who takes his ease in his Inn, instead of keeping watch all night with the rats, fleas, and musquitoes, as do the poor "officers of the Guard."

We have completed the Inventory of Ordnance etc. etc. which I wrote you in my last letter that we were engaged in making at the Castle of San Juan d' Ullua. Although our duty was somewhat laborious I was glad to have an opportunity of examining thoroughly the "Gibralter of America" which independent of other reasons of interest, is considered the most complete fortification of the Western Continent. I regret to add that my friend Morris has been ordered to the castle to supply Lieut. [John B.] Gibson's [22] place and I am therefore almost entirely deprived of his society, which grieves me much.

There are six new Regular Regiments encamped at "Sergara" three miles from the city, also one brigade of the Division under command of General Kearny, who is himself

---

[22] John Bannister Gibson (    –1856), a Pennsylvanian, had been breveted lieutenant after Contreras and Churubusco. He was probably the son of the Pennsylvania Supreme Court Justice of the same name.

quartered in town. Captain [Joseph] Hooker of our Regiment, is his Adjt. General.[23] I have met with Lieut Walker of the voltigeurs, his Regiment will rendezvous at Fort McHenry near Baltimore.[24] But Maj. Genl. Lane leaves for New Orleans this evening. It is currently reported here that the "Warrior of the Army" has been offered the command of the Mexican forces by their Government. The Parades party are hourly gaining strong accessions and very little doubt is now entertained of the present Government being completely overthrown. The well known "San Patricio Brigade" composed chiefly of Deserters has gone over to the Paredes faction as might have been readily expected.[25] The Carlist renegade and Guerillero, Padre Jarauta, is also with this faction.[26] Paredes in his late pronunciamento says nothing of monarchy as was his wont of old, but enveighs against the Government for selling their brethren of California and New Mexico, for a few paltry dollars etc. He is sustained by the priesthood and the officers of the Regular Army. The Government on the

[23] Joseph ("Fighting Joe") Hooker (1814–1879), of Massachusetts, West Pointer, breveted lieutenant colonel at Chapultepec, where, however, his record was preliminary to his better known exploits in the Civil War, especially at Malvern Hill and Manassas and later in command of the Army of the Potomac.

[24] William Stephen Walker ( –1899), from Pennsylvania and Mississippi, became lieutenant in the Voltigeurs (light skirmishers attached to the infantry). During the Civil War he was a brigadier general for the Confederacy.

[25] The San Patricie Brigade was based upon a nucleus of Irish deserters from the United States Army. They had fought for the Mexicans at Buena Vista and Churubusco.

[26] Cenobia Jarauta, Spanish-born priest and former royalist, was one of the chief guerrilla rebels against the Mexican government. John S. Jenkins (*War Between U.S. and Mexico*, p. 473) is one of those authors who have believed a "Col Zenobio" and Father Jarauta to be two separate people. Jarauta was executed in July, 1848.

other hand, place their reliance on the newly established National Guard, who from the indications already exhibited, appear to have no particular predilection for the smell of villainous saltpeter. It is proposed by the Government to set in motion an ambulating guilliotine, which will be accompanied by a large body of troops, a priest and an executioner, the latter two, are to perform their appropriate functions on all persons who may be found on the road unlawfully bearing arms—a salutary and speedy method of getting rid of all evil disposed persons! Bye the bye, we have more than our share of that class among us now, for besides our resident population of Mexican and American scoundrels, we have now superadded, several hundred retainers and followers of our army, who like foul harpies are found in numerous gangs at the rear of each Division, moving with and preying upon its vitals. The restrictions here on gambling have been removed lately, and in every public house (and there are many of them) are a half a dozen Faro, Monte, and Rouge et Noir tables, besides a thousand other contemptible gambling, picayune, games. The Americans bid fair to rival the Mexicans in this great national vice of theirs. I am glad that the Military Commission has been dissolved for we should have been overwhelmed with business. The weather here is very hot and there have been several coups de soleil lately. I am quite prudent and am happy to say have my usual good health. I suppose you know that the 1st and 2nd Artillery Regiments, rendezvous at Govrs. Island. N.Y. It is quite uncertain now when we shall leave this place, whether we shall sail direct from here to New York or first go to New Orleans and from thence go by land or water carriage to our destination. With much love for Mother and yourself. I am etc. THEODORE

GOVERNORS ISLAND. N.Y.H.
Sept 10th 1848

DEAR MOTHER,

We arrived here last night after a long, tedious passage of forty days. We had during the earlier part of the voyage a constant succession of dead calms. In the Gulf Stream, off the Bahamas, we encountered a most tremenduous Southwesterly hurricane which lasted 20 hours carrying away all our sails, our maintop gallant mast and causing other lesser injuries, all of which we were most fortunately able to repair from our extra supply. The Captain of the vessel died the 26th day out and we came very near crowning our chapter of accidents by being shipwrecked on the shore of New Jersey near Barnegat, our ship striking on a hidden shoal during the night; it was very calm and we got her off with some trouble but I believe uninjured and here we are at last safely arrived at Governors Island. Our detachment was commanded by Capt Nauman. I have command of Capt Winder's Compy. the other officers were Capt. Brannan Adjt.[27] Lts. Morris[28] and Chalfin[29] and Asst Surgn. King.[30]

[27] John Milton Brannan (1819–92), West Pointer from Indiana, was breveted captain in 1847 for service at Contreras and Churubusco. After the war he served in various frontier posts. He fought in the Civil War, notably with Sherman in the Georgia campaign.

[28] Lewis O. Morris (    –1864), a New Yorker and second lieutenant, was a good friend of Talbot's. In an earlier letter from Vera Cruz, Morris's younger brother is mentioned (May 8, 1848). On July 2, 1848, Talbot wrote his regrets that his friend Morris was transferred. He narrowly escaped being sent out to Oregon with Talbot. A colonel, he was killed in the Civil War at the battle of Cold Harbor, Virginia.

[29] Samuel F. Chalfin (    –1891), from Illinois, West Pointer, was breveted colonel for service during the Civil War.

[30] William Shakespeare King (    –1895), a surgeon from Pennsylvania. He remained an army surgeon through the Civil War and till he retired as a colonel in 1882.

79

Governor's Island is a scene of no little bustle and confusion nearly all the Companies of the 1st and 2d Regt of Arty being encamped on it besides the permanent party of the Rectg. Depot. . . . I shall have a great deal to do the whole responsibility of the Company devolving on me of discharging men, etc. etc. There are now Nine Companies of the 1st Artillery here. . . .

YOUR AFFECT SON THEODORE

[OMITTED *here are six letters written from Governor's Island and Fort Columbus in New York Harbor between September 14 and October 31, 1848.*]

# IV.

# TOWARD THE WEST BY SEA, 1848-49

*W*hen *Talbot left New York* on November 9, 1848, he expected a four-month voyage across 18,000 miles of "watery waste." He sailed on the *Massachusetts*, a steam and propeller-driven bark of 750 tons, built in Boston and fully equipped with sails to compensate for the unreliability of steam. The submerged screw was her most interesting feature. Since she had no sidewheel or sternwheel, which until very recently had been the identifying marks of steam, one gallant ship rushed to the side of the *Massachusetts* believing her engine smoke to be a fire at sea. Talbot declared the *Massachusetts* to be the first screw-propelled vessel ever to visit Hawaii and only the second steamer. His accuracy is doubtful, however, for by 1848, some forty years after Fulton demonstrated the *Clermont*, no fewer than forty-five American sailing ships had already been converted to steam, not to mention those newly built. It was nearly ten years since John Ericsson had built the *Robert F. Stockton* with a screw propeller. Though Talbot probably exaggerated, he nevertheless sensed correctly that he was living through the first dramatic decade in the expansion of steam navigation.

The *Massachusetts* sailed the long, exotic route around South America, visiting such, to him, strangely fascinating cities as Rio de Janeiro and Valparaiso. Talbot gloried in the pomp of a Christmas midnight mass with the young emperor of Brazil, Pedro II; he was later intrigued by the regal court of the Hawaiian King Kamehameha III. Royalty always appealed to Talbot, but there was an essentially Burkean or Romantic bent to his patrician sensibilities. The church and the gentry should rule but always in the spirit of equal opportunity for all. In Rio, for example, he was glad to find Negroes in the upper classes, riding in plush carriages escorted by flambeaux and outriders. On another occasion he noted the commendable assumption of equality before God while the highest government officials knelt on the same marble floor beside the poorest peasant.

Talbot was unquestionably a Romantic. For him, as for Wordsworth, nature was an informing and purging force, "a presence far more deeply interfused." Deserts were "sublimely desolate." The Straits of Magellan were framed by "impenetrable forests, barren precipices, and impassable morasses." "Seated alone on the rude moss-covered rocks which overhang this wild seashore, with no other sound than the sullen swell of the tide to break upon the stillness, my mind reverted homeward with a melancholy pleasure." No more Byronic image could be invoked than by the young Theodore moved to a satisfying melancholy by a moody and sullen sea.

Beyond the reveries, his letters more often spoke of the immediate present. Everywhere on the Pacific Coast in the Spring of 1849 men's minds dwelt on California gold. In that year 775 ships cleared Eastern ports for California, and no fewer than 50,000 people poured into the Sacramento Valley. As early as February, in Valparaiso, Talbot heard the familiar tales of abandoned ships in San Francisco Bay and troops deserting their regiments. To an officer heading for a frontier outpost, this latter thought was particularly troubling. But he also noted a general decline in morality, and a rising rate of piracy as a result of the gold mania.

Talbot was unquestionably a Romantic. For him, as for Words-lude between his confrontation with Mexico and his later years in Oregon, a kind of sea-shanty intermezzo. It is a mistake, however, to think of the North American land frontier as one series of events and U.S. expansion overseas as another. Within the young nation, deep forces which pushed men across the prairies also impelled them across the seas. And at least one of these drives was the spirit of Romanticism which, although international, nevertheless found a peculiarly congenial soil in American expansive energy. Talbot believed that Cuba and Hawaii as well as California would someday belong to the United States. For him as for his contemporaries the prairie schooner and the commercial steamer were embarked upon similar seas.

FORT COLUMBUS. N.Y.H.
Nov. 7th 1848

DEAR MOTHER,

We are just embarking, all our stores and goods and chattles have already been sent off and we are now waiting for the steamer to take us alongside of the Massachusts which is lying in the stream, opposite to the Island. she looks beautifully, having been handsomely painted and put in order both inside and out. Being a propeller her paddle wheel is in the stern and submerged, which makes her less liable to injury and were it not for her smoke pipe, she could not be recognised as a steam vessel. As we are to go, it is pleasant at least to know that we go out as comfortably equipped as any Expedition could be, going such a distance.

I will try and write to you again before I leave, which will not be until the day after to morrow. I will write to you from Rio Janeiro, and by every opportunity which may occur on our route. Write to me by all the steamers, for we may make a quick trip and I must have letters waiting for me when I arrive in Oregon. Direct your letters to me "1st Reg. U.S Artillery" "Columbia River, Oregon Territory." We do not know where we will locate yet, but letters sent to any part of Oregon will be forwarded to us whereever we may be in the Territory.

My heart is too full to write. My best love to Sister. God Bless you both. Adieu, Dearest Mother.

Your Affect. Son.
THEO. TALBOT

On Board Ship Massachusetts
New York Nov 9th 1848

Dear Mother,

We embarked, as I wrote you was intended, day before yesterday. To morrow at noon, we set sail on our long voyage. We have to pass over Eighteen Thousand miles of watery waste, to reach our destination. We shall be at sea at least four months. It will take about twenty-five days to reach Rio Janeiro. So that you will hear from me in two months time. I will write to you again from Valparaiso or wherever I may find another opportunity.

I hope that you may get acquainted with Lt. Morris, for he is a most sincere friend of mine. You will probably see him, as he will take his wife on to Washington as soon as he gets married, which will be in spring. Remember me to all our kind friends. . . .

Your Affectionate.

Theodore

At Sea, off the Coast of Brazil
Dec. 21st 1848

Dearest Mother,

We shall have been much longer in getting to Rio Janeiro, than I wrote you that we would be, or in fact than any of us expected when we left New York. Soon after sailing however, Captain Wood informed us that he had received special instructions from Genl. Whiting, the Quartermaster in New York,[1] restricting him in the use of the steam power of

---

[1] Henry Whiting ( –1851), from Massachusetts, emerged from the War of 1812 as a brevet captain. He was decorated for bravery at Buena Vista in the Mexican War, becoming a brigadier general in 1847.

the ship, to certain parts of our route, where it was deemed to be most necessary. Moreover we have on board but a very small quantity of coal for a voyage of such long duration and the Captain was not given authority to purchase more, so that in so much as steam is concerned, we find ourselves almost reduced to the level of ordinary sailing vessels. Fortunately however our ship is a very excellent sailer entirely independent of her steam power, which was always intended to be auxiliary to her sails—to be used only during calms and unfavorable winds. Being constructed with a screw propeller after the patent of Capt. Ericsson,[2] with her engines in the lower hold, we are not inconvenienced by her machinery, while at the same time we know that in case of need we have ever a powerful agent at command, for the management of the ship. We can also easily distil an abundance of fresh water for the whole command, by means of the engines, which as you know is no slight advantage at sea, where the want of good [water] is so frequently a source of great privation.

On our first leaving New York we had head winds and much stormy weather for several days, the winds gradually more favorable, although generally light, until after we crossed the Equator, since when, we have had fair winds. On the 27th of November, we spoke the fast sailing British bark "Pursuit," in North Lat. 23° bound from Cork to Mobile, she promised to report us there, all well, and I hope that you saw it in some of the newspapers. On the 6th instant we spoke the U.S Store ship "Relief" but she had left Norfolk for Rio,

[2] John Ericsson (1802–89), Swedish inventor, patented the screw propeller in England in 1836. He came to America in 1839 to build ships for the navy, the U.S.S. *Princeton* (1844) being the first naval ship propelled by screw. He is chiefly remembered as designer of the *Monitor*. *DAB*.

long before we started from New York. This vessel is a notor-
iously dull sailer, having once been a hundred days in getting
from Norfolk to Rio. She delayed the movements of Wilkes'
Exploring Expedition so much, that he was obliged to send
her off home, as soon as he could get rid of her.[3] I understand
that she is now bound to Monterey, Cala., if such be the case
I pity those who are in her. Knowing the character of the vessel we all had a hearty laugh when our Captain, after passing
the customary salutations offered her commander some late
papers, with all the results of the late presidential election.
He replied, "that he was very much obliged indeed, but that
he had not time to stop"—as if fifteen *hours,* much less fifteen
minutes delay, would certainly make him rather late in getting
somewhere. We have come up with and passed several vessels bound to the Southward. We have so easily run by every
ship that we have yet met with, that we may safely consider
ours to be a very fast ship. We have not found it near so hot
as we expected that it would be in the equatorial regions. The
thermometer has never been higher than 86 degrees and most
of the time much lower: we have been lucky however in having
very few dead calms. Our accomadations have proved to be
very comfortable in every respect. My own health is much
improved and I am growing quite fat again.

We spend most of our mornings reading and in the
evening play cards in the cabins or loll about our spacious
quarter deck talking and somewhile puffing away our time as
pleasantly as need be. All the upper decks both forward and

[3] Charles Wilkes (1798–1877), naval explorer, though still a lieutenant was
commander of the United States Exploring Expedition to the Antarctic, Pacific
islands, and the Northwest coast between 1838 and 1842. He later commanded
the *San Jacinto* in the *Trent* affair, 1861. *DAB.*

aft, are covered with awnings, which conduce much to the comfort of the soldiers as well as the officers. We have about a score of soldiers wives, who go out as company laundresses and who manage to make themselves as troublesome as all the rest of the command put together, but I suppose they are necessary appurtenances to a military colony. We are just so far south that the sun passes vertically over our heads and in a little it will pass to the northward of our zenith. Each night, new constellations make their appearance in the heavens and we gradually lose sight of those we have so long been accustomed to see in the north. The Southern Cross which is considered a very handsome constellation is now visible, but I do not think that the stars of the Southern Hemisphere compare with our Northern groups. . . .

We expect to arrive at Rio, day after to morrow, in time for the Christmas festivals, which as Brazil is a Catholic country will I suppose be very extensively celebrated. We will not leave before the first of January so that we will have an opportunity of seeing many of the sights, which I shall not fail to describe to you and in my next letter I promise you to be more cheerful for I fear I have written in too gloomy a strain. Thinking of home I have insensibly grown melancholy. We will probably meet at Rio some of the 2d Infantry. They are under the command of Genl. Reilly[4] but sailed in several different vessels. some of their transports sailed some time before we did the others were to sail after we left. The ship Fanny Forrester was to take out two companies of the 3d Artillery to California and to start just after us.

[4] Bennet Riley (1787–1853), from Maryland, began his military service in the War of 1812. In the Mexican War he was breveted brigadier general at Cerro Gordo, and major general at Contreras. After the war he was military governor of California. He died a few years later of cancer.

87

I think my dear Mother that it would give me more pleasure to have a good miniature of you than the daguerrotype which you promised me. The latter is so easily taken that I might have both. I am sure you will not refuse me. Dec 23d. We have just arrived in Rio. There are two American Men of War here, whose officers immediately boarded us. They tell us that a ship will sail for New York to morrow morning. I shall send this letter by it and write again. It is excessively hot here now it being midsummer, but is quite healthy  My best love to Sister.

Your Affec. Son<br>THEODORE

RIO JANEIRO. Dec. 25th 1848

MY DEAR SISTER,

Immediately after our arrival here I wrote a letter to Mother by the Ship "Courier," which we found on the point of sailing, bound for New York. On entering the Harbor we were hailed from Fort "Santa Cruz," which commands the entrance; finding that the "Massachusetts" was a Government vessel, we were directed to proceed to the Man of War Anchorage, which is directly in front of the City. We had hardly dropped our anchor when we were boarded by a boat from the "Brandywine," the flag ship of Commodore Stover.  he tendered to us the usual civilities and proferred us the use of one of his boats during our sojourn, which however we declined having good boats and oarsmen of our own. We were also boarded by a boat from the French Man of War Steamer lying here, offering us the usual civilities. The officers of the U.S. Brig "Perry" called on us in like manner. We brought with us decisive news of the issue of the presidential contest which was of course a matter of much interest to most of the American Residents who eagerly crowded on board to learn the Result.

Being pretty well tired of the confinement of the ship most of us dressed ourselves and went on shore in the afternoon to stretch our legs. On landing we directed our steps to the "Hotel Pharoux," a fonda situated on the waters edge and the general resort of the foreign naval officers. We met here a Surgeon of our Navy, who kindly offered to act as our Cicerone. We were glad to avail ourselves of his offer and accordingly forth we sallied for a sight seeing stroll. Crossing an open plaza, we first passed the palace or town residence of the Emperor. This building fronts on the water and is of a very unpretending appearance but covers a considerable extent of ground; it has no garden or other enclosures about it, opening directly on the public streets. It is two stories high and a large portion of it was formerly a Carmelite Convent. In the lower part of the palace is kept the main guard in front of which were pacing some sentinels dressed in trim blue uniforms while their officers lounged lazily about the portals. The next place we bent our way was to the "Rua d'ouvidor," the Broadway of Rio Janeiro. In it are the fashinable stores, which are many of them very handsome, making a rich display of jewelry, gold, silver, military equipments, flowers etc. But this street is so narrow that two carriages cannot pass each other without one of them driving over the trottoirs [sidewalks], which are only four feet wide; the houses towering up three and four stories make the way appear still more confined. We were glad therefore to emerge into an open plaza where we actually felt that we breathed more freely. I cannot think what can induce people who live under a *vertical* sun to

89

exclude so perseveringly the slight breezes which might otherwise find their cooling way through their crowded thorough-
fares. In the lower end of the plaza in which we found ourselves, was a large and very handsome fountain round which
thronged hundreds of negroes all carrying water jugs or kegs,
some filling their jugs others waiting for their turn at the
fountain and the whole of them, both men and women, keeping up the most infernal jabbering that I have ever heard.
As their supply is obtained they file off homeward in a trot[?],
singing some monotonous portuguese or African song. The
number of negroes here is immense, about every second person being either a negro or a soldier. Continuing our walk we
entered a public garden handsomely enclosed and neatly orna-
mented with trees, shrubs and flowers. It had also its arbors,
statues and I noticed a very finely designed fountain of
bronze, representing huge monsters of the deep, spouting
forth columns of waters and apparently disporting themselves
in the liquid element. We met here a few ladies enjoying the
promenade. The Brazilian ladies are seldom to be seen in the
streets being kept almost as much secluded as the inmates of
harem.

Returning home we passed the Cavalry Barracks
where we saw the troops drilling, they presented a neat and
cleanly but by no means imposing appearance. Their quarters
seemed to be in most excellent condition. Many of the soldiers are Negroes and even the officers, those too frequently
holding high rank. After having taken a cup of coffee and
sundry Koblers we felt ourselves sufficiently recuperated after
our unaccustomed exercise, to visit the Portuguese Theater of
"San Januario." Our object was more to take a look at the
people then to derive much amusement from a play spoken

in a language which none of us could understand. The portuguese much resembles the Spanish but still differs too much
for one who understands Spanish alone, to follow the thread
of a discourse. Uniforms preponderated here to a greater extent than in the streets [ ; ] there were not a great number of
the weaker sex present and those who did honor the theater
on this occasion appeared to be plain in dress as well as in
features. The audience loudly and in most noisy manner displayed their relish for the performance, which was low comedy.
They displayed more vivacity than I had imagined that they
possessed.

On Christmas eve we visited several of the churches
Midnight Mass being celebrated here with much pomp and
ceremony. The first church that we went to was that of San
Benedict which is attached to the Convent of friars of that
order. We had with us an English gentleman a catholic who
was well acquainted with many of the friars and through him
we were enabled to see the interior of the establishment. The
revenues of this Convent are said to be immense and everything appertaining to the church is of the most magnificent
description. The interior of the Church is covered with the
most elaborate fretwork the whole richly gilt. There are eight
altars in this church besides the high or main altar each dedi-
cated to some particular saint whose statue surmounts the altar.
There is one to the Blessed Virgin under the title of the
"Gloriosa," representing her as a beautiful woman clothed in
the richest robes and wearing a rayed crown of silver and
precious stones. Another bears the effigy of a Brazilian Saint
martyred for his faith in the early settlement of the country.
There was one to St Lawrence who was broiled on a gridiron
and to others that I now forget. In different parts of the church

were suspended huge lamps of silver, gold and glass chandeliers etc. The pavement of the church is of marble richly adorned in different parts with the finest mosaic work. We passed from the church to the robing room or sacristy there is a large beautifully inlaid row of low presses on either side, in the drawers of which are placed the vestments. Handsome oil paintings alternate with the most splendidly framed pier glasses that I have ever seen. The window frames were heavily gilt Adjoining the principal room was a smaller one separated by doors with curtains of cloth worked in gold and silk. In the centre of this apartment was a very large marble fountain with handsomely designed gold figures holding faucets. The priests wash here previous to the ceremonials of the altar. In the lobby between the sacristys are placed cenotaphs of marble and the rich dark woods of the Country, bearing urns, which contain the bones of certain distinguished individuals, Marquises, Generals etc., whose virtues are inscribed on plates of Gold. adjoining the church are long cloisters beneath the pavements of which rest the bodies of the deceased brothers of the order. When we first entered the church they were chanting Matins and soon after the abbot of the order entered the sacristy accompanied by a large train of brethren. The Abbot himself was a fine looking man of venerable appearance. We were much struck by the remarkably intelligent faces of most of the others. Being robed by their attendants they entered the church in a showy procession, the effigy of the infant Christ being borne in a gold cradle and placed near the high altar. The Churches here are said never to be crowded because indiv[id]uals are required to attend their parish churches and there are near *sixty* churches in the City alone. The congregation was principally composed of women, the rich and titled ladies of the land seated side by side on the stone pavement with the dirtiest negresses. With all the splendor and outward solemnity I could not but feel shocked to see the very evident want of devotion amounting to levity almost, in every one present, not excepting the priests themselves. It appeared to be regarded as a superb pageant not as a solemn act of religious worship.

We were invited by the priests to come and see their observatory and library which are said to be very excellent. Ascertaining that I was a Catholic I was asked several questions about the Catholic Clergy in the United States

Leaving the Convent we hurried to the Imperial church to witness the Emperor and his consort receive the Sacrament during Mass.[5] This church was not more filled than the one which we had left we found no difficulty therefore in reaching a position near enough to have a good view of the royal pair. They were seated in a box or balcony on the side of the altar The Emperor was dressed in a dark blue uniform somewhat like that of a general officer. he had a large star on his left breast and a blue net silk scarf over the right shoulder; he also wore a light sabre. he is of medium height rather inclined to corpulency and of light complexion wears red whiskers and is altogether of a most decide[d]ly ordinary appearance. His movements are abrupt and totally undignified. he is now about 24 years of age I believe. Next to him sat his wife dressed in deep black with a black headdress which partially concealed her face. She is older than the Emperor and is by no means handsome. She is at present

[5] The popular and scholarly Dom Pedro II who ruled from 1831 to 1889 and his wife, Teresa Cristina María, daughter of Francisco I, king of the two Sicilies.

93

however in bad health and is in great affliction in consequence of the death of her Mother. Those who are acquainted with her say that her manners are very attractive and that she is beloved by all who know her. In rear of the Emperor sat a lady attendant dressed in deep mourning and three Chamberlains in uniforms. In the body of the church were distributed some of the Emperors body guard wearing gold and blue uniforms with chapeaux and armed with halberds. There were also other soldiers with muskets who were posted among the crowd. The singing was very fine accompanied by orchestral music. The Emperor and his consort descending from their balcony knelt at the foot of the altar receiving the Sacrament from the hands of the Bishop. At the end of the Mass they retired into the palace with which the back part of the Church communicates. Soon after the royal carriages three in number each drawn by eight mules and accompanied by outriders with flambeaux, left the palace for the customary royal residence at San Cristobal 4 or 5 miles out of town. Were it not that the Court is in mourning there would have been immense display during the usual joyous season of Christmas.

The Brazilians are said to be quite republican in their feelings as the Government is in most of its institutions. They have two houses of assembly and during the minority of Pedro II they had an elective regency. . . .

THEO. TALBOT

RIO JANEIRO. Dec 30th 1848

MY DEAR MOTHER,

We dined Christmas day on board the Brandywine frigate, the officers of that ship entertaining us in a most hospitable manner. . . .

94

I have derived much pleasure from a visit to the Imperial Botanical Garden situated on the waters edge five miles below the City. Here are collected trees, plants and shrubs from every quarter of the Globe. It is laid out very neatly in groves, alleys, parterres and walks with numerous grottos, alcoves, cascades fountains etc. They have large *tea* and coffee plantations, groves of mango trees with the ripe fruit growing, bananas shaddocks, pomegrantes, avocado pears limes, oranges, belle apples, coitas, chirimoyas, bread fruit and so on through the whole catalogue of tropical productions; they have likewise all the fruits and plants of the temperate zones which will admit of cultivation in so warm a Climate. The trees and plants indigenous to Brazil are many of them very remarkable either for their growth or the peculiar brilliancy of their hues. Even the birds that hover around among these frag[r]ant groves are of more resplendent hue than any of our own. The whole face of nature animate as well as inanimate, which is independent of man, has here assumed a bolder or more exaggerated type. We found all the spice trees growing here in great perfection, such as the nutmeg cinnamon cloves besides the camphor sago, gamboge and thousands of other curious plants of which even our guide could not give us the names. Dr. Holden our Surgeon[6] who accompanied me was as much delighted as I although with me it was like meeting with old acquaintances to see growing with my own eyes trees and plants that I have so often heard you describe. This garden is planted out after the Linnaen System.

We adjourned to a neighboring cottage half hidden in a grove of bamboo, where we refreshed ourselves with

---

[6] Levi R. Holden (      −1874), Rhode Island army surgeon, breveted lieutenant colonel for meritorious service in the Civil War.

some delicious pineapples and then betaking ourselves to our Cabriolet á postillion, returned to town absolutely tired and surfeited with novelties.

As I have before remarked the negroes are a great feature of Brazil, it being a common saying here that every second person that one meets on the road is a negro and every third a soldier. The free negroes wear shoes by which they are distinguished from the slaves to whom this luxury is not allowed. Many of them arrive at distinguished positions in society and attain great wealth. It would surprise one of our Southerners after passing a gang of negroes loaded like mules, to meet perhaps in the next street another Ethiopian, lolling back in a splendid carriage, with his outriders and all the other accessaries of pomp and wealth and perhaps clothed in the uniform of a General. Apropos Genl. Reilly arrived in the Iowa three days since as has also the Rome another transport of the 2d. Infantry, who are bound to California. So there are no lack of American officers and troops in Rio. We expect to start to morrow, going through the straits of Magellan. Our next port is Valparaiso which is said to be a very pleasant place. From there we hope to go to Callao the port of Lima although that is uncertain. We shall go much faster now for we have taken coals here and will get more at Valparaiso. I do not think including stoppages that we will get to Oregon much if at all before the end of March. We do not expect to go to the Sandwich Islands but still it is possible that we may, it will depend much on the information we receive on reaching our next port which will be in about thirty five days. If any opportunity occurs I will write to you from Valparaiso. . . .

Your Affec. Son

THEODORE

AT SEA, OFF THE COAST OF CHILI
Feb. 7th 1849

MY DEAREST MOTHER,

Having obtained water and such other supplies as we needed, we resumed our voyage from Rio Janeiro on the 1st day of January. The Brazilian Court having laid aside their mourning on that day, the New Year was welcomed in with great rejoicings. as we steamed down the harbor the grim Forts on either hand were thundering forth their noonday salvos, these again answered by all the Men of War the whole echoed and reechoed back among the steep, rocky dells, until the sound fell on the ear like distant thunder. The lofty precipices of barren rock skirting the entrance and in a manner surrounding the Bay of Rio, give to it a most magnificent character which added to its mercantile advantages have caused many to pronounce it the most splendid harbor in the World.

When a short distance out at sea to the Southward, looking back at the mountains near the entrance of the Harbor, they present the appearance of a huge giant lying extended along the shore, the head and upper part of the body being very well defined and reminding one of the stern effigies we see pictured from the warrior tombs in old English Cathedrals. Bye the Bye, I don't think that I wrote you that I had seen Pettrich the Sculptor, several times, while I was in Rio.[7] He appeared to entertain very warm and friendly remembrance of the United States. He said that he had written many times to the gentlemen of G. Town College but had never

[7] Ferdinand (Frederick August) Pettrich (1798–1872), whose models for the west front of the U.S. Capitol were rejected in 1838, was in Brazil in 1847. He may have been back in Philadelphia in 1852. He died in Rome.

97

received any answers to his letters. He has been assiduously engaged at his art during his residence in Brazil. I saw several fine statues executed by him, in the Imperial Museum. He has been well patronized, owns a farm etc. etc.

Life at sea, as you have experienced, is the one, same, unvarying routine. We made Cape Virgen, one of the headlands of the entrance of the Straits of Magelhaens on the 19th of Jan. The same evening a British bark called the "Rover," ran down to us from the entrance of the Straits; when within hail, her Captain begged us to heave to and lend him some aid for his vessel had sprung a leak and with all hands at the pumps the water was still gaining on them. We were very glad to comply with his wish and the poor fellows being reassured by our presence, examined the leak more thoroughly and succeeded in stopping it so effectually that the ship could proceed on her voyage.

The straits of Magelhaens is an intricate passage leading from the Atlantic to the Pacific Oceans, between the main continent of America and the numerous islands which constitute the "Tierra del Fuego." It is occasionally traversed by navigators as it materially shortens the route and the boisterous weather usually encountered in doubling Cape Horn is also avoided. This passage however is very narrow in some parts and is not altogether safe except to steam vessels. In consequence of head winds we lay at anchor all day on the 23d Jany. in Fortescue Bay the Southermost part of Patagonia and some of us went on shore. We found the country exceedingly barren and rugged and although it was here midsummer, yet snow capped mountains and a cold, bleak aspect, surrounded us on every side. How little did I imagine a few months since that I should ever wander on the inhospitable shores of Patagonia! Creatures of circumstance, wafted like chaff before every wind, yet each day we plan and indulge visions of the future, but "Coy to morrow cometh not with prophesies fulfilled." Seated alone on the rude moss covered rocks which overhang this wild seashore, with no other sound than the sullen swell of the tide to break upon the stillness, my mind reverted homeward with a melancholy pleasure. . . .

On one of the numerous Islands in the western part of the straits we saw a party of the Native Tierra del Fuegians. They are an ugly illshapen race of small stature, with low foreheads, broad flat noses, large mouths and the usual Indian characteristic, high cheekbones. Their huts were constructed in the rudest manner, of young trees, interlaced with bark and offering but a poor defence against the inclement weather. Neither men nor women had any other covering than a piece of seal skin, thrown across the shoulders. They were much pleased, fairly dancing with delight on receiving the little presents we made them. as with all Savages tobacco appeared to be the prime want. We were astonished at their great facility for mimicry, all of them imitating the most difficult words of our language, even to the very *tone* of pronunciation. Their canoes were constructed of bark fastened with shreds of seal-skin and small twigs and are very frail, but they seldom venture in them outside the kelp, by the aid of which they pull themselves along the shore. They live almost entirely upon mussels and other shell-fish.

The Chilians have a small settlement at "Port Famine," near the middle of the Straits. The name admirably indicates the character of the place. It is supported by Government principally I suppose with a view of sustaining their claim to these Regions, though I do not think that they will ever find any nation inclined to dispute with them the proprietorship of these impenetrable forests, barren precipices and impassable morasses.

We left the Straits on the evening of the 26th Jany. in company with the Steamer Edith, which vessel we had overtaken on the previous day. We had hardly got beyond the shelter of the land when we encountered a heavy gale of wind, with a boisterous sea and stormy sky. We were soon separated from our new consort. This storm lasted for about a week alternately lulling and becoming more furious: accustomed to the sea and rough weather I did not suffer from sea-sickness, but I stood a good chance of having my brain addled by the continual pitching. Some of our officers found it still more unpleasant, being unable to stay either in or out of their beds. Our good Ship fought her way bravely through this stormy region into a more genial clime and with a favoring breeze we shall anchor in the harbor of Valparaiso to morrow.

Wed. 8th. Valparaiso. We reached this place safe and sound this afternoon. The US. Steamer Oregon, left here yesterday which I regret very much as it would have enabled me to send you a letter very direct if I could *only* have written to you by the opportunity. I send this by Mr Keller in the Edith, by the way of Francisco Bay where he will put it in one of the Mail Steamers. You can tell Mr K. that I saw his son in excellent health and spirits. The Steamer Panama has not arrived here yet although she left the United States some time. She is said to have a large mail. The only news that I have heard by the Oregon, is that the Cholera has appeared in New York. I hope that it is not true, but we feel very anxious.

I saw a Captain, this evg. just come from California, his crew all deserted at San Francisco and he was compelled to sell his vessel. 20 vessels have just gone from this place with provision to California. $80,000 was sent on board of a vessel to day for the purchase of the virgin ore at the rate of $10 an ounce. The quantity of gold found is incredible. The U.S Soldiers have all deserted in spite of every effort to prevent them. The Oregonians are said to be emigrating by hundreds and if we ever get to Oregon I suppose that our soldiers will be off to the mines and that we will have no other resource than to follow the rest of the folks. It will take us about two months and a half to get to the Columbia. It is not decided yet whether we are to stop at Callao en route.

I am very much pleased with the *very* little that I have seen of this place. The population is about 40,000 I believe. The site is very irregular, some houses perched up on lofty ridges, others ensconced in narrow, deep gorges. The people seem to be polite and obliging. There are no Amn. men of war here but many English, French and native. The weather is very pleasant and abundance of every kind of fruit in the markets. We change our seasons very rapidly. Well, if we are spared to each other I shall have some long yarns to spin, for you know that I am better with the tongue than the pen. Remember me to Mrs Thornton the Larneds and all our good friends. How I long to hear from you! but I will try and be patient, ever hoping the best. My best love to Sister. May God watch over and preserve you both. It is my constant prayer, my hourly thought. Your devoted Son.

THEODORE TALBOT

[*A long letter, dated March 15, is here* OMITTED. *It covers in great detail a side trip from Valparaiso to Santiago. The last part of the letter is dated March 16 and picks up as follows.*]

March 16th.

... A word of our present whereabouts. This morning we passed to the North of the Equator near the hundredth degree of West Longitude. "Crossing the line," is no longer an occasion of boisterous merriment as it was with our older mariners nor in these degenerate days does the Mighty Monarch of the vasty deep deign to appear personally before presumptuous wanderers in his watery realms, modern discipline saving novices in the nautical art from the rude initiation to which they were formerly subjected.

Since we left Valparaiso we have had a constant succession of almost dead calms and had it not been for our steam we should have made but small progress. A few days since we passed the Gallapagos Islands famous for their fine terrapin. We saw three American whale ships here. The captain of one of them who was at some distance from seeing only the smoke rising from the after deck thought that our ship was certainly on fire and getting out his boats made for us in all haste and it was not 'till he had approached quite near that he found out his mistake and that it was a bona fide steamship. He excused himself for being somewhat nervous about fire as he said only a short time previous when in the port at Tumbos, his crew had put fire in the hold of his own ship, hoping thereby to get rid of a voyage which they had conceited would be unlucky, but fortunately their attempt was discovered in time to arrest its progress. These whalers remain out at sea four and five years at a time to obtain their cargoes and the men are exposed to constant hardship and danger.

On one of the Gallapagos Islands are the Captain and passengers of a Chilian Brig bound to San Francisco, California. It seems that they went on shore to hunt and amuse themselves and the mate and crew took the opportunity to run off with the ship which contained goods and money in her to the amount of $60,000. This occurred only three weeks ago. I fear that all this gold finding in California will lead to acts of piracy, among its other attendant evils. . . .

Your Affectionate Son

THEODORE

AT SEA, OFF OAHU. H.Y.

April 18th 1849

MY DEAREST MOTHER,

We are once more at sea after a week's pleasant sojourn at Honolulu, the Capital of the Hawaiian Islands. I sent you thence via Cala., a letter written at sea before my arrival, in which I also enclosed a slip informing you of my safe arrival at Honolulu. The mode of conveyance was somewhat uncertain but I hope that it may reach you in safety as I know full well the value of any tidings from those we love. I now sit down to transcribe some account of our visit to Honolulu while the impression is yet fresh on my memory. On every side we met with objects entirely novel and highly interesting. To pretend to give you any sketch of the wonderful rise and progress of these Islands in the arts of civilization, would take me far beyond the limits of an ordinary letter, but should you take interest in the subject, I would refer you to Jarves' or other late Histories of the Sandwich Islands,[8] I will endeavor to confine myself to the little incidents and matters which came under personal observation during our short stay, although the numerous chances and changes of this newly civilized nation are a constant temptation to digression.

On Monday the 9th instant passing Diamond Point we came in sight of the harbor and town of Honolulu situated on the south side of the Island of Oahu. The sea being calm we approached the entrance of the little Harbor quite rapidly with all sails furled and under steam, much to the astonishment of the natives, who not seeing our propelling power could not imagine by what mysterious agency we were thus safely gliding into port. The town of Honolulu presents a very pretty appearance from the sea. It extends back from the water's edge a considerable distance and is regularly laid out in streets and lanes. There are three churches and many very handsome public and private edifices, ranges of stores, etc. constructed of wood, stone and adobes. Most of the private houses have large gardens with shrubbery attached to them and there are rows of trees planted in some of the streets. Interspersed among the more substantial buildings are numbers of the native grass houses, which contribute very happily to the pleasant and varied Coup d'oeil. Behind the town rises a high steep ridge on which are some fortifications and on the right hand side as you enter the harbor is a quadrangular fort. We found no foreign men of war in port but several Amn. Whalers and merchant vessels of different nations. Many foreigners came on board of us as soon as we had come to anchor, to learn our news and also to proffer to us the usual

---

[8] James Jackson Jarves, *History of the Hawaiian Islands*, (Boston, Tappan and Dennet, 1843). There were three editions by the time Talbot wrote.

civilities. We found that our ship was a great object of curiosity as no propeller had ever visited the Islands before, and but one Steamer, The "Cormorant," an English vessel. Hundreds of boats and canoes filled with natives were crowded around us, admiring the noble ship and the strange wheel in her stern armed with "shark fins." Nearly all of them were well clothed after the European fashion; some few had only a shirt and the maro. They were exceedingly noisy all talking together in the native tongue and making the greatest hubbub imaginable. These Islanders are accomplished swimmers and dozens of them both men and women were in the water entirely nude, diving under the ship and the propeller, in order to make a more thorough inspection of this new wonder.

On going ashore we were at first followed everywhere by a crowd of native idlers of which class there appears to be no lack in any part of the town. We took tea the evening of our arrival at Judge Turrell's, the American consul.[9] The next day no natives were around the ship the Govr. having given orders to that effect, supposing that it might be unpleasant to us to be so surrounded. We went in the evening accompanied by Judge Turrell, to a party at the house of Mr Wyllie, Minister of Foreign Affairs to H.M.[10] He lives about a mile and a half from the town. We found assembled a very agreable party of foreigners both ladies and gentlemen, we had dancing and altogether a very pleasant evening.

[9] Joel Turrill, consul of the United States.

[10] Robert Crichton Wyllie (1798–1865), a Scotch M.D. who resided long in Latin America, had come to Hawaii in 1843. Two years later he had sufficiently impressed the Hawaiian king to be appointed his minister of foreign relations, a position he held until his death. Harold Whitman Bradley, *The American Frontier in Hawaii: The Pioneers, 1789–1843, passim.*

The British and French Consuls, Dr. Judd,[11] Minister of Finance to H.M., Mr Bates,[12] Atty. Genl. Judge Lee, Chief Justice,[13] and other foreigners holding office under the King together with many respectable merchants and residents were present. The only natives there were Alexander Liholiho, the adopted son of the King and heir apparent to the throne and his brother Lot Kamehameha. They are the sons of Keku-anara, who is the Governor of Oahu. They have both just finished their education at Mr Cook's Chiefs School and are studying law with Mr. Bates the Atty. Genl. They are both very accomplished and gentlemanly young men, speak English perfectly and with the greatest fluency. Lot is 17 years of age, Alexander is only 15 but they are both very tall and manly for their ages. Alexander I saw a good deal of as he was on board of our ship several times. He is very sociable and pleasant in his manners and appears to be well informed on most subjects. His great passion is to travel but the King is reluctant to part with him fearing that he might fall a victim to the change of climate, as did King Liholiho, his queen and many of their suite, who died whilst on a visit to England. Alexander is said to be of a decided character and I think is of

[11] Gerrit P. Judd (1803–73), a New Yorker sent as a medical missionary to Hawaii in 1828. In 1842, having long been a counsellor of the Hawaiian court, he was placed on the Treasury Board and shortly thereafter was made secretary of state for foreign affairs. These and other prime positions kept him in the center of the Hawaiian government till he was forced out in 1852. *DAB.*

[12] Asher Brown Bates (1810–73), born in New York and married in Michigan, arrived in Hawaii in June, 1848. Shortly afterward, he became a legal adviser to the crown. For fourteen years he held various governmental positions, including a seat on the Privy Council. *DAB.*

[13] William L. Lee (1821–57), New York jurist, was en route to Oregon for his health when he landed in Hawaii in 1846. The Hawaiian government invited him to head the judicial system, and he accepted. His subsequent draft of the penal code remains to this day the basis of Hawaiian law.

much more intelligence than the heir apparent of Tahiti whom I saw in Rio Janeiro. Mr Wyllie had the King's band in attendance at his party; it is composed entirely of natives and performed very well. His Majesty Kamehameha III was absent on a visit to the island of Maui, whither he had gone to celebrate his birthday.[14] The day after our arrival one of the royal yachts was despatched for him as it was confidently expected that he would desire to see our ship having been absent on a former occasion when a Steamer visited this Island. There are one or two very genteel Hotels in Honolulu and it was quite agreable to us to take an occasional walk, a game of billiards, or even a mere lounge ashore, after being so long confined to the limits of our ship. We had horses always at our command and when inclined to pay visits, innumerable hospitable invitations to be complied with. Wednesday evening we spent at a party given by the Amn. Consul's lady. We met here Mr Hill a noted English traveller who has wandered through Siberia and other out of the way places,[15] Mrs. Lee a *poetess* etc., but the most interesting persons to me, were two native female chiefs, scholars of Mr. and Mrs. Cook's Seminary, Misses Bernice Pauahi and Mary Ii. They are both of light color, very pretty and very well educated. They were fashionably dressed wearing colored muslin dresses with some trifling articles of jewelry. I conversed with Miss Bernice and found her very agreable and full of polite conversation. She is 17 years of age. She played several difficult airs on the piano but declined singing on the plea of having a cold, being out

[14] Kamehameha III (1813–54) ruled from 1825 to his death. He was responsible for the introduction of constitutional monarchy into Hawaii. Bradley, *The American Frontier in Hawaii*, 142–44, 274–76, 309, 419.

[15] S. S. Hill, English traveler and author of *Travels in Siberia* (1854) and *Travels in the Sandwich and Society Islands* (1856).

of practice or some such excuse, for all the world like the pretty asseverations [assertions] of one of our own fashionable belles. I am told that only nine years since, she was a little girl running about half naked and wholly *wild!* All the protestant missionaries, who are assembled at this time at Honolulu, from the different Islands of the Hawaiian Group, at a general meeting, visited the ship en masse, accompanied by their families. They appear to be very prolific for they had a whole troupe of children in their train, all looking very grave and demure, miniatures of their papas and mamas.

I was at the native mission church a large stone edifice built by the *compelled* labor of the natives. In its vicinity are several comfortable stone dwellings inhabited by the missionaries. The mission has an extensive printing establishment and bookbindery at which are yearly published great numbers of school and religious books. There is no question but that the missionaries have done an immense deal of good among these Islands, that they have elevated and improved the body of the people both socially and morally speaking, yet there is still much to be done and their labors are in a manner just begun.

The French Catholic Mission under charge of the worthy Bishop Maigret is improving rapidly, new proselytes being gained every day and new schools constantly established. The natives are said to be becoming more favorably disposed towards the religion because they find they are not heavily taxed to support its teachers, nor are they compelled by royal edicts to build its churches. *The fact is,* they are impressed by the pure, exemplary self abnegating character of its priesthood, men who instead of ever seeking their own personal aggrandisement, humbly devote their *whole* energies to the welfare of their pastoral charges, aiding and counselling in prosperity, cheering and consoling in the hours of sickness and adversity. The Catholics met with great opposition on their first arrival here, were once expelled and finally landed under protection of the guns of a french frigate. But they are now treated with more tolerance by their protestant brethren. The French Cathedral is a very handsome edifice built by funds from the Soc. prop. fid.

There are many very pleasant rides in the vicinity of Honolulu. One is to the "Pali," a steep precipice over which the victorious Kamehameha I is said to have driven hundreds of the natives in fatal and inglorious flight when he conquered this Island. Kamehameha I was originally only King of a part of Hawaii or Owyhee but by his prowess succeeded in bringing all the other Islands of the Group under his sway. There are many very fine Coffee and sugar plantations, Cattle ranchos and farms scattered about in the plain of Honolulu, owned by foreigners and natives. The population of Honolulu and its vicinage is 9000. Of the Island of Oahu 20,000, of the whole group, over 90,000, but I regret to add the native population is everywhere fast decreasing. The soil of the Islands generally is rich and productive. The fruits of all countries appear to succeed well by planting them in the Climate to which they are naturally adapted. This can be easily done by selecting different elevations from the even, constant warmth of the lower plains up to the very snow covered peaks of Hawaii. These Islands all bear the marks of volcanic action: there are several extinct craters on the island of Oahu, but I believe that the only active volcano is on Hawaii. I rode one evening with a party of gentlemen to a very large cocoa nut grove four miles from the town. We passed a chain gang on the road. The police system of this island appears to be excellent, crime is promptly and severely punished, law and order reign everywhere. Arrived at the grove, it was absolutely wonderful to see the agility with which the young natives climbed or I should rather say ran up the smooth limbless trees like so many monkeys, showering down the green cocoa nuts in all directions. I here, for the first time tasted these nuts in that delicious pulpy state, nearly all milk, in which I have so often heard you say that you have eaten them in the West Indies. After a long gallop at full speed, California fashion, we found them peculiarly refreshing. Returning, we met the young princes Alexander and Lot at the race course. Riding on horseback is the favorite amusement of all classes of the natives, and is about the only one which the missionaries permit them to enjoy. Saturday is the great gala day. Hundreds of the natives both men and women mounted on horseback, collect on the course just beyond the town. The natives are fearless but many of them not very expert riders and the wild racing, tumbles, noise and general confusion which invariably take place at these gatherings, beggard description. Notwithstanding all this tumult there is strange to say, no drunkeness, fighting or even quarrelling. Foreign gentlemen who have been long resident here tell me that they have never seen a native drunk. They certainly have not learnt this virtue from the example of the majority of whites who have visited their shores. The native sports and dances are discountenanced and forbidden by the prot. missionaries but during my stay I had an opportunity of seeing the ancient spear exercise and some of the native dances. The dexterity with which they were formerly taught to handle the spear was truly wonderful, using it alike as a complete means of defence and a formidable weapon of attack.

I examined the Fort in company with the Consul and the Act. Govr. Ii.[16] It is a miserable structure mounting some 70 iron and brass guns and offers no kind of protection to the harbor but it serves as a town prison and as barracks for the Kings Troops. It also serves to fire salutes and I heard one fired from it the other day in very excellent style, in answer to the salute of a Russian Man of War Brig which came in to port a few days after us. The Governor of Oahu, Kekuanaoa is absent, Ii, the Actg. Govr. is a very smart gentlemanly person, he is not by *birth* of high rank but has risen in the state by the Aristocracy of talent. The Consul in accordance with the request of our officers gave an invitation to all the native population, through the Governor, to visit the ship on an appointed day when we would be prepared for their reception. The Govr. was much pleased at our desire to gratify the native curiosity and our invitation being generally made known, crowds were in waiting on the wharves at appointed time. Govr. Ii accompanied by some fifty officers of the army and navy etc. in the full blaze of their dress uniforms came off to the ship first and were soon followed by a miscellaneous multitude of all sizes, sexes and conditions. They soon pervaded every part of the Ship. There was no nook or corner which escaped inspection on that day, but the engine-room was of course the grand focus of attraction. The men, as I have before remarked, conform as nearly to the European dress as their

[16] Probably John Ii, long adviser to the king, member of the Treasury Board, judge of the Superior Court, and member of Commission to revise the Constitution in 1851. *Ibid.*, 132, 332, 414.

means will permit; the women usually wear two long loose gowns the upper of silk or muslin sometimes confined at the waist by a sash or ribbon. On the head are worn becoming wreaths of natural or artificial flowers. The hair is usually left about 18 inches long is black and glossy, flowing into ringlets. They vary in color from almost Congo black, to the lightest shade of Mulatto. Many of them are tall and commanding in their carriage. As they grow old they appear to become very fat. Their faces are generally broad and flat with a pleasing expression and many are very pretty. Among the natives, fatness was formerly and I believe is yet considered one of the attributes of Beauty. Notwithstanding the great number on board all behaved with the greatest propriety, although they had access every where not a pin's value was stolen and when the time came for their departure they returned in the utmost good order. I did not remain on board during this descent of the natives but extricating myself from the throng early in the day, made my escape to the shore preferring to pay my devoirs to the pretty Miss D.—a native of this place born however of foreign parents, who has been educated in the United States and has just returned home. *I* think that she is decidedly the belle of the village. But you need not entertain any fears on account of my too great susceptibility.

During our stay we were invited to three parties by Mr S. Reynolds[17] an Amn. Merchant and old resident of this place. He was married I believe to a native, but she is dead and his children are all grown up and absent. The old gentleman is very wealthy, lives in a large house and has undertaken

[17] Stephen Reynolds, a New Englander who had come to Hawaii in 1823, was well established as a retail merchant by 1830. He later added sugar plantations to his economic interests. He became insane in 1855. *Ibid.*, 92, 118, and *passim.*

to educate a number of half caste girls entirely at his own expense. He spares no pains in their education having governesses to teach them all ladylike accomplishments, music, fancy work, painting etc. etc. He has pursued this charitable whim for many years and some of the young ladies brought up by him have married foreigners and done very well. Two of his parties were given especially to us, one of which I attended and enjoyed myself very much. I found him to be a complete original. The old gentleman wears huge shirt collars of such size that only his nose, eyes and the top of his head are visible. He always acts as Master of Ceremonies at his parties and sometimes dances himself. Round his large dancing room are hung portraits in oil of his favorite pupils some of them full length pictures executed by American Artists.[18] There were some thirty young ladies present and several foreigners among whom was our amiable Commissioner Mr. Ten Eyck.[19] He has just returned from a short visit to California and gave me some interesting information about my old acquaintances there. Mr. Ten Eyck has become involved in some difficulty with the Hawaiian Government and is at present interdicted from all official intercourse.

Although exceedingly anxious to reach our ultimate destination, yet the time has passed so rapidly during our

[18] In a duplicate fragment, not here reproduced, Talbot says that all of these paintings were done by John M. Stanley "an artist who came to the country from Oregon and California having been with General Kearney." He is perhaps best known to Americans for *Portraits of North American Indians* . . . . Smithsonian Miscellaneous Collections, Vol. II, Article III, Publication 53 (1852).

[19] Anthony Ten Eyck was appointed as commissioner to the Hawaiian Islands in 1845 by the new Polk administration in Washington. About the time of Talbot's visit he was ending years of frustrated efforts to negotiate a treaty with the Hawaiians giving the Americans special prerogatives there.

pleasant sojourn at Oahu, that it was with a feeling nearly akin to regret we heard it announced that our ship was in readiness and that we must again resume our course 'oer the trackless world of waters.

Your Affec. Son<br>THEODORE

PACIFIC OCEAN<br>April 20th 1849

MY DEAR SISTER,

I commenced a letter to you before my arrival at Honolulu but no good opportunity offering for its transmission, I cast it aside, glad to save you the infliction of a very dull letter all about the sea, and in its place will send you these following Sandwich Island *notes*. I have already spun Mother a long yarn on the same subject and will there fore let you off easily, writing in continuation.

The King arrived at Honolulu from the island of Maui, on Saturday night, landing amid salvos of Artillery, with banners flying, drums beating etc. His Majesty having intimated his desire to visit the "Massachusetts," an invitation was extended to himself and suite to come on board on Monday at 3 O'clock P. M. when we would take a trip outside the harbor. It was our intention to have given a party to all the foreign residents from whom we had received civilities, but in consequence of the difficulties existing between the Ministers of H.M. Government and Mr Ten Eyck we found that it would not be agreable for them to meet and we could not give any ball at which the U.S. Commissioner was not an invited guest, so we had to let the matter rest, our time not permitting us to make the delay necessary for another trip in compliment to Mr. Ten Eyck.

It was quite rainy in the early part of Monday afternoon and a heavy shower was falling when the royal procession arrived at the water's edge. Shortly previous to coming on board, the King sent a message requesting that he might be received without any military parade or ceremony whatever. The royal barge containing the King and Queen was the first to come alongside of us closely followed by the others of the regal train. In the hurry of Embarkation from the shore, one boat filled with some of the King's Military Officers was upset, to their no little discomfiture I presume, for they lost the jaunt and spoilt their handsome uniforms. All the rest of the party being safely on board, we weighed anchor and steamed out of the harbor in style, with the Hawaiian flag flying at our main. The sky in the meantime had cleared off and the sea being calm we had a very pleasant afternoon for our excursion. Thousands of spectators were assembled on the beach and in the fleet of boats and canoes ranged from the wharves to the entrance of the harbor. His Majesty Kamehameha the Third is a man of moderate height but is robust in his make with a dark complexion and intelligent cast of countenance: he is 37 years of age. His manners are simple yet dignified, he speaks English passably and is said to be a man of much natural talent and acquired information. His dress on the occasion was a full suit of black with a silver star on his left breast and a white hat bound with black crape. His Queen, Kalama, is a large unwieldy personage of dark color, by no means handsome but with an amiable expression of face. She is 32 years of age and has no children. She was dressed in a fashionably made black silk, with a black bonnet and trimmings and she wore a large black mosaaic brooch. Her Attendants were all in black the Court being in mourning. The King and Queen are usually attended by pages and maids of honor but on this occasion they were dispensed with. John Young the Premier is a tall and very handsome man.[20] He is the son of an English Sailor of that name who together with his messmate Isaac Davis, were taken prisoners more than 50 years ago by King Kamehameha the First, who aware of the superior talents of the whites took this means of availing himself of their knowledge, for his own and the national benefit. They were both married to females of the highest rank and soon became reconciled to their condition. They no doubt materially influenced the happy fortunes of that victorious King. It is the custom that a female Chief should be Premier but since the death of Kekauluohi, Young has held that position. Victoria Kamamalu, the heir apparent to the premiership, is a very intelligent little girl, ten years of age. She is a sister of Alexander and holds the highest female rank in the Kingdom. Mr Wyllie Minister of Foreign Affairs is next in rank of the King's Cabinet. He is a Scotchman by birth but has sworn allegiance to the Hawaiian Govt. as all must do who hold public offices. He was formerly partner of a mercantile firm in London and is said to be wealthy. He has only resided out here 4 or 5 years but during that time has become so much enamored with the country as to have expatriated himself. Dr. Judd, Minister of Finance, has resided at the Islands a long

[20] John Young and Isaac Davis were not messmates, as Talbot calls them, but they had been detained from two separate English vessels at the same time in 1790. The two sailors were so well treated by the Hawaiians that they were eventually happy to remain as trusted advisers to the government. For ten years after 1802 Young even served as governor of Hawaii during the king's absence. Davis died in 1810. Bradley, *op. cit.*, 16, 33–34, 37–38, 55.

time, having come out as physician with the first Amn. Missionaries. He is married to an American lady and has a large family. Dr. Judd exercises unbounded influance over the King, in reality, holding in his hands, the entire administration of the Government. Several other foreigners holding office under the King were present with their families. Many of the native Chiefs who accompanied His Majesty were splendid looking men. I noticed particularly Paki, one of the King's Chamberlains and father of Bernice Pauahi. He was over 6 feet 6 inches in height and exceedingly robust.

We went out to sea 10 miles and then returned into the harbor. The King who is quite a conoisseur in naval matters was highly interested, examining all the machinery and receiving the explanations of the Engineers with much attention. On leaving, he had himself rowed round the Ship, in order to obtain a full view of her fine proportions. Next day a very complimentary letter was received from the Foreign Office, expressing His Majesty's thanks for the polite reception etc. etc.

Emerging from the shadow of Royalty, I remain ever,
Your Affect. Brother,
THEO. TALBOT

# V.

## OREGON, 1849-52

*When Talbot received orders* for Oregon, his heart sank. It was a land, he felt, which at its best was a "terra incognita or a genteel Botany Bay for Army Officers." And he knew of what he spoke, since he had been there five years before on his first trip West with Frémont. Then Oregon had been a diplomatic conundrum, a joint occupancy with England bearing a question mark for a future. But as time went on, the British had shown less interest in the area and more preoccupation with the anti-colonial doctrines of Adam Smith. Also, in 1846, soon after Talbot's 1845 visit, the Hudson's Bay Company had moved the headquarters of its Columbia Department from the banks of the Columbia to the northern island of Vancouver. The United States had waited until increasing numbers of settlers should strengthen its case. In 1846, that *annus mirabilis* for American expansion, the time was judged ripe along the Columbia as it had been so judged along the Río Grande and San Francisco Bay. The chief difference between the Oregon and the Mexican areas was that England would negotiate; and in 1846 the territory of the United States was stretched to a new Northwest, to the shores and into "the continuous woods," as Bryant memorialized, "where rolls the Oregon." The date was June 15, and the cession was embodied in the Oregon Treaty.

The territory stood in 1849 as a glaring example of the problems faced by the army. A third of the continental United States was suddenly dropped into its lap, and when the new scale of distances was imposed upon the existing problems of supply, finance, and recruitment, the burden was staggering, as France and Spain had earlier found, in the eighteenth century. The new country to be protected seemed full of displaced and misplaced people—wandering families looking for

118

Eden, Indians being expelled from their Garden for reasons they could not appreciate, and, perhaps hardest to cope with, irresponsible spoilers of all kinds, especially the miners and land speculators, forever restless, tempted, and tempting.

Looking outside the barracks on the Columbia, Talbot saw a rather miserable picture. Many new immigrants were disgruntled, he believed, because they had been shunted off to Oregon by a failure of grass on the California route. Others were frustrated because, for one reason or another, they could not rush to the California mines. They may have been the foundation for the future, but the settlers nevertheless seemed vile to Talbot. He called them "beggars on horseback," and "purse-proud, illiterate mobocrats." "You can't imagine how disgusting it is to be compelled to have intercourse with such people." The Indians were equally unfriendly. They would hardly have left unnoticed the fact that the post had been built on an Indian graveyard. Not even the missionaries had been that thoughtless!

Settler and Indian alike hated the army. It was even accused, wrote Talbot, "of being leagued with the H[udson's] B[ay] Company and the Papists to defraud the people of their just rights."

To keep order among these conflicting groups, Columbia Barracks had been built in 1849 near the site of the old Hudson's Bay post on the north bank of the river about eight miles above the present Portland. The men of the regiment were predictably of mixed background and commitment. Talbot related their efforts to beat the black market, their attempts at suicide, their drunkenness, eccentricities, and all the emotional eruptions caused by close confinement during long winter months.

In general, Talbot saw the army as filled with partiality and wastefulness, as ridiculously underpaid, and as hopelessly undermanned. In short, he contended, if Congress did not increase support, it might as well disband the army in the West.

In such moods, Talbot would sometimes engage in self-examination. His future looked bleak; he was saving no money from his $1,000 annual salary. His luck seemed always such that "if I buy a horse, he is sure to go irremediably lame." Oregon had become a "dreary term of service." Still, for a man like himself, he thought the army was probably a good solution.

This bitter satisfaction was consistent with the quietly pessimistic world-view which crept over him in Oregon. The optimism of St. Louis seemed long ago, as if muted by fog along the Columbia. The territorial delegates he saw as scoundrels, the Englishmen traveling in the West were ludicrously "indulging in the romance of a wild woods life," and the great men on the world's stage were passing with none to take their places. He had just heard of the death of Daniel Webster; Clay and Calhoun had died only a short time before. Talbot hoped that a future emergency would call forth new men of like stature to meet the need. Perhaps in that dimly foreseen crisis the army could be counted on to do a better job. Meanwhile it must somehow subdue a Western wilderness. And meanwhile, too, it would provide for Theodore Talbot a refuge from an increasingly troubled and unkempt world.

Astoria, Oregon Territory

May 10th 1849

My dear Sister,

We arrived here this morning from Baker's Bay, having crossed the bar of Colombia River, yesterday. Our passage from the Sandwich Islands to this place has been a very fair one, only occupying twenty-one days. Rev. Mr Damon, Seamen's Chaplain at Oahu, accompanied us as a passenger and we have found him quite an agreable addition to our society.[1] On arriving off the mouth of the river, there was but little wind and the sea was partially calm and favorable for our entering but a heavy haze or fog completely shrouded some of the most prominent headlands and landmarks and a formidable line of breakers apparently extended quite across the

[1] Samuel C. Damon, Congregationalist chaplain of the Seamen's Bethel in Hawaii after 1842, began publication in 1843 of the *Temperance Advocate and Seamen's Friend*, later the *Friend*.

entrance, from Cape Disappointment over to Point Adams, a
distance of nearly eleven miles. We fired guns hoping that
a Pilot would come off to us, although being concerned with
some Indians in the plundering of a H.B. Compy. Ship which
went ashore here sometime since. After waiting several hours
the Captain twice approached very near to the bar, but as
often retreated, (using his own expression,) 'his courage leak-
ing out at his elbows,' on sight of the tremendous rollers and
the raging foam covered breakers. In the afternoon the tide
having changed it became much more calm upon the bar and
we again sought a safe passage, having sent one of our life
boats in advance to sound the Channel. This time we succeeded
in finding an admirable entrance through which we passed
without being endangered by breakers or other obstacles. You
may be sure that we all felt rejoiced to leave this crowning
peril of our voyage behind us and our Captain was naturally
quite triumphant at having accomplished happily without,
what many Captains have failed to do, *with* the most skilful
Pilots.[2] We anchored last night just inside of Cape Disappointment.[3]

Astoria, of which we have all heard and read so much
is a modest little village of a dozen log houses on a gentle

[2] The Talbot Journal covering this same period has been published: Charles
H. Carey, ed., *The Journals of Theodore Talbot, 1843 and 1849–52* (Metropolitan Press, Portland, Oregon, 1931). Throughout this chapter any journal
entry which throws light on the letters will be quoted in the footnotes and referred to as *Journals* with the date of entry.

In the *Journals*, May 8, 1849, Talbot indicates that in crossing the bar and
entering the Columbia River, his ship followed the passage laid down by Captain
Charles Wilkes of the Naval Expedition of 1838–42.

[3] Cape Disappointment was named in 1788 by an English sea captain, John
Meares, sailing a Portuguese ship, the *Felice*, in the Canton, China, trade. Failing
to find the reported great river here, he named the bay Deception and the cape
Disappointment.

declivity towards the River, in front of a steep ridge covered with evergreens.[4] We found here Mr Adair, the newly appointed Custom House Officer.[5] He says that nearly all the male whites are gone to California from this neighborhood and that Oregon generally is nearly depopulated. Great numbers have already gone and are still going to California from here, both by land and water. Gold *has been* found on the Umqua River in Oregon, on the road to California and it is said to exist in other parts of *Oregon*. Many men who were absent some 3 or 4 months in Cala. have returned here with 5 10 and even 25,000 dollars in gold ore or coin. Instead of decreasing the ore is found in new places, in fact the tales told here stagger all credibility. Prices of everything in Oregon have raised to an enormous height. Eggs are $2.00 a dozen, lumber $250. per M, common blankets $16.00 and so with every article of trade.[6] Even the worthless Chenook and other River Indians, charge $10 a day for their trifling labor and expect to be paid in the hard coin. Our soldiers will all have

[4] Astoria began in 1811 as a part of John Jacob Astor's dream of a union between Pacific shipping and the interior fur trade. Dogged by hard luck and finally by the War of 1812, the venture was sold to the British North West Company in 1813 and renamed Fort George. Absorbed into the Hudson's Bay Company in 1821, Fort George became little more than a lookout. About 1826 the Indians burned the buildings. Talbot in his *Journals*, May 10, 1849, calls Astoria "a miserable place consisting of about a dozen log & frame houses scattered over a very uneven hilly spot of open ground. Most of the houses have no enclosures about them, look cheerless & miserable. Fort George is nothing but a long one story log house." Henry J. Warre's contemporary painting of the site agrees with Talbot's description.

[5] Talbot in the *Journals*, May 9, 1849, calls John Adair a general from Kentucky. He was appointed by President Polk as Collector for Astoria, 1849–1861.

[6] Talbot gives other prices in the *Journals*: town lots 25' x 100' $200 (May 10, 1849); jacket cloth, $8 (June 19, 1849); 144 small boxes of matches, $6 (July 18, 1849); barrel of porter, $18 (July 24, 1849).

their heads turned and desert I suppose. I had hoped that we would have been removed from this gold excitement and its influences but we might as well be in California. I really cannot tell how we shall get along. Governor Lane has arrived and is at Oregon City on the Willamette.[7] We are going up to Ft. Vancouver[8] and the mouth of the Willamette 80 miles distant from here, if we can find sufficient depth of water for our ship.

I have been most sorely disappointed not to receive any letters. The Govt Mail Agent for this place has cleared out to Cala. his wife remaining behind to keep the Post Office. None of the mail steamers have come up here and but one mail; which came up in a coasting vessel; dates to Dec 1st 1848. The steamers are said to lie in San Francisco Bay. The crews having deserted. I shall send this to San Francisco in the coasting bark "J. W. Cater" I hope that it will find its way to you tot ou tard. Give my best love to Mother. I shall write by every vessel bound down the coast and pray that I may soon hear from both of you although in the present state of things I fear that I shall again and again be disappointed. Remember me Affectionately to Mrs Thornton, to the Larneds, Markoes and all our kind friends. I feel quite

[7] Joseph Lane (1801–1881), first governor of the Oregon Territory, arrived on the Columbia March 2, 1849, only two months before Talbot. From 1851 to 1859 he served as territorial delegate to the United States Congress, and then till 1861 as senator from the new state. His vigorous southern sympathies during the Civil War effectively stopped his political career. *DAB.*

[8] After the Hudson's Bay Company incorporated the North West Company, it established a new center for the fur trade at Fort Vancouver in 1825, on the north bank of the Columbia just opposite the Willamette River and the present city of Portland. Fort Vancouver was in turn forsaken by the HBC in 1846 when the company moved north to the present Victoria on Vancouver Island. Cf. The Hudson's Bay Record Society, *McLoughlin's Fort Vancouver Letters, First Series, 1825–1838* (London, n.d.).

anxious to learn that Mr. Larned's health has improved. Is it not a hard case that we should be sent out here to starve among the gold like so many misers. Genl Smith[9] is powerless and I hear has recommended to Govt. a *very high* increase of the soldiers pay as troops are *absolutely* required, he also has hinted that officers cannot subsist on honor alone. The "Cater" is dropping down the river past us, so I must say Good Bye.[10]

Your Affect. Brother<br>THEO. TALBOT

[*The following is in the left margin of the last page.*] We expect to be stationed near Vancouver or Oregon City. Astoria is a good direction for the present.

CAMP, NEAR FORT VANCOUVER<br>OREGON TERRITORY<br>May 25th 1849

MY DEAREST MOTHER,

The Columbia River above Astoria is a handsome stream generally thickly wooded with a growth of pine and fir, down to the waters edge. Its channel is in many places

---

[9] Persifor Frazer Smith (1798–1858), a Philadelphian and graduate of Princeton, had moved to Louisiana whence he had fought as a volunteer against the Seminoles. In the Mexican War he served as a colonel under General Zachary Taylor and was breveted brigadier general and transferred to Scott's command around Mexico City. Talbot had briefly come in contact with Smith earlier while the General organized the embarkation of the army leaving Vera Cruz. After the war Smith commanded the Pacific Division, including California and Oregon, until 1850. *DAB.*

[10] Talbot, *Journals*, May 10, 1849: "William was severely flogged for stealing $600 from Lt Wood's iron safe. He was whipped until he fainted but denied with the most solemn asseverations that he was in any way concerned in the theft but $310 of it was found in his trunk. On having it searched a second time besides this, 170$ had been found in a storeroom. He obstinately persisted in his mendacity notwithstanding the tremendous flogging, until it was proved

shallow but we were only detained one day by getting aground, which was rather fortunate for a ship drawing so much water as ours. There are a few settlers scattered here and there on the River and the infant colony of "New Plymouth" near the lower mouth of the Wilhamet River boasts three wooden houses.[11] We reached Fort Vancouver the old Head Quarters of the Hudson B. Compy. on Sunday the 13th of May and anchored abreast of the Fort. We saluted the Fort and our salute was returned by the Fort and the H.B. Compy's bark Columbia, lately arrived here from London. The Fort is situated in an extensive level plain running several miles along the north bank of the River. It consists of a high quadrangular stockade with bastions, surrounding the numerous warehouses, shops, and dwelling houses of the Company and its officers. In its vicinity is a Catholic Chapel and a village of 40 or 50 houses occupied by servants of the Compy. Mr Douglas the resident Governor[12] received us very politely and Major Hatheway determined to encamp near Vancouver, in which opinion he was confirmed on the arrival of Gov. Lane. A requisition will be made however by Gov Lane for one company to go to Nisqually, a place on the Southern end of Puget's Sound where the Indians are numerous and a little disposed to be troublesome. Gov. Lane has just returned

on him beyond question, he then acknowledged it. Woods will be about 100$ loser the amount spent by Bill in difft ports."

Other references to flogging in the *Journals*: June 28 and September 23–25, 1849.

For heavy army punishment, see Robert M. Utley, *Frontiersmen in Blue*, 38–39.

[11] An early name for St. Helens, Oregon.

[12] James Douglas (1803–1877), as an executive of the Hudson's Bay Company, founded the settlement of Victoria, British Columbia, where his name is preserved in the central street. For Major Hatheway see note 41 *infra*.

from a visit there since our arrival. As soon as a store ship arrives and means of transportation can be obtained, Capt. Hill's Company[13] will embark for Nisqually, but that may not be for two or three months yet. We find the Territory in a completely disorganized state. Two thirds of the settlers of Oregon have left farms and families behind, and gone to the California gold mines. Every thing like regular labor has ceased. Those who have been to the mines and returned with their bags of gold and have turned the heads of those who have not been, the most exorbitant prices are paid for provisions and goods of all descriptions, and it is next to impossible to get a white person to work steadily, for the highest wages. The H.B. Company have lost nearly all their employees being obliged to hire Indians and even they charge 4 and 5$ a day for their paltry services. Mr Douglas the R. Governor of the H.B. Compy. has left this place since our arrival to assume command of their new Head Quarters, at Victoria, Vancouver's Island. Peter Ogden Esq. succeeds in the charge of Fort Vancouver.[14] We have found them very kind and willing to

[13] Bennett Hoskin Hill was a West Pointer from the District of Columbia.

[14] Peter Skene Ogden (1794–1854), the son of Anglo-American loyalists resettled in Canada, began his fur-trading career with the North West Company and by the time he was twenty had incurred the disfavor of the Hudson's Bay Company in the bitter competition between the two organizations. With the absorption of the North West Company into the Hudson's Bay Company in 1821, Ogden found himself obliged to travel to London for a reconciliation with the proud governor and committee of Hudson's Bay, in which he was successful in 1823.

Assigned to the Far West, Ogden led a trapping expedition in 1825 and in the course of his travels encountered Great Salt Lake in May of that year. He was not its discoverer, however, since Jim Bridger, the American mountain man, had seen it either in the fall of 1824 or in the early spring of 1825. Étienne Provost, still another mountain man, saw it in the fall of 1825.

Ogden's ensuing career for Hudson's Bay Company was characterized by intense competition with American trappers and fur-trading interests and a

furnish us every assistance, but the present state of things renders them almost helpless. They are very anxious to leave the American part of Oregon. They think that the United States must have bought them out the last session of Congress, the matter being in negotiation. I hope this may prove true, for the United States will not be able for 10 years and even for the same price, to provide half as good depots for the troops which they are sending out here. No Quartermasters or Commissaries have arrived here, nor has the slightest arrangement been made for the reception of troops, so that we are thrown back on our own resources, for those of the country may be put down as Zero. But I suppose that storeships etc. will soon arrive from home. A portion of the Rifle Regt. is expected here this summer. Lt. Hawkins[15] of that Regt. who commanded the escort of Gov Lane has 8 of his men still with him. He is now at Oregon City on the Willamette River 25 miles from here. He has kept these men by allowing them to work in some saw mills there, when not on duty, by which they each easily earn a $100. per month. I am indebted to Lt. H. for a letter from you which he brought me from Ore-

high measure of respect and distinction, which led to his appointment as the company's chief factor at Fort Vancouver on the Columbia in 1846 in succession to Dr. John McLoughlin and as one of a board of three superintending the Columbia District. Talbot, *Journals*, May 17, 1849: "We called on Mr. Ogden who takes charge of the Fort Vancouver & were introduced to Mrs. McKinley a half breed his daughter. Ogden is a rough old man but quite hospitable in his manners." Ogden's retirement in Oregon and the acceptance of his U.S. residence at the end of his life brought him back to his ancestral country full-circle. There is no historical evidence to sustain Talbot's statement, *infra*, that Ogden was at John Jacob Astor's Astoria, 1811–13, or in the Far Northwest earlier than the decade of the 1820's. Cf. The Hudson's Bay Record Society, *McLoughlin's Fort Vancouver Letters* (First, Second, and Third Series, 1825–46); the same, [*George*] *Simpson's 1828 Journey to the Columbia*.

[15] George Washington Hawkins, a West Pointer from North Carolina, was dismissed from the army in 1853.

gon City. It is dated Nov 24th and came in the 1st mail. Since then no mails have been sent here, the Mail Agent appointed by Government for Oregon, having remained at the gold mines. So the Oregon mail has been kept at San Francisco, in consequence of there being no one here to whom it could be consigned. The trading, coasting vessels too, are unwilling to bring letters from California for fear that their speculations might be interfered with. This is very hard for I am sure many of your letters of late date must be lying in the San Francisco Post Office. I was very agreably surprised, for as I wrote from Astoria, I thought all the letters of the 1st mail had been left there, but it seems that mine and some others had been sent up the river. I wish indeed my dear Mother that I could make you custodian of a goodly heap of the precious metal but instead of my profiting by the mines, my pay which was small enough before for the position in all conscience, has now dwindeled down to nothing, where dollars pass as dimes. We cannot even draw our pittance when it is due, for there are no paymasters. I might for a time obtain much greater pay than I do now, out of the Army, but this state of things cannot last and the fact is that in nearly all cases it is only merchants and men of Capital who are making fortunes after all said. If a man gets 20$ a day in the mines and it costs him *that* amount to live he might as well get a dollar a day elsewhere and live better for that dollar. This gold mining to say the best of it is a kind of desperate *gambling* in which even life itself is set at stake. We have as yet lost none of our soldiers. It is expensive, difficult, and dangerous, to go by land from here to California, and I suppose that they have found it out. I have no doubt though that many of them will attempt it, for the temptation is very great. Six of Capt Woods[16] crew have deserted here and he has raised the pay of the others from $9 to $100 per month to induce them to go to San Francisco with the ship. We are messing in soldiers rations, rather rough fare but we are glad to get even these. Our encampment is on a rising ground directly in rear of Fort Vancouver, to which place you had better direct your letters. My best love to Sister and to you my dear, dear Mother.

Your Affec. Son<br>
THEO. TALBOT

CAMP, NEAR FORT VANCOUVER<br>
June 11th 1849

MY DEAREST MOTHER,

Since my last letter, Capt Ingalls[17] of the Quartermaster's Dept. has arrived here from California and we are about making preparations for Winter Quarters. It is in contemplation to finish two new wooden buildings in the immediate vicinity of the Fort and to erect others for the use of our Company (L). Capt Hill is to go to Nisqually as soon as practicable. Major Hatheway is not sure though, that his arrangment will hold, for Genl. Smith may possibly order L Compy. down to Astoria. I came very near going to Fort Hall with Mr Grant of the H. Bay Compy. who is Comdr of that post.[18] Mr Grant was down here on business and Major

16 The *Journals*, like the letters, is peppered with entries on desertion, covering an estimated thirty-eight men: entries for 1849, May 16, May 25, July 6, July 7, July 8, July 10, July 20, July 28, August 8, September 23; entries for 1850, March 5, March 29, June 13, November 17; entries for 1851, July 31.

17 Rugus Ingalls was a Maryland West Pointer, veteran of the Mexican and Civil wars.

18 With Frémont on the 1843 expedition, Talbot had met Richard Grant, who was in charge of Fort Hall for the HBC. Talbot *Journals*, September 13,

H. intended to send me there in order to purchase supplies if it were possible to obtain them in that vicinity for the Rifle Regiment—but he afterwards abandoned the idea. Fort Hall is more than 800 miles in the interior and I was not sorry to avoid this long and tedious trip. Mr Grant is an old acquaintance of mine and it afforded me much pleasure to meet with him. I have also met with Mr. Campbell a young gentleman of good family who came as far as the Dalles in the capacity of Voyageur,[19] with Fremont in the Expedition of 1843. He settled in Oregon, has married a handsome wife, had a fortune left him by a deceased relative and is now a wealthy resident of Oregon city. I met him in Philadelphia in the fall of 1847, and again our paths cross.

We shall have no society here hardly, except that of the gentlemen of the Fort. They are very polite and sociable and many of them interesting men. Mr Ogden the gentleman in charge is an American by birth, was connected with Astoria, when that place was first founded by J.J. Astor. He joined the H.B. Compy and has since been distinguished for his energy and daring in the command of trapping and exploring parties in every portion of their territories and the countries adjacent. He has also travelled in Europe. When I am down at the Fort sometimes, the old gentleman says "Come here Talbot, let's have a Smoke and a glass of wine, you are one of us," and carrying me into his quarters sits down and spins

---

1843: "Grant is a good looking gentlemanly man talks of the country as British, the Indians in it as serfs of the Hudson Bay Compy, and so forth, in the same strain."

[19] J. G. Campbell had come to Oregon in the fall of 1843 on the Second Frémont Expedition with Talbot. Campbell had stayed on the Columbia as a pioneer businessman in the firm of Campbell and Smith, mercantilists in Oregon City.

long yarns about the Rocky Mts. and mountain adventures. Some of the gentlemen have lived for years in Russia, England, France etc. etc. The Regulations of the Company are very strict and methodical in every Department of its affairs. The Officers of the Company mess at one table, at which no women are allowed to be present. Quite a Cavalier Regulation that, is it not? Few of the officers are married.

I have seen but little of the American Society of Oregon. There are a few families of Amn. settlers on the opposite side of the River and at different places in our vicinity, but they are all of the lowest class of frontier Settlers. Good enough sort of folks, but not very agreable Society. I understand however that there are many very agreable, fine families residing about Oregon City and up the Wilhamet River. I have not seen them. I need not tell you that most of the accounts which you see of the high social conditions and agricultural advantages of Oregon etc. are gross exaggerations.

We hear to day, that a mail has at last arrived at Astoria. This is glorious news; we may not get our letters for a week yet. The dates I believe will be up to Feb 4th from the U.S. It is said that the next mail will come direct in the line steamer; I hope that this is true. I send this letter by a vessel [the *Massachusetts*] which sails for California this day. I do not write you any of the Cala. News as I suppose that you hear all news from that quarter almost as soon as we do here. I regret to learn that such strong rumors prevail that Col Frémont and party have perished on their way from the Rocky Mts. to California.[20] I hope that they have no

20 Talbot, *Journals*, July 15, 1849: "Capt Grant Brit Army arrived here from Cala Comes out in charge of the Compy of Emigrants to Vancouver Isld. Saw Fremont in Cala Came from Chagres in Stmr with Mrs. Fremont. does not

foundation in truth. Gentlemen recently arrived from Cala. tell me that town sites, mill seats and other land speculations are in vogue there just now. A man buys lots in a town in which there is not at this moment a single house for $5000, sells to morrow for $10,000 and buys perhaps elsewhere, "et ainsi va tout le monde." A repetition of our land speculations of 1836.[21] The accounts of the dissipation and disorder are disgusting in their details. We are nearly free from those evils here, but our *high prices* are on the increase. In many

admire her. King, Proulx, Scott, Wise &c of Fremont's party dead of starvation poor fellows."

Frémont, after his court-martial in 1847, had mounted a tragic effort in the winter of 1848–49 to justify himself and also prove the feasibility of an all-seasons railroad route across the central Rockies. Pitching over Robidoux Pass in the Sangre de Cristos into the San Luis Valley from Pueblo, with Old Bill Williams as his reluctant guide, Frémont and his party became trapped in the deep snows of the La Garita Hills, losing one-third of their number before Frémont admitted defeat and retreated down the Río Grande Valley to Taos for refitting. Williams returned to the scene of the disaster in the spring of 1849 to recover scientific equipment and baggage but lost his life either to a party of Utes or to muleteers accompanying him, the cause of his death remaining to this day obscure.

Frémont continued on to California but with inconclusive results, to be followed by Lieutenant John W. Gunnison's Expedition of 1853, many of whose members, including its leader, were massacred by Ute Indians in the Sevier Valley of Utah; and by Frémont himself in the winter of the same year, but again with inconclusive results and with great hardship to his party. Favour, *Old Bill Williams, Mountain Man*, 145–82; Charles Preuss, *Exploring with Frémont: The Private Diaries of Charles Preuss, Cartographer for John C. Frémont on His First, Second and Fourth Expeditions to the Far West*, trans. and ed. by Erwin G. and Elisabeth K. Gudde, 143–53; S. N. Carvalho, *Incidents of Travel and Adventure in the Far West with Colonel Frémont's Last Expedition*, ed. by B. W. Korn; Allan Nevins, *Frémont, Pathmarker of the West*, 408–20; Micajah McGehee, "Rough Times in Rough Places," *Century Illustrated Monthly Magazine*, Vol. XLI, No. 5 (March, 1891), 772–78.

[21] Talbot would have been only eleven years old during the speculative mania centering around Western lands and wheat in 1836. It was probably the panic of the following year which etched the phenomenon on his memory.

cases the market is even higher here than in San Francisco. I will give you an item from a late importation. Dried Apples $45. per Bbl. value in N York $2.00. The prices for clothing too, are outrageous.

Some of our men have attempted to desert. Their plan was discovered and frustrated. Out of some 30 or 40 concerned in the plot only seven got off. They were pursued the same night and retaken without loss. This complete failure and the many known obstacles, will I hope deter them from future attempts. The Quartermaster I believe intends to employ some of our men in the erection of buildings etc. giving them the high market wages for labor, the Captains of Companies giving them short furloughs for that purpose. This plan may have a good effect towards keeping them. I doubt it myself. It is certain that it will have a ruinous effect on military discipline. The only true way is to increase their proper military pay. Give my kind regards to all our good friends. I can hardly think of anything now but that *Astoria mail*. My best love to Sister.

Your Devoted Son,<br>THEO. TALBOT

[A twenty page report on a side excursion to the Alcea River is deleted here. It was reprinted in Philip T. Tyson, *Geology and Industrial Resources of California: To Which is Added the Official Reports of Generals Persifer F. Smith and B. Riley, including the Reports of Lieutenant Talbot, Ord, Derby, and Williamson, of Their Explorations in California and Oregon* (Baltimore, 1851).]

FORT VANCOUVER. O.T.
Nov 9th 1849

MY DEAREST MOTHER,

... We have been in Winter Quarters about a month. The Company Officers all live in a long one story *log* house built by ourselves. It is partitioned off, each officer having a sitting and bed room to himself, with a general mess room. Our accommodations are rude enough, but still they afford us a good protection against the winter rains which have already commenced to pour down upon us.

Genl. Smith and Staff arrived here in the latter part of Sept. on a tour of inspection. The Genl. hurt his foot in disembarking from the vessel which brought him here and has been confined to his room nearly ever since but is now getting well. The Officers of his Staff who accompanied him, are Lt. Col Hooker (late of our Regt.)[22] Adjt. Genl. Pacific Divn., Maj. Lee Chief Commissary,[23] Maj Leonard, C. Paymaster,[24] and Maj Vinton C. Quartermaster.[25] I have been quite agreably disappointed in Maj. Lee, against whom I had rather taken a prejudice from our slight acquaintance at St. Louis Mo. Being on duty as commissary when he first arrived I was frequently brought in contact with him and have found him very kind and desirous to advance my wishes in every way that lay in his power. He is also a very agreable

[22] Joseph Hooker of Massachusetts had fought valiantly in the Mexican War, but his historical position rests more firmly in the Civil War as "Fighting Joe" Hooker, who followed Burnside as General of the Army of the Potomac.

[23] Richard Bland Lee of the Virginia Lees was a West Pointer and later a colonel in the commissary for the Confederacy.

[24] Hiram Leonard served as paymaster from the Mexican War to his retirement in 1872 as a brigadier general.

[25] David Hammond Vinton, a Rhode Islander and West Pointer, served in the Quartermaster Corps from ten years before the Mexican War until his retirement in 1866.

134

Lieutenant Theodore Talbot. A Drawing by Anthony Forbus from an Early Photograph.

Christopher (Kit) Carson and John Charles Frémont (COURTESY
DENVER PUBLIC LIBRARY)

Joseph Reddeford Walker, from the Portrait
by Alfred Jacob Miller, 1837.

Bent's Fort on the Arkansas, from the Perspective Drawn by Lieutenant J. W. Abert, 1845.

A Frémont Camp, from the Drawing by Edward Kern, 1845.

Astoria, from the Wilkes Expedition *Report.*

H.M.S. *Beaver* off Fort Vancouver, 1850 (COURTESY WASHINGTON
STATE HISTORICAL SOCIETY).

Colonel B. L. E. Bonneville.

companion being possessed of an almost inexhaustible fund of story and adventure and is withal quite an eccentric.

The Regt. Mounted Rifles arrived here in detachments early in October and have gone into winter quarters at Oregon City. Bvt. Col Loring[26] commands the Regt. and supercedes Maj Hathaway in the Command of the Dept. Col L. has only one arm having lost the other in Mexico. He intends coming here with the Majority of the Rifles early in the spring and we shall probably have to take up a new position somewhere about the mouth of the Columbia. Vancouver has been made the Commisary Depot for the Territory and an officer specially detailed to take charge of it. Maj. Lee endeavored to get me the appointment but Bvt Capt. McLane[27] of the Rifles who ranks me in the line and as a Commy. made application for it and Col. Loring gave him the preference, so that I am now returned to Company duty. The place was only desirable as an *independent* position, for the additional pay is not a fair compensation for the trouble and responsibility incurred.

Maj. Crittenden son of Gov C of Ky. is under arrest and charges for drunkeness, the same offence for which he was dismissed from the service a short time since.[28] Bvt Major

[26] William Wing Loring (1818–86) from North Carolina joined the army while still in his teens to fight against the Seminoles. After becoming a lawyer and sitting in the state legislature, he returned to the army in the Mexican War, losing an arm at Chapultepec. He commanded the Military Department of Oregon from 1849 to 1851. He joined the Confederacy in the Civil War and afterward fought for the Khedive of Egypt.

[27] George McLane, enlisted from Maryland, decorated at Churubusco and Chapultepec, would be killed by Navajos in New Mexico in an Indian campaign of 1860.

[28] George Bibb Crittenden, West Pointer and Kentuckian, after gallantry in the Mexican War was cashiered in 1848, but was restored the following year. He later fought for the Confederacy.

Simonson[29] and Lt Julian May,[30] are also awaiting trial, in
fact there appears to be but little harmony existing among the
Officers of that Regiment. We have had no desertions lately.
It is very unhealthy in the Cal. gold mines and many of the
Oregonians have returned. I hear of many Washingtonians
in California, Bomford, Jones, Blair and etc. Midshipman
Denny a relation of the Jeseps came overland with the Rifles
and is now staying with us. Col. Hooker was also in Washington last spring. He says that Loo Adams is engaged to Mr
Thorn, is it so? We have just heard that the French have
seized upon the Sandwich Islands.[31] The United States will
probably interfere and we should all be very glad to be ordered
there. I brought over with me a Kanaka, (the common name
given to Islanders here) as a servant, but I find it as much as
I can do to keep myself, in the present state of things, so that
I was glad to get rid of him, which I did a few days ago.[32]
By the bye who is now Chef de Cuisine and femme de chambre
of your establishment. I am most truly sorry to learn that our

[29] John Smith Simonson (1796–1881), native Pennsylvanian, sat in the Indiana state legislature before serving under Scott in the Mexican War. He fought
with the army against the Indians in Texas and New Mexico after his service
in Oregon.

[30] Julian May, from Washington, D.C., had joined the service at the beginning of the Mexican War. He was to die shortly before the Civil War.

[31] On August 25, 1849, armed forces from two French frigates occupied the
fort, government offices, and the customs house in Hawaii. The action resulted
from a series of French grievances, including a heavy Hawaiian duty on brandy
and Hawaiian decision to prefer the English language over French in commerce.
The French invasion lasted until September 5.

[32] Talbot, *Journals*, April 17, 1849 [Honolulu]: "My own boy Frank was
on board in time with all his traps. He has lived with Macfarlane & bears an
excellent character for honesty &c. Give him $6. p month." *Journals*, May 11,
1849: "My boy learning English fast." *Journals*, September 23–25, 1849:
"Detected my boy stealing—Had him whipped & he ran off."

kind friend Mr. Larned is declining so rapidly. Give my best love to Mrs Thornton—and remember me to Mr Mathews, the Gentlemen of G. T. College, and to all our friends. I am glad to learn that there is a prospect of realising something from the Arkansas property and hope that you will soon be enabled to live more comfortably. For me, I believe that I am growing every day poorer instead of richer but where is the Subaltern who is not? I must therefore fain be content with the general lot of that restless discontented race of individuals. Cultivate every kind of political influence if you ever want me to come home again. Is it not a pity that some of our cousins with such high military rank are not in the American Army  I might then talk of Oregon as a sort of Terra Incognita or a genteel Botany Bay for Army Officers. I should like to know my Spanish cousin very much. Why does she wish to immerse herself within the walls of a convent? I think that Convents are institutions of which the present age has but little need. They were in former times the safe guard of the innocent and helpless against rude oppression but certainly my cousin does not require that protection. If she is influenced solely by religious motives with her talents and true piety might she not perform all the worldly duties alloted to her station and in saving her own soul contribute to the Salvation of many others by a brilliantly virtuous example. If her worldly path is beset with dangers and trials, it is the Divinity himself, in his wisdom, who has placed those difficulties in the way rather that she should triumph over than seek to avoid them. My ideas may surprise you my dear Mother, and perhaps I am wrong, but I cannot reconcile myself to the idea of any friend thus burying themselves in a living tomb.

My best love to Sister. May God bless and preserve
you both in health and happiness.

I am Ever
Your Devoted Son.
THEODORE TALBOT

FORT VANCOUVER OREGON
Dec. 25th 1849

MY DEAR SISTER,

. . . To day, is bright and clear, the first we have had
for many days or rather weeks. We have had first continuous
heavy rains and then incessant snow storms. It has been much
colder thus far than it usually is here and the Colombia R. has
been partially frozen over, a circumstance of rare occurrence.
Notwithstanding the damp and wet weather I have not been
at all troubled by my old enemy the rheumatism and my
general health has been excellent. I spent the latter part of
last month at Oregon City, being there on duty as a member
of a General Court Martial. During the sittings of the court,
Bvt. Lt. Col. Backenstos its President, was deemed by the
Court to have been guilty of gross disrespect in the face of the
Court, and was *arraigned* and *tried* by the Court.[33] This is a
procedure almost without precedent in the records of Military

---

[33] Talbot, *Journals*, November 17, 1849: "Court assembled . . . Col. B. declared the Court adjourned until Monday, members objecting Col B. still persisted in adjourning the Court & left the room. Court continued in session,
arresting Col B & directed him to appear at 2 oclock & apologise for his con-
tempt of the Court. Judge Advocate stated to Court when it reassembled at 2
oclock after a short recess that Col B refused to appear before or recognize the
arrest of the Court. The Court then directed charges to be made out against Col
B. & he cited to appear & answer to them. He claimed his seat on Monday &
was ejected, not answering or appearing to defend himself." Backenstos resigned June 30, 1851.

Courts and the proceedings of the Court have been referred
to Washington where I have no doubt that they will create
some sensation as they have done here. Since, Col Backenstos
has had a violent personal affray with Asst. Surgeon Moses,[34]
for which he is now in arrest. Majors Crittenden and Simonson still remain in arrest awaiting trial. May who was in arrest
has been released without trial (the affair which was trifling
having been satisfactorily adjusted) Col Loring is here spending his Christmas. He has his hands or hand full (he has only
one arm) in managing his command, of which *this post* as you
know, is a part. Lt. Talmadge of Hill's Compy. has been promoted to the 4th Arty. and is ordered home.[35] Happy fellow!
Genl. Smith and staff left here for California the end of last
month. We are quietly waiting for the opening of spring,
sometime in May when we shall take up our abode at Astoria.
These I believe are the principal items of the Mil. intelligence.

We have received a newspaper mail from the United
States up to the end of August but no letters. The terrible
devestation created by the Cholera in all parts of the United
States is really alarming. I see that a few cases are reported
to exist in Washington and I feel exceedingly anxious to hear
from you. My last letters from home are dated in the beginning of June nearly six months ago!

Jan 4th 1850.

Yesterday the long desired letters reached me, one
from you, dated Aug 25th and one from Mother, July 12th.
It seems that they arrived in Oregon nearly a month ago and
had come as far as Portland on the Wilhamet, when they

[34] Israel Moses, New Yorker, served in the Army from 1847 until the end
of the Civil War, at various times in the medical service and in the infantry.
[35] Grier Tallmadge was a West Pointer from New York.

were taken down the River again with the rest of the letter mail by some daring speculators, who had got news of a sudden rise in flour at San Francisco and were afraid that the same intelligence might be contained in some of the letters, which have just arrived from Astoria a second time. By this trick a large quantity of flour was bought here at 20$ per bbl which will be sold at 60 or 70$ at San Francisco. This is but a single instance of the lamentable condition of our mail arrangements. The mail to the states is still more uncertain for we have to depend almost always on private conveyance as far as California.

. . . You seem to entertain the same opinion as I do about our cousin Joanne entering a Convent and I cannot regret that she has not suceeded in her intention. I wish that I could become personally acquainted with her. Remember me to her and give my regards to our friends one and all. You must send me a pair of slippers if you have an opportunity. I have been wearing the nice pair that you last made me ever since I left home until about a week ago when some confounded rogue took into his head to steal them. I had a very handsome pair of velvet slippers embroidered in gold and floss silk sent me two months ago but I would prefer to wear a pair made by yourself. . . .

Your Affectionate Brother
THEODORE TALBOT

*[The following letter is a fragment. The missing portions are not available in the original collection.]*

ASTORIA. Aug 2d. 1850

MY DEAR SISTER,

. . . The jesuits must be getting along finely with their school, I hope it may prosper. There are but few jesuits in this portion of Oregon. There has been and still exists a very strong sectarian feeling among the people of this country engendered by the Prot. Missionaries who formerly exercised much control, but the conduct of the majority of them has been such as to bring them into general disrepute and they are fast losing that influence. The Catholics as a body command much respect. None of them have been very successful with the indians on this coast who are very intractable, and all except the Catholics have abandoned this barren missionary field. There are still some large indian villages in our vicinity but they are the mere remnants of the great nations which dwelt upon this River at the time of its first discovery and occupation by the Whites. It is melancholy indeed to witness the tremenduous devastation which has here so rapidly followed in the footsteps of the strangers. Death and destruction has been dealt out to the Aborigines with an unsparing hand, even those diseases which we are accustomed to considered the most trifling extending to the indians have become fearful epidemics sweeping off whole tribes. It is but a few years since that the measles swept off thousands of the poor natives. Quite near our camp is the last resting place of King Cloncomely the great chief of the Chenooks. Little did that formidable warrior dream of the fatal spell that would be wrought on his people by the strangers, when full of confiding friendship he came in savage pomp to Astoria, at the head of a great fleet of canoes bringing with him his only and beautiful daughter an offering in marriage to the Chief Agent of Astor. As dowry was brought an immense quantity of rich furs worth many thousand dollars. these were strewn on the path from the landing place to the new Fort, a considerable distance, the girl stepping from her canoe walked on them followed by a numerous retinue of slaves who gathered up these costly presents as she passed over them and bringing them on laid the rich piles at the feet of her future husband. Not forty years have yet elapsed and the nation of Cloncomely has only a few straggling representatives to tell of its former greatness.[36] We have changed our camp since I wrote last finding it impossible to clear a spot and erect suitable quarters before the advent of the rainy season and are now occupying the old site of Astoria. Our temporary camp rests partly on an old indian grave yard which same I suppose has set me moralizing on the strange fatality attending the contact of the antagonistic races and at the expense of your patience I have written what came to my mind first.

The Massachusetts has been here some time with the Army and Navy board of commissioners, who are examining the coast with regard to defences etc. Lt Knox commands her, he and some of the others have been in Oregon before with Wilkes.[37] It has been quite a treat to us to have the society of these gentlemen. The Army officers are Col Smith,[38] Maj. Ogden,[39] Lt. Leadbetter[40] all of the Engrs. We were quite sorry they left us so soon: having sailed yesterday for Cali-

[36] Concomly, a one-eyed Chinook chief, first appeared in white history when met by Lewis and Clark. After his friendship with the British was established, he became a link between the Hudson's Bay Company and the natives.

[37] Samuel R. Knox from Massachusetts joined the navy in 1828. He commanded the schooner *Flying Fish* during most of the explorations led by Captain Charles Wilkes throughout the Pacific, 1838–42. The Wilkes Expedition examined the Columbia River in the spring of 1841.

[38] John Lind Smith, South Carolinian, decorated for Mexican War bravery, died in 1858.

[39] Edmund Augustus Ogden was a West Pointer from New York.

[40] Danville Leadbetter, West Pointer from Maine, resigned from the army in 1857 and after 1861, in spite of his origins, fought for the South.

fornia. Tell my dear Mother for it will tickle her vanity that
Mr Leadbetter told me that Col Smith said, (mind how particular I am) that he was very pleased with my report on
the Alce[a] Expedition (where I went last summer) that it
was just what it ought to be and very creditable to me &c.
Col. Smith afterwards said the same thing to me himself. A
propos of Col. Smith, He is a rich jolly old bachelor with a
very white head & a very red nose & has travelled all over
Europe again since the Mex. War in which he was brevetted
& was in Paris during the Revolution. He has always abundance of good wine, good jokes & the best military library
in America, all of which are at the service of his friends. The
opinion of such a man is worth   something.

The Mail Steamers from the Isthmus are to come up
here in the future so we shall have a speedy communication
with home. I did not get any newspapers by the previous mail
but the steamer arrived yesterday and I got a number of my
own and indemnified myself for former losses by securing
sundry others. Genl. Adair of Ky is Collector and Postmaster
his wife is a very nice lady and he has two half grown daugh-
ters, altogether a very pleasant family. I am still poor as ever
and no good chance yet of getting rich. Mess bill last month
(food alone) 48$. Washing 15$. not surplus enough to keep
me in shoe leather, to say nothing about cigars sundries etc. I
gave for painting the outside of a house which same I could
do much faster myself and cheaper too were it not for my
shoulder straps. I feel sometimes tempted to resign for I am
sure that I cd make money but I do not like to enter into the
contest with the scoundrels that I see round me and with
whom I must be in constant contact to succeed. Now that I
have many business transactions for Govt. I find out more

than I ever knew before with regard to most business on this Coast. Give my love to Friends. I am Ever

Your Affect. Brother,<br>
THEODORE TALBOT

ASTORIA. OREGON TERRITORY<br>
Sept. 25. 1850

DEAR MOTHER,

You may be surprised at my not having mentioned Maj. Hatheway's sad attempt on his own life; but I as well as other officers had promised him not to mention it in our letters, in the vain hope that the circumstance might be concealed from his friends.[41] It was done as I see it stated in the papers, whilst laboring under delirium tremens, a species of low nervous derangement produced by excessive drinking. He had been in this condition several days when taking advantage of the temporary absence of his servant in an adjoining room late in the night, he got hold of a razor and would undoubtedly have killed himself had not his servant providentially suspected something wrong and suddenly entering his bedroom seized him before he could consummate the horrible deed. The servant's cries for assistance aroused Mr. Woods[42] and myself who were sleeping in the next sets of quarters and the Major was soon mastered. Fortunately his ignorance of anatomy saved him for he had given himself two terrible gashes, but in such a manner as to cut merely the thick muscles

[41] John Samuel Hatheway, West Pointer from New York, saw meritorious service in the Mexican War before his troubles in Oregon. Talbot in the *Journals*, October 19, 1850, tries to conceal the problem by writing in French, here translated by Charles Carey: "[Major Hatheway] wants to kill himself again; he had the delirium tremens for three days previously." Hatheway did finally commit suicide in 1853 in New York.

[42] Either Lt. Joseph Jackson Woods or Captain Wood of the *Massachusetts*.

144

of the neck. Dr. Holden immediately sewed up his wounds and in three weeks he was as well as ever. He was of course much shocked on recovering fully his right mind and I hope will eventually abandon all indulgence in a habit over which he can exercise no control and which if persisted in must inevitably terminate his career disgracefully. Heretofore all remonstrances or advice have had no effect upon him. he acknowledges the justice of all said and seems to feel sensible of his faults and the infinite trouble and annoyance which he causes to those round him, but still cannot resist his sad propensity. As you say it was unfortunate that he was sent out here, where there are many temptations and none of the restraints which exist elsewhere. His habits were well known, for he was tried in Vera Cruz just before I joined the Regt. for habitual drunkeness and escaped dismission by a mere quibble in consequence partly, no doubt, of his popularity among his brother officers. Hatheway when sober is considered an excellent and agreable officer to serve with. You will of course appreciate my motive in not mentioning this matter before, for I have all confidence in your prudence. And it is necessary to be prudent. You would be surprised did you know how the private remarks of officers often get to ears, and create impressions which they were never intended to do. I have had experience on that score myself.

Lt. Fry has gone home having received orders transferring him to a company in New York.[43] I shall not miss him much as we were never on intimate terms. Haines[44] who

[43] James Barnet Fry, West Pointer from Illinois, was a frequent companion of Talbot's during the company's stay in Hawaii, though the *Journals* does not reveal Talbot's feelings about his fellow officer.

[44] Thomas Jefferson Haines, New Hampshire West Pointer, was mustered out of the army as a colonel at the end of the Civil War.

was to have been transferred with Fry, came out here but managed to get orders from Loring and has returned to the United States. This was contrary to Smith's orders and also those from home, so Haines will probably have to come back and be in trouble about it besides. I wish indeed that the State of Kentucky or anybody else could succeed in bullying old Crane[45] or coaxing him into getting me ordered home.

As quartermaster, I am rapidly becoming quite a proficient (I flatter myself,) in the arts of Carpentry, bricklaying, blacksmithing and in a word of tinkering generally all at the expense of Uncle Sam. From motives of economy we are not allowed to employ regular mechanics, the soldiers being required to construct their own quarters. I frequently have a quiet laugh to myself when the men who dont know much about it themselves, refer some important point to me, as, whether the "Lieutenant" thinks that a certain piece of timber had better be "mortised or rabated," or something else be done to it, I, (knowing nothing about it,) as in duty bound, look very sagacious and give a truly oracular and dubious decision, or if I can't evade it, decide sometimes right, and very often wrong—but that cant be helped, for I find that carpenters and various other mechanics, unlike poets, stand no chance of being born such, but must be fashioned by a longer or shorter apprenticeship. I should like my present duty well enough though, (because it gives me *occupation* and I pick up some useful information,) were it not for the money and property responsibility which it involves and of which like all "green 'uns" I am much afraid. In fact it is not very agreable to be responsible for all sorts of things at a post,

[45] Ichabod Bennett Crane from New Jersey moved from the marines to the army in 1812. He died as a colonel in 1857.

from a ten penny nail up to a six horse team and perhaps have besides some 15 or 20,000$ in cash, of which some kind rogue may relieve you, much to your detriment. Luckily I have two good soldier clerks who save me much trouble for our accounts are very voluminous and somewhat intricate, requiring much writing—admirable traps for men with honest intentions and not very formidable to those reversely inclined. I stand much in awe of the 3d Auditor who has the final settlement of my accounts and who can have my pay stopped any day if he can detect any informality. Although I am getting a 1000$ a year now I can barely keep my nose above water. I hope that we shall get into comfortable quarters before the rains of the winter season set in. We have already had one or two rainy spells which have served as practical hints to us that tents are not the pleasant places in which to spend an Oregon winter. The death of Genl. Taylor has created much sensation and great anxiety is felt to know the policy cabinet etc. of his successor.[46] The Cuban affair seems somewhat ominous of war. Have you subscribed to the Herald for me yet? if not *please to do so*. I lose many of those you send and they are always behind the rest of the mail in date which is important. We suffer much for the want of reading matter, especially the light current literature of the day. Bookstores are unknown and but few individuals have any books and those not readable. We officers have more valuable books among us by half, than all the other inhabitants of the Territory. This statement does not accord well with that of our Honble delegate in Congress who attributes the highest degree of literary

---

[46] Zachary Taylor, President of the United States from 1849 until his death from cholera on July 9, 1850; succeeded by his vice-president, Millard Fillmore.

intelligence to his constitutents, it is true nevertheless.[47] He is not over brilliant himself, as you may have perceived if you have ever taken the trouble to read his speeches. The prices of labour produce goods etc., still remain much higher here than in California. Everything which might be termed luxuries and even many articles of necessity are very scarce and command enormous prices. I was amused the other day to see brooms which cost 8 cents in New York and certainly would not average one cent more to bring them out here selling readily at 3$. Axe Handles at $2.50 and so with a thousand other articles. I understand that there will be a large overland emigration to this country this year. Some hundred have already arrived. People are also coming here from California. I cannot say much for the new appointees. Strong[48] and Hamilton:[49] they stopped here some weeks not being able to get transportation up the River for the immense quantity of pots and pans, stores and goods of all sorts which they brought out with them (even down to chickens) at the expense of the United States and in a man of war. The hens being removed to shore, commenced laying eggs and a citizen who had been very polite to Strong casually expressed a desire to have 2 or 3 eggs for hatching as the breed was somewhat better than he had himself, but Judge Strong who is a prudent, nasal whining Yankee, "guessed his eggs might be worth more than a dollar a piece up country and he guessed he'd keep 'em." I

[47] Samuel R. Thurston (1816–51) represented the Oregon Territory in Congress from 1849 to 1851; he died at sea on a return trip to Washington. He was a Dartmouth graduate and a Democrat, but also, in David Lavender's words, "a demogogue" who spent much time trying to extinguish Indian titles to land.

[48] William Strong came on a federal appointment to the district court. He was a Whig and most of his district was north of the Columbia.

[49] Charles Smith Hamilton, New York West Pointer, was a brevet captain in the Mexican War and was decorated for bravery at Churubusco.

think that he will do well. Egg peddling may not redound much to the honor of the Supreme Judiciary, but at any rate promises to be profitable. Hamilton hasn't too much talent. He was an Editor and a Capt of vols. in the war and is now dubbed Genl. He feels much the importance of "mine office" and is so military withal in his appearance as to cause considerable anxiety lest he should fall over backwards. They begged and borrowed me out of all patience. Give my best love to the Larneds Mrs. Thornton etc. The young ladies need not trouble themselves about me as I intend to remain a bachelor. I will not be *too* positive about it *yet* or I might have to make poor Benedick's excuse. "When I said that I should die a bachelor, I did not think that I should live 'till I were married." I hope that you carried out your intention of spending some time at Piney Point. I am sure the change would do you good. I have written in anticipation of the arrival of the Mail Steamer daily expected. The last steamer was in such a hurry that letters all ready could not be mailed in time. Give my best love to Sister.

Your Affectionate Son.<br>THEODORE TALBOT

ASTORIA. O.T.<br>Oct. 24th 1850

MY DEAR SISTER,

We are pursuing the even tenor of our way in the quietest manner imaginable. I have been as well as usual. The rainy season has caught us in our tents in consequence of our being disappointed in receiving lumber, the mill with which we had contracted for our supply having most perversely broken down at the very time when we would have had it working hardest. In a very few days though we shall all be housed a most desirable object now, for when it once commences raining here in good earnest, there is no predicting when it will ever stop again. I am going to have very nice quarters, as in duty bound, according to Genl. Twiggs theory. He on one occasion having heard of the appointment of an officer of his command as a quartermaster sent for him and asked him if he was familiar with his new sphere of duty. The officer making some modest reply, the General proceeded to give him advice: "Let it be your duty Sir, in the first place," said he, "to make *yourself* comfortable, secondly make yourself more comfortable, and when you have done that, make everybody else as *uncomfortable* as you can." With which excellent maxims for his guidance he dismissed the young quartermaster. I need not add that most Officers who are *not* quartermasters, think that all who are, obey Twiggs rules very implicitly. I have just returned from up the River where I have been for some days past. As yet we have only one very small steamer but still at this season of the year that is a great improvement over open boats in our river travel.

We have had lately a considerable emigration from California by sea, mining proving less successful than heretofore and the prices of labor being also very low. Many overland emigrants have been compelled to come [to] Oregon in consequence of the failure of grass on the California route. This will be beneficial to Oregon, several new localities are being settled and are thriving. Most of the old settlers have become so suddenly enriched that they lost all their energy and are completely verifying the old proverb, "Set a beggar on horseback etc. etc." You can't imagine how disgusting it is to be compelled to have intercourse with such people. No aristocrat with the blood of the Howards coursing through his veins, ever swelled or strutted with half the importance of some of the purse proud, illiterate mobocrats round about us. The uses to which they put their newly acquired wealth are in many instances fully as ridiculous as the extravagancies of any farce. I understand that a law has passed lately in the Sandwich Islds. permitting aliens to hold real estate, this will have the effect of attracting thither a great number of Americans and I have no doubt that in a very few years these beautiful islands will become completely americanized and perhaps be annexed to our already brilliant galaxy. We lost one of our men a few days ago, the first man who has died since the company left New York now nearly two years. How long these two years have seemed to me who have only being looking forward to the expiration of my dreary term of service in Oregon. For your's and Mother's sake how I long to be with you.

Thurs Evg.

I commenced my letter none too soon. The Oregon came in quite unexpectedly. I have just read a very interesting letter from my dearest Mother for which please to thank her, with my most affectionate love. It was singular that she should have encountered Señora Barton. She is a very pleasant lady and of excellent family. We have not got our papers yet but have heard some of the principal items of news. I received a *very splendid* card of invitation to a "Grand Celebration Ball in honor of the Admission of California into the Union" to be given at San Francisco 29th inst. I am not sorry that they have suspended our new uniform. [John Charles] Fremont is in the *senate* for the short term however, [William Mc-Kendree] Gwin having drawn the "Long straw," six years.

Capt Patterson U.S.N. commands the Oregon,[50] he is going home to marry Miss Pearson. Capt Ingalls Capt. Morris etc. have just arrived from Vancouver which will prevent me from writing any more before the mail closes. Morris is a son of the Comd. his family live in the City. Give my regards to Larneds Jesups and etc.

> Your Most Affectionate brother,
>
> THEODORE

ASTORIA. Dec 25th 1850

MY DEAR SISTER,

I received by the Nov Steamer a letter from yourself of Sep 23d and one from Mother of Oct 9th, with many papers. I also found at the Post Office your package which had been deposited there by Capt. Budd, to whose care it had been entrusted by our friend Mrs Blair. The old shoes that were wont to do the duty have been cast aside, and as I now write I am luxuriating in your beautiful slippers—they fit me perfectly and in taste and workmanship you could not possibly have pleased me better. Accept my best thanks for yourself and thank Mother for the nice socks. I am very glad that you receive my letters regularly. I have the same happiness. The Mail Steamers arrive here generally between the 26th and the end of each month but under the present arrangment their stay here is so short that letters intended to go in them must be mailed beforehand, but an arrangment is proposed by which letters can be received and answered by the same steamer. I was much surprised and pleased to hear that Congress had

[50] Carlisle Pollock Patterson (1816–81) retired from the navy in 1850 to assume command of the Pacific Mail steamship *Oregon*.

increased our pay, the addition will prove none the less welcome that it has been unexpected. It has only been by the most strict economy in dress and debarring myself of many comforts that I have been able to get along at all.

The Oregon land bill which we got by the last mail is going to make a great change in the state of affairs in this country.[51] Hundreds of poor fellows whose brilliant visions of the land of Gold have been dissipated by its stern realities, have wandered hitherwards in the hope of acquiring that wealth which has as yet eluded their grasp. Many land here penniless, with shattered healths, and some have died of diseases previously induced by poverty and neglect and even have had to be buried by us. Sickness and poverty meet with but little sympathy, for the eager pursuit of wealth makes men hard hearted. At home you hear only of those who have been successful in heaping up a handsome fortune; but a sad reverse may be found to all these bright pictures: thousands perish miserably among strangers, dying uncared for and unwept. Every one in this part of the world, obeys none other than the sneering injunction of Horace,

> "Get money; get a large estate,
> By honest means; but get, at any rate."

But besides the poorer persons, many men of Capital have lately come to the country with the intention of investing. Three Steam Mills are being erected within sight of us, one bye the bye on the Govt. Reserve. It is still undecided whether the President will confirm this place as a reserve. In the meantime we are in a state of uncertainty by no means agreable.

[51] The Donation Land Law, in effect from 1850 until 1855, originally provided 320 acres for all white or half-blood male citizens plus the same for wives.

The people here detest us and are straining every nerve to have us removed, I for one am nothing loth to go, unless we can have all of them removed, of which there is not much chance. I am afraid it will be compromised by circumscribing our limits in such a manner as to leave us in the closest vicinage to very unpleasant neighbors. It would be a hard matter for any class of people to be more unpopular than Army Officers are in this country. This principally arises from their having done their duty in selecting the most elegible points in the Territory for Govt. purposes. In the last Oregon City paper I see a string of resolutions, passed at some little town on the Wilhamet, denouncing us in most unmeasured terms and praying that we may all be sent out of the country, (a resolution I most heartily second and I suppose you would too). We are accused in the vilest language of being leagued with the H.B. Company and the Papists to defraud the people of their just rights and etc. . . .

> I am as Ever, Your Affecte Brother.
> THEODORE TALBOT

> ASTORIA. OREGON
> Jan. 25th 1851

MY DEAR SISTER,

I have already written to Mother for this mail but I could not refrain from inflicting one of my cramped epistles upon you, to thank you for your own lively and pleasant letters. I am very glad that your health has been so good. We are always healthy here. Some of the Doctors say abominably so. Like Othello, *our* Doctor's occupation clean gone but instead of getting into a passion about it he has merely gone to California to make some speculations there. He is a Jew and not a Moor however, and retains at least, one of the grand characteristics of his nation, the desire to make money, an inclination which I must confess that I share with him but I do not know how to go about it and must therefore fain content myself with a little, consoling myself with the Horation Maxim "parvum para decent," in other words, "petites gens peu de bien." [52]

It has been raining like a young deluge for ten days past. We have not much occupation or amusement except in reading. I find that my taste for reading has much improved. There is certainly a most delightful species of companionship in a good book. You have always had an inclination that way. I hope that Mother does not extend her awful economy into the book dept. Apropos, I have some slight misgivings and would really like to know for certain, if Mother does dress respectably and for the honor of the house, if warm fires are kept in the parlors and if they are comfortably furnished. Mother also writes very pleasantly about riding in the Omnibuses, perhaps it is the fashion, all I know is that it was not exactly the mode when I was last in Washington. If you will, make purchases for me of such useful books as you yourself would like to read, I will reimburse you and whenever I come home I can get them. We have had quite a treat lately in some new books which Dr. Moses received from New York. We are indeed very well off for the better sort of books and only miss the light literature (or current trash as you may choose to call it.)

My friends Mr and Mrs Campbell have just returned to Oregon after spending the summer (and some $10,000) at the Eastern watering places. They brought back with them

[52] Small things from small people.

Mrs. Tucker wife of Major Tucker of the Rifles.[53] The Major
was married only a month, when he had to leave his bride to
come out here. She is the daughter of a hotelkeeper at Cleave-
land or somewhere on the Lakes where the Major was recruiting. The officers do say, that "Old Dan" took so many
mint juleps that he found marrying mine host's daughter was
the most convenient way of paying his score. This is scandal,
Mrs. T. is a very nice little woman. I read in the paper to day
that a Lt Harrison of the Navy had just married the daughter of a tavern keeper at Oregon City.[54] I do not know either
of the parties, who have both lately arrived in the Territory,
but from what I have heard I should judge that the young
lady possesses some spirit of her own. The Captain of the
Steamer in which she went up to Oregon City told me that
on the passage some unfortunate individual all unconscious of
the relationship, was abusing in good set terms her Publican
father, (who indeed is not sans reproche) when the young
lady hearing him, informed the gentleman that he was "a
mean, nasty puppy" and made such formidable digital demon-
strations that the unwitting offender deemed it prudent to
retire precipitately to a place of safety, there to reflect, no
doubt, on the imprudence of making personal allusions in
mixed companies. You can relieve Mrs. Thornton's anxiety
by informing her that I am positively not going to be married.
In the first place I am too poor to marry, secondly, there is no
one here to marry, thirdly, I wouldn't if I could—three co-
gent reasons, each more conclusive than the other.

[53] Stephen S. Tucker, a Vermonter decorated in the Mexican War, resigned
from the army shortly hereafter in 1851.

[54] Probably George W. Harrison of the *Cyane*, who had served earlier on
the Wilkes Expedition.

I have felt much better reconciled to remain here since I have met or heard of so many persons who have come and gone to the states from here, in such short periods of time, often even far in advance of the mails. We no longer appear so isolated as we were a year ago when we had only the remembrance of our own long voyage and letters came so few and far between. You must not be uneasy however when you do not hear from me, for the mails are still very irregular and Mail Agents most culpably negligent. Sometimes too, I am away from the Post and out of reach of the mail. We enjoy a great advantage at this Post over all others in the Terry. in sending and receiving our mails, which I for one duly appreciate. We are now expecting the regular monthly Mail Steamer. Remember me to all friends and write frequently to Your Affect. Brother.

THEO. TALBOT

COLUMBIA BARRACKS, O.T.<br>(VANCOUVER). May 20th 1851

MY DEAR SISTER,

Your letter of March finds me pretty busy at my new post. I am rejoiced that you are able to report an improvement in Mother's health for I have been much troubled about her. I gave Mrs. T's message to Bomford—he frequently comes to see me. He is, as you probably know a clerk to Capt. Ingalls a Qm. I cannot but admire the stamen of the man, he takes hold like a good fellow and performs his duties well, no one would suppose that he had ever been in the region of white kid gloves.

Col Loring left here two weeks ago. The rich Maj. Kearney of the 1st Dragoons is here now, in command of this post.[55] He was sent here to take the horses of the Regt. M. Rifles to California by land. Enough of the men of the Rifles were transferred here to 1st Drags. to make two companies. Three Lieuts of the Rifles were left here to assist Kearney. He will start on his journey in three or four weeks. I do not admire Kearney much. Vancouver is looking very beautiful and I am delighted at the change of stations. I think now that I shall remain here for several months as we hear nothing of any troops being ordered out to supply the place of the Rifles. I had some difficulty in getting here. Hatheway had offered me the command of the Company and Post at Astoria which would have increased my pay between 30 and 40$ per month, but I preferred this post and less pay. It was rumored that the 7th Infy. were on their way out here but now it seems to be doubtful whether any troops will come and I believe Hatheway is sorry that he did not take this post himself. I do not think however that he will order me away as I have receipted for a large amount of public property and have been at considerable personal expense consequent to my change of station. Beside the future Charge of the Post I will be actg. Ordnance Offr and Dept. Commissary. I am now allowed a clerk from civil life and employ a young gentleman from Carlisle Pa by the name of Noble. I pay him a very low salary for Oregon $120 per month. (About my own pay.). Col. Backenstos and Maj Tucker of the Rifles have resigned and remain in Oregon much to the gratification of those under them who are eager for promotion. I received the Living Age etc. which you sent

[55] Philip Kearny (1814–62), "rich" because he had inherited a million dollars from his grandfather, endeared himself to the Oregon settlers by chastising the Indians in two battles near Medford. His more distinguished uncle was Stephen Watts Kearny.

158

me and am much obliged. I do not now want the Cath. Mirror regularly, I get all the religious intelligence in other papers which I take and do not feel any interest in its stories, poetry, accounts of fairs etc. Please not to write my name in ink on covers of magazines, papers etc. I got 2 Army Registers. I am climbing up the ladder of promotion poco poco. Well! let us hope for a war or at least a pestilence. I was much pleased with the able phamphlet of Archbishop Hughes. He is a learned, eloquent and fearless advocate worthy of the true church.

Ex. Gov. Lane is canvassing for the delegateship and will be elected without opposition. The news from the gold mines on the Umpqua is flattering, about 8000 people are at work there. Oregon is improving rapidly population fast increasing. We have now four river Steamboats plying on our waters. The Surveyor Genl. Preston has at length arrived with his corps and is at work here. He has no easy task before him.

I was so unfortunate as to sprain my left arm the other day and have not yet quite recovered the use of it which prevents me from enjoying the fine weather as much as I otherwise might. My general health and spirits are better than usual. Give my love to our friends. Is Loo Adams' marriage, un fait accompli? The probable union of Mrs. Larned appears to me to be very sensible, if it is not very romantic, they have both however outlived such juvenile notions. Genl Jesup I should think must have been much mortified by Willie's conduct. Remember me affectionately to the Kearneys. I have always felt the strongest attachment to Mrs Kearney despite of all her amiable oddities and in fact to all the family. Give my respects to Father Mathews. May he live many long years in the enjoyment of his earthly reward, the grateful prayer of thousands who bless his name, yet indeed, it is only to wish him detained from that imperishable recompense promised the just man in heaven. My best love for Mother and yourself.

Your Affec. Brother.

Theo. Talbot

You need not alter my direction, my letters come straight and I have just heard news which may make my stay here uncertain.

Columbia Barracks: O.T.

Sep 22d 1851

My dear Sister,

"Delays are dangerous, procrastination is the thief of time."

A school-boy text, but true as preaching. I have delayed writing to you until the evening that the mail closed hoping that something would turn up more worthy of record than the ordinary hum drum tenor of our daily life. At length, despairing of any catastrophe great or small wherewith to enliven a stupid letter, I had just set me down and commenced thinking (a serious operation for me, you will say) in how many words I shd. write you, that I had *nothing* to write, when in pops an orderly, with Genl. Hitchcock's[56] compliments and a note containing a long passage from Spinoza, which the Genl. says he would be obliged to me to translate and make out the sense of if I can. Rank unfortunately controls merit, so I have to push aside "My dear Sister," for the nonce and work away some hours trying to understand

---

[56] Ethan Allen Hitchcock (1798–1870), a Vermonter and grandson of Ethan Allen, commanded the Pacific Military Division from 1851 to 1854. His journal, *A Traveler in Indian Territory*, ed. by Grant Foreman, is a first-hand account of considerable historical importance.

what very likely the Author himself did not, no uncommon thing, it is said with metaphysicians. This job accomplished, I despatch the orderly, when my clerk who is sitting in the room asks suggestively if I have written to Major E.[57] about *that* draft and "Great Antonio! It escaped my memory entirely and must be attended to immediately." Thinks I to myself you wont be bored with a long letter this time my dear Sister. La voici! I hope that you are truly thankful. Why have you not written to me this long, long while? I got no letter from home last mail and was as mad as a hornet. I had a fit of the blues and was patiently waiting for a pleasant home letter to dispel them—none came so the blues had to cure themselves. We expect to hear of the annexation of Cuba by the coming mail. Our "Manifest destiny" bids fair for fulfillment.[58]

Give my best love to Mother keeping a share for yourself. I am afraid of losing the mail so must bid a hasty Adieu
Yours Affectionately—
THEODORE

COLUMBIA BARRACKS, OREGON
Jan 20th 1852

MY DEAR SISTER,
I have just received a letter of yours dated Nov. 8th missent, as I see by the Postmark, to Monticello, Oregon: where that town may be, I have not the remotest idea, its

[57] Possibly Brevet Major William Hemsley Emory, a graduate of West Point, class of 1831, who distinguished himself with Stephen Watts Kearny in the Southwest and California during the War with Mexico and in other commands during the Civil War. *DAB*.

[58] Against a backdrop of diplomatic efforts to purchase Cuba, a series of filibustering efforts occurred in the early 1850's. Talbot here is responding, most likely, to an invasion in July, 1851, under Narciso López.

Postmaster whoever he is, like an honest fellow, has forwarded your letter intact to its true destination. Direct in
future to Columbia Barracks.

Deprecation some well deserved reproaches on my
part for your long neglect of me, you ladylike, take the in-
itiative and hoist me with my own petard. *My* short letters,
and *my* shortcomings generally, forsooth! very well done!!!
I have a precious gift of gab I most humbly confess and it is
well for you indeed, that I cant make my *tongue* perform the
office of my pen for the nonce or you might expect a regular
stunner,—as it is, I surrender at your discretion, please to
consider me essentially used up. I would only suggest mildly,
that to write ones "Doings" when one is doing nothing is not
*quite* such a fruitful topic to an unimaginative mind, as you
would have it appear—and for the news—Well never mind
about the news. I had almost forgotten that I had just agreed
to consider myself very naughty. Your next charge though,
I must beg leave to deny most emphatically. My modesty is
great no doubt, but my sense of justice, on this particular occasion at least, is still greater. Honor to whom the honor is due.
*I* am not the author of any of the poetry (?) which you attrib-
ute to me, I pray you then in the words of the song which you
quote, "let me up, let me up," and cease to tax your sisterly
affection at the expense of your better judgment by endeavoring to find pretty conceits in all the rhyming doggrell of the
Oregon newspapers. What put such a notion in your head?
I wrote sometime since that I had a soldier for a clerk, who
used to expend his poetical afflatus on the fly leaves of my
account books, and meeting with some of these productions in
print, innocently sent them to you, never dreaming that most
unwittingly, I should be made to play jack daw in the fable

to a select circle of admiring friends. Your neat simile however about Homer, is not wasted being equally appropriate to the true author. the same idea had occurred to me, but that might have been expected, les beaux esprits se rencontrent toujours.[59] Once for all, know ye, that I am no poetaster and that Mr. Theo. Easy is not the flimsily disguised nom de plume of your good brother, so no more of that Hal and thou lovest me.

Loo Abert [née Loo Adams?] is married; I am sorry for her but suppose it couldn't be helped. It was very considerate of her to wait for me so long, no wonder indeed that she should get tired of enacting Patience on a monument and abbreviate her sorrows by descending into the arms of Pat. Byrne. I hope that she has bequeathed her maiden constancy to some equally fat and rosy cheeked damsel. I should be quite despairing were it not for the reflection that,

> "There are fish, and no doubt 'ont
> as good *in* the river as ever came *out* 'ont"

I think that you are mistaken about Gibson's[60] intending to

[59] Happy spirits always meet one another, or, birds of a feather flock together.

[60] Talbot, *Journals*, February 8, 1849: ". . . Lt. Gibson was brought on board by Mr. Wheeler, a citizen of Valparaiso, from the *Edith* where he had a row & being knocked down by Capt. Couillard He behaved very badly after coming on board I understand & was put under arrest. he was drunk." *Journals*, February 13: "Maj. Hathaway & Capt. Hill asked me to speak with them on the quarter deck. Maj. H. told me to tell Lt. Gibson that charges had been preferred against him by Capt. Hill & that he Maj. H. wd afford him every facility to effect a transfer from the 1st into some other Regt with any of the officers, that in case that he did so Capt. Hill would withdraw the charges but otherwise that if he still chose to remain in the Regt we wd be compelled to urge the charges. Capt. Hill who was standing by corroborated these remarks. I told Lt. G. He said he preferred 'to let things take their course—' " *Journals*, May 11, 1849: "Lt. Gibson's charges are suspended & he is restored to duty for the present." John Bannister Gibson resigned from the army in 1854.

resign; he is at present in command at Steilacoom, Capt. Hill being on sick leave. Hill is in wretched health and has gone to the Sandwich Islands. Lt Beltzhoover[61] has been resigning for the last two years but I suppose continually thinks better of it. Who gave you these items? Mother mysteriously intimated to me that some officer of my Regt. was going to resign shortly, not mentioning his name and recommending me to say nothing about it, which advice (of necessity) I have religiously followed. was it one of these? There is an old Spanish proverb which says, 'Fraile que pide for [*sic*] Dios, pide por dos,'[62] so it is with Crane and his "looking out" for the Regt. Genl. Childs[63] is in command of the Regt at the last advices. Col Whiting[64] is on sick leave I suppose. Two companies have gone to Texas, where they are endeavoring to concentrate a large force. Our present army is totally inadequate for the protection of our extended frontier, not even enough to maintain a respectable game of bo-peep with the Indians. On this side the land, the military force is still more contemptibly ineffective. Fortunately as far as Oregon is concerned every thing is quiet and it is well that it is so, for there are not men enough at the different posts to protect the public property at them, to say nothing about growing cabbages or carrying on Campaigns. I hope that they will increase the Army this winter and make a Capt. or a Genl. of Your Affectionate Brother,

THEODORE

[61] Daniel M. Beltzhoover, Pennsylvanian West Pointer, fought for the Confederacy in the Civil War.

[62] A monk who petitions to God, petitions for two.

[63] Thomas Childs, West Pointer from Massachusetts, was breveted Brigadier General in the Mexican War. He died of yellow fever in 1853 while in command of East Florida.

[64] Levi Whiting from Massachusetts died eight months later in August, 1852.

COLUMBIA BARRACKS. O.T.
March 16th 1852

My dear Sister,

I thank you for your letter of January 8th. At your request I have carefully read the articles on Hungary in Brownson's Review. The facts stated there, although as a matter of course, highly colored by the violent prejudices of the writer, are quite enough to prove conclusively that Kossuth[65] has not *always* been the "consistent Champion and greatest living exponent of Democracy" and utterly demolish his claims to the title of "Luther the Second," a soubriquet which Brother Beecher and other fast Clerical demagogues still persist in bestowing on M. Kossuth, notwithstanding that he himself modestly (?) declines the honor. To us, Spectators at a distance, wholly removed from the contagious enthusiasm of the pit, the Kossuth Demonstration has appeared at best, to be only a shabby political farce, but one indeed which if not checked in its progress will inevitably wind up with a most serious denouement. I see however by the latest news that the sober second thought is coming over the peoples and as the Maygar hat is handed round they cease clapping and commence buttoning up their breeches pockets. Perhaps before this letter reaches you the republican descendant of Attila will have given place to the "Aztec Pigmy" or some cheaper and less dangerous lion, who instead of frighting the ladies out of their wits with warlike growlings will so aggravate his voice as to roar you as gently as any sucking dove.

[65] Lajos Kossuth (1802–94), radical nationalist Hungarian leader, championed such reforms as independence of Hungary from Austria, taxation of the nobility, and emancipation of the serfs. At the time of Talbot's letter, Kossuth was in the United States seeking assistance for his cause following the failure of the revolutions of 1848.

Brownson[66] is an able, pungent writer, but as you say, he is indeed "ultra." The true spirit of religion, I take it, does not consist in bigotry nor should a holy zeal ever degenerate into mere intolerance: like most newly fledged converts, Knight-errant to do good,

> "He hasteth to teach and preach, as the warhorses
>     rusheth to the battle,
> "And to pave a way for truth, would break up the
>     Appenines of prejudice:—
> "His sword is edged with arguments, his vizor
>     terrible with censures;
> "He goeth full mailed in faith, and zeal is flaming
>     at his heart.
> "Yet one thing he lacketh—*Discretion.*"

I sincerely deprecate all unnecessary admixture of politics with religion, for however much these religio-political attacks may serve to display the caustic wit and wordy talents of the disputant, they rarely promote the true interests of the church and too often have the reverse tendency, awakening the strongest personal and political hostility, where religious conversion was alone intended.

The news from France and the rest of Europe is highly interesting. The prediction of Napoleon 1st that Europe within the next 50 years would become republican—Cossack, bids

[66] Orestes Brownson (1803–76), New England religious writer and reformer, moved successively through Presbyterianism, Universalism, and Unitarianism, before his conversion to Catholicism in 1844. In his *Quarterly Review*, first published in 1838 and then beginning again in 1844, he followed his social doctrines, such as support for Robert Owen, the workingman, and Brook Farm. *DAB.*

fair to be verified. The tone of many of the ablest English papers, by no means given to crying Wolf! is rather ominous of an impending struggle, in which circumstances may compel us to perform an important role without even the promptings of a friendly Kossuth. The very awkward attempts of John Bull to fraternize with his much beloved and long-despised Brother Jonathan are rather absurd.

To change the subject to personal matters. I see a corner of my new shoulder straps sticking out of my writing desk, so I will just return thanks while I think of it. They came last mail, all safe, are very neat and I am much obliged.

You must have had an unusually severe winter and to this cause may probably be attributed Mother's repeated attacks of neuralgia   I have sympathized most sincerely with her sufferings and your own cares and anxieties. I hope that I shall very soon have better accounts of her health. The season in this country though inclement has not been very cold. I have led a life of the utmost seclusion this winter—a very hermit, less all the goodness. I live in a house by myself and for days and days, indeed almost weeks, have only ventured out of my shell or cell for a few minutes each day to get my meals, not having the society of a living thing except at these times. . . . This retirement has been part voluntary, partly enforced, from bad weather and want of sociability or inclination for out door wanderings. I was amused yesterday by a stray savage who stalked into my quarters and after taking a quiet survey of their utter loneliness gravely asked me, if I was not afraid of evil spirits. Verily, I should fear, that some long and silent winter evg. I might fall a prey to dull goblins and gloomy fancies, did not your affectionate letters so often assure me

that *you* are 'ever with me in spirit.' With such goodly protection,ˣ "Skookoms"[67] can never get hold of Your Loving
Brother

THEODORE

ˣ Anglice. Blue devils.

COLUMBIA BARRACKS
May 7th 1852

MY DEAR SISTER,

  . . . . My clothes from Owen have arrived and as far
as he is concerned are in all respects quite satisfactory. Our
new cap is rather a preposterous sort of affair but I suppose
that when we become better accustomed to it we shall admire
it more. Have you seen it yet? I doubt whether any of the
officers will wear it until they are obliged to do so. It is however the cap worn in the French and many other services. The
Mexicans wear a similar truncated cone minus the visor, which
renders it still more imposing. I came near offending Genl.
Hitchcock last summer by laughing at the invention, not
being aware that he had been a member of the Board which
had successfully eliminated its graceful proportions. I am
much obliged for the file of papers, "The Golden Legend"
etc. I hope that Col Merrick may be appointed Charge to
Rome. It is very desirable more especially in the present state
of European Affairs that the U.S. should be represented there
by a Catholic. Capt. Miller of the Qmr Dept[68] stopped here
a few hours last steamer on his way to Port Orford. He is
lately from Washingn. and I understand said that he was very
well acquainted with some of my friends there. I only saw

[67] Skookum: a Chinook deity, a god of the woods.
[68] Morris Smith Miller (1814–70), New Yorker and West Pointer, received
special distinction for his Quartermaster Corps service during the Civil War.

168

him a few minutes before he started and did not have time
to talk with him. Capt. Howard, formerly a Dutch Admiral
etc and whose name lately figured in the Forrest trial[69] has
been staying here for the last few weeks. He was of opinion
that Col Fremont was a swindler and as I could not agree with
him we did not cultivate our acquaintance. I see by late papers
that Fremont has made large sales of his mining property
and that his wealth has by no means been overrated. He is said
to be in miserable health

I know Gibson[70] of the Navy very well and he is a very
good fellow: we were together a good deal, two years ago,
when he was at the mouth of the Columbia on the Coast Survey. I have received two of the new Army Registers and still
find that there is quite as much truth as poetry in the words
of a favorite army song "Oh in the army is promotion very
slow". Well! it might be worse and we must hope, as we have
been doing during our present cloudy weather, that we will
get a glorious streak of sunshine after a while. The spring has
been very backward in Oregon, cold, with incessant rains. May
day was just about as dreary and stormy as you can comfortably
imagine. Last week was court term here and the Judges, Sher-
iffs, learned Busfurs [Busbys] and "intelligent juries," etc
gave an unwonted appearance of bustle and activity to our
usually quiet, sleepy neighborhood. Oregon is going to be,
(if not already) a great country for lawyers and rogues. All
courts in new Countries abound in amusing scenes and inci-

69 William A. Howard (1807–71), served long as a revenue officer and
helped the German government in the same capacity during the late 1840's.
Howard was involved in the 1851–52 divorce trial of actor Edwin Forrest
through alleged affairs with Mrs. Forrest.

70 Probably William Gibson, who was a midshipman on the *Ewing* during
McArthur's survey of the Columbia in 1849–50.

dents, and we have no lack of, to relieve the dull proving or trashy declamation which our not over talented lawyers inflict upon their audiences. A soldier [Hurdman] of this command was tried for the murder of an Indian and sentenced to confinement and hard labor for life. I was amused at the reply of a Juror in this case, who on being asked among other questions usally put to Jurors, "Whether he had any conscientious scruples as to punishment by death etc?" naively and no doubt honestly answered "No, that he had no conscience." Another juror called, (himself on trial under an indictment for murder) had of course, very serious scruples about the propriety of hanging folks, and was excused. A third had 'formed no opinion and had no prejudices' but thought the man ought to be hung. So much for "Trial by Jury that bulwark of our liberties." Oregon is still safe.

I attended last evening the first and the final rites of our church and in compliance with the dying request of the Mother who had been a friend of mine stood godfather to her poor little half-orphaned babe. I am at present in command of the post, Major Hatheway having broken his leg by a fall from his horse three or four days ago. He is doing well however and will be about again in a few weeks. We are hourly expecting the arrival of the mail. Give my best love to Mother and my kind remembrances to all our friends.

Your affectionate Brother

THEODORE

[P.S.] May 17th . . . Mother wishes to know if I get the papers which she sends. I receive only part of them I think and those come usually two or three months later than they should. I cannot account for this delay if you mail them at any time near their dates. This is one reason why I prefer to have papers from the Office of Publication as these seem to come more direct and *all* the postage is saved, for they have never condescended to charge newspaper postage in Oregon as yet. It is very provoking to receive some dollars worth of papers which I know have given you much trouble to put up, and all of them from 4 to 6 months old and so much waste paper, as I have long since read the same news in other papers. I do not therefore wish you to trouble yourself to send me papers unless it is some particular news that I might not be likely to see otherwise. I hope that before many months roll round that instead of having to complain of the irregularities of Oregon Mails I may be my own messenger of love etc.

Your THEODORE

COLUMBIA BARRACKS. OREGON<br>July 9th 1852

MY DEAR SISTER

You should not feel any uneasiness because you do not hear from me regularly, for any one of fifty causes, (and never a single one of them at all connected with my well-being), may for the time, interrupt our communication. The arrival and departure of mails on this side of the land, has been very uncertain in consequence of accidents to the Steamers and still remains entirely out of proper train. Several mails also have been badly damaged or lost lately in transit over the Isthmus. So I must beg you not to distress yourself because Messrs. Howland, do not perform their mail contracts faithfully or because your very good brother is too lazy and fancies himself too busy, to write as often as he is in duty bound.

Washington must have improved in appearance very much of late. No wonder that your genius loci should be

aroused by the unwonted stir and commotion on his premises
and give you all a hearty shaking as he stretches himself after
his long undisturbed slumbers. I am pleased to hear that the
Kearneys are settled down again comfortably as I am sure
it must be very agreeable to all the family. Medora ought to
be quite a belle by this time. Give my love to them. the same
to Mrs. Thorton and you may tell her that I have *now* the
pleasure to wear a very pretty pair of epaulettes, her present
to me, and which I had not before purchased in compliance
with her request to that effect. I have just come in from drill.
Nothing very strange that for an officer, nevertheless it has
been a matter of such rare occurence as to deserve record, for
since we have been in Oregon there has been so much of other
work for the men that there has been no time left to play at
Soldiers. The secret of this warlike zeal is that we are expecting
the arrival of an Inspector Genl. and wish to get up all the
"milingtary" possible in a short space of time, in order to
throw dust into his worthy eyes. I have been in command of
the post for the last two months but the Major having got
well of his broken leg has resumed command. We see by the
mail from the states which arrived to day that the 4th Infy.
are ordered to this Division. whether any of them will be
sent to Oregon we do not yet know. *We* may be ordered to
some other post in Oregon. half our company is now at Port
Orford and as many of our men are to be discharged this
summer unless this detachment rejoins us, we shall not have
much more than a corporal's guard here. Our old post at
Astoria is to be abandoned as a military post. This will probably throw Geo Bomford out of employ for the time as he
has been hired as an Agent in charge of the public property

at that post for some time past. I received a letter from Maj Reynolds[71] this mail, dated Fort Smith Ark. He writes that Irwin Bomford is married and living there. I am sorry to see in the papers a notice of the death of Mrs [J.] Q. Adams.

Although no politician I have been anxiously expecting the nominations of the Conventions for the Presidency. As yet it is very difficult to make a shrewd guess as to who they will be. Judge Pratt[72] who is a great politician (and not in very high standing as one either) gave it to me roundly the other day because I told him that I had *no* politics hoping by the avowal to escape the infliction of a deal of twaddle. He thought that I might consider it politic to have no politics but did not believe it possible that I should not have some decided bias of opinion at my mature age. Such however in truth is the melancholy fact. Speaking patriotically, I do not know whether the one or the other of the great parties would be most likely to benefit the Nation if their measures were fully carried. It has always resolved itself in my mind into a simple case of the "In's" and the "Outs." Are you a politician? If you are come to the rescue. Say shall I be Whig or democrat. As the hour for closing the mail has nearly arrived I will not risk farther delay at present but will give you some of my crude ideas on this weighty subject at some future period. In the meantime I bid you Adieu

With much love for yourself and our dear Mother

Your Affect. Brother

THEODORE

---

[71] Robert B. Reynolds from Tennessee.

[72] O. C. Pratt, Democrat from Illinois, was appointed by President Polk as an associate justice of the U.S. District Court in Oregon.

A Receipt for Washing Clothes expeditiously and with but
little labor.

| | |
|---|---|
| 1 Pint Alcohol. | Mix together and keep in |
| 1 Pint Spirits of Turpentine | a bottle well corked. |
| 1 oz. Liquid Ammonia | |
| 1 oz Gum Camphor. | |

Two table-spoonfuls of this mixture to five gallons of water
adding about one pound of brown Soap or more if you choose.
Rub the clothes a little if very dirty but this is generally not
necessary. After the Clothes have soaked one hour in this
mixture then boil them in clean water for an hour and wring
them dry, which completes the process.

NB. probatum est. My washerwoman uses this in getting up
my clothes, with much comfort to herself, great economy of
buttons and expletives on my part, and I believe no serious
detriment to the linen. Any druggist can make up the receipt.

//As you are such a great housekeeper I give you a
chance to avail yourself of my experience.// [// . . . // are
Talbot's symbols]

[This recipe belongs with the July 9, 1852, letter.]

COLUMBIA BARRACKS. O.T.

August 7th 1852

MY DEAR SISTER,

. . . . Indeed I sometimes feel very sorry that I ever
entered the army, then again I think it is all for the best, for
under any case it would be easier for me always to spend than
to make money. With some people it appears as though everything that they touched was by some magic power transmuted
into gold, with me it appears to be directly the reverse, whatever the thing may be, let it glitter as favorably as possible

before, as soon as it comes into my hands, it turns to worthless dross. If I buy a horse he is sure to go irremediably lame, if I enter into an almost certain speculation, the moment I get my finger into it, off it goes like a bomb shell, a regular burst up. Could I sing I should certainly chant as my favorite ditty " 'twas ever thus etc". However, who knows, there may be a good time coming.

I have already commenced to receive Harper and Balto. Sun and am also very much obliged for "Ivar" and the "Journey to Iceland," papers etc recd. this mail. Your kindness keeps me fully posted in the news and literature of the day. I promised in my last letter to Mother to send her $200. and very unexpectedly received the money the *same* day just after I had mailed my letter and now hold it waiting her disposal and a convenient opportunity for transmittal. Unless she writes to that effect I may not send it for some months. We expect the arrival of 4 Companies, with the Head quarters band etc of the 4th Infantry at this post about the end of the month. The whole Regiment is to be stationed in Oregon. One Compy at Steilecoom 1 at the Dalles 1 at the Umqua. others at Port Orford etc. I will probably be relieved from duty as Commissary at this post. We shall not be ordered home at present, whether we will remain here or go to Cape Disappointment at the entrance of the Columbia River we do not yet know.

The large increase of military force in the Territory will render the prospect of our being ordered homewards more favorable—though indeed apart from the hope of being able to pay you a short visit en passant it is hardly desirable. The army is so small as to be wholly inadequate to the wants of the Country and we should probably be sent off immediately to some miserable post ten times worse than any in Oregon. Congress had better increase or disband the present Army.

I write you these hurried lines subject to much interruption but they will at any rate assure you of the well being and affectionate remembrance of your devoted Brother.

THEO. TALBOT

COLUMBIA BARRACKS. O.T.
October 6th 1852

MY DEAR SISTER,

I have the pleasure to acknowledge the receipt of your letter of Aug. 18th. I was quite surprised to learn from your letter that Mr. Stonestreet had been appointed Provincial of the Jesuits as I had not seen any notice of it elsewhere. It appears to me that he is rather young for the position, but he is a man of much talent and will undoubtedly fill it with honor to himself and advantage to the Order. It is evidently their desire to Americanise the Order as much as possible. I am glad to learn that Mrs. Thornton is still able to enjoy with so much zest all the fashionable discomforts of a gay watering place. I think that you are mistaken in supposing that Congress have passed finally a law with regard to our extra pay. In newspapers of later date than your letter it is said that such a bill passed the H. of Rep. but had not been acted upon in the Senate. We almost hope that it may be defeated rather than passed in the shape which it at present has. The increase of pay proposed amounts to just nothing at all when considered as an act of justice to Officers or an attempt to equalize their compensation with the pay established for them as just and proper under the old order of things. In my case the extra pay would only be $15 per month. It is still hoped that the

Senate will be more liberal and allow the previous uniform rate. The increase of pay that the House would allow us sounds as contemptibly to people in this country, as it would at home if they were to propose to add five cents a day to officers pay as an act of splendid generosity accompanied by the usual flourishes of trumpets and the conscientious qualms of honorable economical members. Congress are really too shamefully mean. We anxiously hope the next mail will bring us some better news on this subject and that Congress will open their hearts and the public purse to more liberal or I should say, just views as the Session draws to a close.

We heard positively that a sailing V. was to leave San Francisco for Port Orford and thence to Vancouver in order to carry us to our new post, we shall now expect her every day until she arrives and my next letter will probably be dated from "Steilacoom." I am rather sorry to leave Vancouver as it was our first resting place is a very handsome spot and central in position. But on considering the move in all its bearings I have come to the conclusion that it will rather be agreable than otherwise from the novelty if not other cause. I do not know of any positive disagreabilities of the post itself and the chief objection to a residence there is the isolation. If we can get our mails regularly that is all I care about: this I understand we can do but they will be two weeks longer in transit than here.

Col Bonneville the officer in command of this post is the same old fellow whose journal of travel in the Rocky Mts etc rewritten or edited by Wash. Irving.[73] He is per-

[73] Captain Benjamin Louis Eulalie de Bonneville (1796–1878), a graduate of West Point, on his return from leave to "explore" and, as it turned out, trap for furs in the Rocky Mountains, in 1835, more than a year overdue for re-

fectly, what is popularly termed an "old fogy." All the officers belonging to the companies here are young Lieuts. except Capt Wallen who is an old acquaintance of mine. Not that I would have you understand that I am so old myself although I do now draw my "young" first fogy ration. All the older officers of the company here appear to have absented themselves as long as possible. Col Buchanan, Mrs Adams cousin joined his company in California last mail I understand.

I have this very day closed up all my accounts as disbursing offr. and having found them all correct feel very much relieved I assure you. I have yet to await the final decision of the accounting officers of the Treasury but I am

---

assuming his army duties, met Washington Irving in late August or early September at Hellgate, the country estate of John Jacob Astor. From the meeting emerged in 1837 the only connected record of the vicissitudes of the Captain and his party we are likely to have, Zenas Leonard's (*Adventures of Zenas Leonard*) being confined largely to the record of the detached party of trappers Bonneville sent under Joseph Reddeford Walker in 1832–33 to California. That Irving was, in *The Adventures of Captain Bonneville* and *Astoria*, much more of a reliable historian than subsequent generations of scholars have credited him is made clear in Edgeley W. Todd's massive editing of both books, published respectively in 1961 and 1964 in the *American Exploration and Travel Series*. The internal and external evidence now makes clear that Bonneville was, in his Oregon probings and in his assignment to Walker to go into California, a searcher after future U.S. positions in both areas: his letter of July 29, 1833, from the Crow Country to Major General Alexander Macomb is a highly significant document in this respect. Up to that time, no official investigation of the Northwest region had been made since the explorations of Lewis and Clark.

The contrast between Irving's and Talbot's reactions to Bonneville and his reminiscences here and *infra* is revealing. Irving, who had visited Montreal at the age of twenty in 1803 and had met the partners and clerks of the North West Company, "listened with astonished ear to their tales of hardships and adventures" (Irving, *Astoria*, I, 25). He had "felt anxious," he wrote, "to get at the details of their adventurous expeditions among the savage tribes that peopled the depths of the wilderness" (Irving, *Astoria*, 3–4.) And therefore with gusto he later heard Bonneville out. Talbot in his subsequent description of Bonneville seems merely amused.

sure that I must come out all right. This being responsible for public money under the low tone of feeling which has prevailed in Oregon and California and in the Army here is anything but agreable. It has occasioned me a private loss of 200$ even before my accounts were settled but I would rather have it this way than that the U.S. should lose a cent by me. My position has been such that from the latitude allowed me I could have easily made some thousands of Dollars without almost the possibility of detection and the very knowledge of this has compelled me to be more strict even too my own loss rather than the slightest suspicion should rest upon me. I could explain myself very fully to you on this subject but I do not like to trust it to a letter. I think that all things considered that the best thing to be done is for Mother to marry me to some rich heiress and let me resign.

I write you in great haste as usual. Give thousands of love to Mother and keep a few for yourself.

Yours Affectionately,<br>THEO. TALBOT

COLUMBIA BARRACKS. O.T.<br>Dec 1st 1852

DEAR SISTER,

Although the M. Steamer which arrived last night brought us two mails, I was so unfortunate as to receive no letter from home. I hope that Mother and yourself are well. The Anita in which we were to have sailed for Puget's Sound has been wrecked we learn, at Port Orford, in attempting to leave that place. No lives were lost. We shall receive orders relative to our destination probably by the next mail from Head Qrs of the Division, news not having reached there yet of this disaster. I think that we will be ordered to remain here this winter. We have had incessant rains now for nearly a month and it is still raining and storming bravely as I now write, so that there is not much going on out of doors. Last week was the "Court week", and the visitors brought by the occasion, have served to vary our monotony a little. I thought that I would have had to figure in their Court proceedings myself, as an attempt was made to prosecute me for having destroyed two whiskey sellers stock in trade and burnt down their shanties. Nothing came of it however. A son of Earl Fitzwilliam came over with the Hudson Bay Express this fall. Every year some English Officers or men of note, avail themselves of this chance of indulging in the romance of a wild woods life. Fitzwilliam,[74] is a member elect of the new parliament. He has been travelling in the U.S. for the last two years and spent part of the previous winter in Washington. You may have heard of him. Our Comdg. Officer, Bonneville, retains many of the feelings and habits contracted in his trapping adventures. Nothing would please him better than to be ordered far interior again with all his command, a wish which you may be sure none of his officers share with him. I mess at present with the Col. and am often amused as much as the others are disgusted by his accounts of the fare which he used sometimes to have in the mts. Not always the most delectable in the world, as I had fuller experience than himself. Mrs Collins a young lady from Green Bay, Wis. Superintends the Col's mess. her husband Lt Collins[75] is a citizen

[74] George Wentworth Fitzwilliam (1817–74), third son of the fifth Earl Fitzwilliam, member of Parliament from Richmond, 1841, and from Peterborough, 1841–59. *DNB*.

[75] Joseph Benson Collins, a native of the District of Columbia, was breveted three times before he retired as a colonel after the Civil War.

appt. and is from Washington City. If all the married officers of the 4th Infy had brought their families with them we would have had quite a number of ladies here. Several intend sending for their wives. Lieut     Floyd Jones[76] who was married only a few days before starting, heard this mail the sad news of the death of his wife. Since I last wrote another officer, Capt. Augur,[77] has joined his company at this post. The 4th Infy. men have been deserting a good deal since their arrival here and the companies are already very much reduced. Congress will find it cheaper to pay their soldiers better on this coast. Provisions are very scarce in Oregon at this time. Flour is $35 and Pork $60 a barrel in consequence partly of the very large emigration and also the scarcity in California. The news of the Presidential election is looked for with intense interest. As yet we have only heard from Cala. which has gone for Pierce. The opinion here, is now strongly in favor of Pierce. Webster's death may give some additional votes to Scott. One after another the great men of this country and England are passing from the world's stage and it appears as though there were none to take their places, this may only be because the crises are yet wanting to call forth new and as talented actors upon the scene. The Cuban difficulty looks suggestive of a war with Spain. a consummation most devoutly wished by a large portion of the people of the U.S.

I hope that our friends the Larneds and Mrs Newman are enjoying better health than when you last wrote. Do you ever see the Jesups. Willie, I understand has grown up a

[76] Delancy Floyd-Jones, West Pointer from New York, retired as a colonel after the Civil War.

[77] Christopher C. Augur (1821–98), West Pointer in the class of Ulysses Simpson Grant, aside from his services in the Mexican and Civil wars, fought Indians in Oregon and on the Plains.

wild fellow and has given his family much trouble. In the event of Scott's election is it thought that Genl. Jesup[78] will command the Army? Please to remember me to Mrs. Thornton. Father Mathews has been endowing a new Academy in Washington say the papers I judge therefore that he is enjoying good health of mind and body. May he long live to witness his many good works bearing fruit a hundred and a thousand fold. Present to him my most affectionate respects. . . .

I am Ever.

Your Affectionate Brother.

THEODORE. TALBOT

[78] Thomas Sidney Jesup (1788–1860), Virginian, was best remembered for his forty-two years as quartermaster general.

# BIBLIOGRAPHY

Abert, J. W. *Journal of Lieutenant J. W. Abert from Bent's Fort to St. Louis, in 1845,* 29 Cong., 1 sess., *Sen. Doc. No. 438,* 1846.
———. *Report of Lieut. J. W. Abert of His Examination of New Mexico in the years 1846–'47.* 30 Cong., 1 sess., *Sen. Exec. Doc. No. 23,* 1847.
———. *Western America in 1846–1847: The Original Travel Diary of Lieutenant J. W. Abert, Who Mapped New Mexico for the United States.* Ed. by John Galvin. San Francisco, John Howell, 1966.
———. *Through the Country of the Comanche Indians in the Fall of the Year 1845: The Journal of a U.S. Army Expedition led by Lieutenant James W. Abert of the Topographical Engineers . . .* Ed. by John Galvin. San Francisco, John Howell, 1970.
Albion, Robert Greenhalgh. *The Rise of the New York Port.* New York, Charles Scribner's Sons, 1939.
Alexander, William D. *A Brief History of the Hawaiian People.* New York, American Book Company, 1891.
Bancroft, Hubert Howe. *California Pioneer Register and Index.* Baltimore, Regional Publishing Company, 1964.
Bent, George. *Life of George Bent Written from His Letters by George E. Hyde.* Ed. by Savoie Lottinville. Norman, University of Oklahoma Press, 1968.
Berthrong, Donald J. *The Southern Cheyennes.* Norman, University of Oklahoma Press, 1963.
Bingham, Hiram. *A Residence of Twenty-one Years in the Sandwich Islands.* Hartford, Hezekiah Huntington, 1849.
Bradley, Harold W. *The American Frontier in Hawaii: The Pioneers,*

*1789–1843.* Stanford, Stanford University Press, 1942.

Carson, Christopher (Kit). *Kit Carson's Own Story of His Life.* Ed. by Blanche C. Grant. Taos, n.p., 1926.

Carvalho, S. N. *Incidents of Travel and Adventure in the Far West with Colonel Frémont's Last Expedition* . . . New York, Derby & Jackson, 1858.

Caughey, John Walton. *Gold is the Cornerstone.* Berkeley, University of California Press, 1948.

Clark, Robert C. "Military History of Oregon, 1849–1859," *Oregon Historical Quarterly,* XXXVI (1935), 14–49.

Clemens, Samuel Langhorne (*pseud.,* Mark Twain). *Roughing It.* New York, Charles L. Webster & Co., 1872.

Conner, Daniel Ellis. *Joseph Reddeford Walker and the Arizona Adventure.* Ed. by Donald J. Berthrong and Odessa Davenport. Norman, University of Oklahoma Press, 1956.

*Dictionary of American Biography.* Ed. by Allen Johnson, Dumas Malone, et al., 22 vols. New York, Charles Scribner's Sons, 1946—.

Downey, J. T. *The Cruise of the Portsmouth.* Ed. by Howard Lamar. New Haven, Yale University Press, 1958.

Dupree, Anderson Hunter. *Science in the Federal Government.* Cambridge, Massachusetts, Belknap Press of Harvard University, 1957.

Emerson, Ralph Waldo. . . . *Emerson's Essays.* New York, Books, Inc., n.d.

Espasa, J. (Publisher). *Enciclopedia Universel Illustrada.* Barcelona, J. Espasa, [1907]–1930.

Favour, Alpheus H. *Old Bill Williams, Mountain Man.* Norman, University of Oklahoma Press, 1962.

Franchère, Gabriel. *Adventure at Astoria, 1810–1814.* Ed. by Hoyt C. Franchère. Norman, University of Oklahoma Press, 1967.

Frazer, Robert W. *Forts of the West: Military Forts and Presidios and Posts Commonly Called Forts West of the Mississippi River to 1898.* Norman, University of Oklahoma Press, 1965.

Frémont, John Charles. *The Expeditions of John Charles Frémont, Vol. I: Travels from 1838 to 1844.* Ed. by Donald Jackson and Mary Lee Spence. Urbana, University of Illinois Press, 1970.

————. *Memoirs of My Life*. Chicago, Belford, Clark & Co., 1887.

————. *Report of the Exploring Expedition to the Rocky Mountains in the Year 1842, and to Oregon and North California in the Years 1843-'44*. Washington, D.C., Gales & Seaton, 1845.

————. *Narratives of Exploration and Adventure*. Ed. by Allan Nevins. New York, Longmans, Green & Co., 1956.

Goetzmann, William H. *Exploration and Empire: The Explorer and the Scientist in the Winning of the American West*. New York, Alfred A. Knopf, 1966.

————. *Army Exploration in the American West, 1803-1863*. New Haven, Yale University Press, 1959.

Grinnell, George Bird. *The Fighting Cheyennes*. Norman, University of Oklahoma Press, 1956.

Grivas, Theodore. *Military Government in California*. Glendale, California, The Arthur H. Clark Company, 1963.

Groce, George C., and David H. Wallace. *Dictionary of Artists in America, 1564-1860*. New Haven, Yale University Press, 1966.

Hawgood, John A., ed. *First and Last Consul: Thomas Oliver Larkin and the Americanization of California*. San Marino, Huntington Library, 1962.

————. "John C. Frémont and the Bear Flag Revolution," *University of Birmingham Historical Journal*, Vol. VII (1959), pp. 80-100.

Heitman, Francis B. *Historical Register and Dictionary of the United States Army*. 2 vols. Washington, D.C., Government Printing Office, 1903.

Henry, Robert Selph. *The Story of the Mexican War*. New York, Frederick Ungar, 1950.

Hine, Robert V. *Edward Kern and American Expansion*. New Haven, Yale University Press, 1962.

Hitchcock, Ethan Allen. *A Traveler in Indian Territory: The Journal of Ethan Allen Hitchcock*. Ed. by Grant Foreman. Norman, University of Oklahoma Press, 1930.

Hittell, Theodore Henry. *History of California*. 4 vols. San Francisco, 1885-1897.

Hodge, Frederick Webb, ed. *Handbook of American Indians North of Mexico.* 2 vols. Washington, D.C., Government Printing Office, 1907–1910.

Ide, Simon. *The Conquest of California, a Biography of William B. Ide.* Oakland, Biobooks, 1944.

Irving, Washington. *The Adventures of Captain Bonneville, U. S. A., in the Rocky Mountains and the Far West.* Ed. and with an introduction by Edgeley W. Todd. Norman, University of Oklahoma Press, 1961.

———. *Astoria: or Anecdotes of an Enterprise Beyond the Rocky Mountains.* Ed. and with an introduction by Edgeley W. Todd. Norman, University of Oklahoma Press, 1964.

Janssens, Don Agustin. *The Life and Adventures in California of Don Agustin Janssens.* Ed. by William H. Ellison and Francis Price. San Marino, The Huntington Library, 1953.

Jarves, James Jackson. *History of the Hawaiian Islands.* Boston, Tappan and Dennet, 1843.

Jenkins, John S. *History of the War between the United States and Mexico from the Commencement of Hostilities to the Ratification of the Treaty of Peace.* Auburn, Derby and Miller, 1851.

Johansen, Dorothy O. *Empire of the Columbia.* New York, Harper and Row, 1967.

Kendall, George Wilkins. *Narrative of the Texan Santa Fé Expedition . . .* 2 vols. New York, Harper, 1844.

Kuykendall, Ralph S., and Gregory H. Kuykendall. *A History of Hawaii.* New York, Macmillan, 1926.

Larkin, Thomas Oliver. *The Larkin Papers.* Ed. by George P. Hammond. 10 vols. Berkeley, University of California Press, 1951–1964.

Lavender, David. *Bent's Fort.* New York, Doubleday & Co., 1954.

———. *Land of the Giants.* Garden City, New York, Doubleday & Co., 1954.

Leonard, Zenas. *Adventures of Zenas Leonard, Fur Trader.* Ed. by John C. Ewers. Norman, University of Oklahoma Press, 1959.

Lytle, William M. *Merchant Steam Vessels of the United States,*

186

*1807–1868*. Mystic, Connecticut, Steamship Historical Society of America, 1952.

Marti, Werner. *Messenger of Destiny*. San Francisco, John Howell, 1960.

McGehee, Micajah. "Rough Times in Rough Places," *Century Illustrated Monthly Magazine*, Vol. XLI, No. 5 (March, 1891), 772–78.

McLoughlin, John. *The Letters of John McLoughlin from Fort Vancouver to the Governor and Committee*. First Series, 1825–38; Second Series, 1839–44; Third Series, 1844–46. 3 vols. Ed. by E. E. Rich. London, Hudson's Bay Record Society, 1941, 1943, 1944.

Miller, Alfred Jacob. *The West of Alfred Jacob Miller (1837)*. Ed. by Marvin C. Ross. Norman, University of Oklahoma Press, 1951, 1968.

*Missouri Republican*, St. Louis, March 20, 1822; May 12, 1845.

Montgomery, Richard G. *Whiteheaded Eagle*. New York, Macmillan, 1934.

Morgan, Dale L., ed., *Overland in 1846*. 2 vols. Georgetown, California, Talisman Press, 1963.

Morison, Samuel Eliot. *The Maritime History of Massachusetts, 1783–1860*. Boston, Houghton Mifflin Company, 1941.

National Archives, Washington, D.C. MSS., Corps of Topographical Engineers, Old Army Section, Record Group 77, Letters Sent.

National Park Service, *Soldier and Brave: Military and Indian Affairs in the Trans-Mississippi West* . . . Washington, D.C., 1968.

Nevins, Allan. *Frémont, Pathmarker of the West*. New York, Appleton-Century, 1939.

New York *Times*, December 1851; January and February, 1852.

New York *Weekly Tribune*, April 10, 1847.

*Niles' Register*. Baltimore.

Parks, Henry Baumford. *A History of Mexico*. Boston, Houghton Mifflin Company, 1960.

Paul, Rodman W. *California Gold*. Lincoln, University of Nebraska Press, 1947.

Pearson, Jim Berry. *The Maxwell Land Grant*. Norman, University of Oklahoma Press, 1961.

Phillips, Paul Chrisler, and J. W. Smurr. *The Fur Trade*. 2 vols. Norman, University of Oklahoma Press, 1961.

Pomeroy, Earl. *Pacific Slope*. New York, Alfred A. Knopf, 1965.

Porrua (Publisher). *Diccionario Porrua de Historia Biographia y Geographia de Mexico*. Mexico, D. F., Porrua, 1964.

Powell, William H. *List of Officers of the Army of the United States from 1779 to 1900*. New York, L. R. Hamersly, 1900.

Preuss, Charles. *Exploring with Frémont: The Private Diaries of Charles Preuss, Cartographer for John C. Frémont on His First, Second, and Fourth Expeditions to the Far West*. Trans. and ed. by Erwin G. and Elizabeth K. Gudde. Norman, University of Oklahoma Press, 1958.

Prucha, Francis Paul. *Guide to the Military Posts of the United States*. Madison, State Historical Society of Wisconsin, 1964.

Rogers, Fred B. *Bear Flag Lieutenant: The Life Story of Henry L. Ford*. San Francisco, California Historical Society, 1951.

———. "Rosters of California Volunteers in the Service of the United States, 1846–47," *Annual Publication of the Society of California Pioneers*. San Francisco, 1950. Pp. 17–28.

———. *Montgomery and the Portsmouth*. San Francisco, John Howell, 1958.

Rolle, Andrew F. *California, a History*. New York, Thomas Y. Crowell, 1963.

Rostow, Walt Whitman. *View from the Seventh Floor*. New York, Harper & Row, Publishers, 1964.

Sabin, Edwin L. *Kit Carson Days, 1809–1868*. New York, Press of the Pioneers, 1935.

*St. Louis American*, May 28, 1845.

Schafer, Joseph. *History of the Pacific Northwest*. New York, Macmillan, 1930.

Simpson, George. *Fur Trade and Empire: George Simpson's Journal*. Ed. by Frederick Merk. Cambridge, Massachusetts, Harvard University Press, 1931.

———. *Part of Dispatch from George Simpson, Esqr, Governor of*

*Ruperts Land, to the Governor and Committee of the Hudson's Bay Company London, March 1, 1829. Continued and Completed March 24 and June 5, 1829.* Ed. by E. E. Rich. The Hudson's Bay Record Society, 1947.

Simpson, Lesley Byrd. *Many Mexicos.* Berkeley, University of California Press, 1952.

Singletary, Otis. *The Mexican War.* Chicago, University of Chicago Press, 1960.

Smith, Justin H. *The War With Mexico.* 2 vols. New York, Macmillan, 1919.

Sunder, John E. *Bill Sublette, Mountain Man.* Norman, University of Oklahoma Press, 1959.

———. *The Fur Trade on the Upper Missouri, 1840–1865.* Norman, University of Oklahoma Press, 1965.

Tabeau, Pierre-Antoine. *Tabeau's Narrative of Loisel's Expedition to the Upper Missouri.* Ed. by Annie Heloise Abel. Norman, University of Oklahoma Press, 1939.

Talbot, Theodore. *The Journals of Theodore Talbot, 1843 and 1849–52.* Ed. by Charles H. Carey. Portland, Metropolitan Press, 1931.

United States Navy Department. *Register of the Commissioned and Warrant Officers in the U. S. Navy.* Washington, D.C., 1848 and 1851.

Utley, Robert M. *Frontiersmen in Blue: the United States Army and the Indian, 1848–1865.* New York, Macmillan, 1967.

Watson, Douglas S. *West Wind: The Life Story of Joseph Reddeford Walker.* Los Angeles, Johnck & Seeger, 1934.

Waugh, Alfred S. *Travels in Search of the Elephant.* Ed. by John Francis McDermott. St. Louis, Missouri Historical Society, 1951.

Wheat, Carl I. *Mapping the Trans-Mississippi West.* 5 vols. San Francisco, Institute of Historical Cartography, 1957–1963.

Wilkes, Charles. *Narrative of the United States Exploring Expedition During the Years 1838–1842.* New York, G. P. Putnam, 1844.

189

# INDEX

Abaco, Island of: shipwreck near, 60–61; life on, 61–62

Abert, Lt. James W. (son): joins Third Expedition, xvii; in St. Louis, 6; reconciled to trip, 9; and knowledge of destination, 14n.; at Westport, 18, 20; messmates of, 23, 24; message for, 24; duty of, 25; description of, 25; on buffalo hunt, 26–27; leaves party, 28, 32; depicts Bent's Fort, 30 n.; message from, 51

Abert, Col. John James (father): recommendation of, xiv; orders of for Third Expedition, xv–xvi; altered orders of, xvi; assignment of, 6n.

Adair, John, custom house officer in Astoria: 122

Adams, Loo, marriage of: 159, 163

Adams, Mrs. J. Q., death of: 173

Alcea River: excursion to, 133; report on trip to, 143

Algonquian Indians: 28n., 31 n.

Allen, Ethan, grandson of: 160 n.

Allen, Lt. Col. George Washington: death of in Vera Cruz, 66–67

Alta California: ills of, 34; Castro position in, 41 n.; government of, 54n.; see also California

Alvarado, Juan Bautista, Castro support of: 41 n.

American River, Sutter's Fort at: xv

*Anchorage* (man of war), in Rio Harbor: 88

*Anita* (ship), wreck of: 179

Antarctic: U.S., exploring expedition to: 86n.

Applegate, Jesse, westward trip of: xv

Arapaho Indians: meeting with, 27, 30; and Kiowas, 31 n.

Archambeau, Auguste: with Frémont, 10; to join Third Expedition, 13; on buffalo hunt, 26–27

Archives, discovery of in California: 50

Arkansas (Arkansaw) River: 29; survey of, xv, 6n.; ascent of, xvii; Bent's Fort on, 7n., 30; Pawnee Fork of, 26; arrival at, 27–28; route along, 33, 35; information on, 35–36n.

Army, U.S.: *see* United States Army

Army Register: 169

Artillery, captured in Mexico: 74

Ashley, William H., fur trade of: 6n., 7n.

Astor, John Jacob: and Astoria, 122n., 127n., 130; country estate of, 178n.

Astoria, Oregon Territory: letters from, 120, 140, 144, 149, 152, 154; arrival in, 120; description of, 121–22, 122n.; Ogden at, 127n., 130; mail arrives at, 131; expected arrival at, 139; Indian chief to, 141; temporary camp at, 142; post at, 158; post to be abandoned at, 172–73

Astronomical observations: 20–21, 23, 25, 29

Augur, Capt. Christopher C.: in Oregon, 181

Bachelor: Talbot as, xii, 149, 156

Backenstos, Col.: court-martial of, 138–39; resignation of, 158

Badeau, François: 13n.

Bahamas: shipwreck in, 59, 60–62; on return trip, 79

Bahia Salada, on route to California: 35

Baker's Bay, arrival in Astoria from: 120

Bankhead, Col.: 75; proposed expedition of, 64; in command at Orizaba, 67; embarks at Vera Cruz, 74

Baptists, and westward move: xii

Barometrical observations: 25

Bartlett, John Russell, as intellectual frontiersman: xi

Bates, Asher Brown, importance of in Hawaii: 106

Bay of Rio, descriptions of: 97

Beall, Lt. Edward Fitzgerald, in California: 47

Bear, supply of in California: 40

Bear Flag Revolt: Frémont involved with, xvii; participation in, 34; Californians captured in, 42n.; Merritt a leader of, 49

Bear River, on Warren map: 37n.

"Beggars on horseback": 119

Beltzhoover, Lt. Daniel M., resignation of: 164

Bent, Charles: in St. Louis, 5, 7n.; partnership of, 30 n.

Bent, George: welcome of, 30; junior partnership of, 30 n.

Bent, Robert, junior partnership of: 30 n.

Bent, William: 7n.; partnership of, 30 n.

Benton, Thomas Hart: western expansion of, xv, xvi; visit to, 5; relative of, 18n.

Bent's Fort: exploration from, xvi; Third Expedition at, xvii; Maxwell arrives from, 6; owners of, 7n.; Carson at, 10; government supplies at, 18; party to be divided at, 20; convoys from, 25; arrival at, 26, 28, 29; peace talks at, 28; establishment of, 30 n.; Indians at, 31; departure from, 33; letter from, 35; on route to California, 35–36n.

Bent, St. Vrain and Company: firm of, 7n.; Carson hunter for, 10 n.; in operation, 30 n.

Black market, in Oregon: 119

Bodmer, Karl, as intellectual frontiersman: xi

Bomford, George: message to, 157; job of, at Astoria, 172–73

Bomford, Irwin: in Fort Smith, Arkansas, 173

Bonneville, Capt. Benjamin Louis Eulalie de: exploration of, xvi n.; fur trappers of, xviii; fur trapping of, 13n.; in Oregon, 177–78; opinions on, 178n.; tales of, 180

Books: scarcity of in Oregon, 147–48; delight in, 155

Brandywine (flagship): in Rio Harbor, 88; Christmas dinner aboard, 94

Brannon, Capt. John Milton, on return from Vera Cruz: 79

Brazil: Christmas in, 87; visit in,

88–97; fruits, plants, and birds of, 95; *see also* Rio de Janeiro

Bridger, Jim: as fur trapper, 7n.; and knowledge of West, 13n.; and Great Salt Lake, 126n.

British North West Company, and Oregon fur trade: 122n.

British Pacific Squadron, off California: 43

British West Indies, as depot of troops: 62

Brook Farm, support for: 166n.

Brownson, Orestes, writings of: 166

*Brownson's Review*, articles in: 165

Buchanan, Col., in California: 178

Budd, Capt., delivers package: 152

Buenavista, lake of, arrival at: 54

Buffalo: hunting, 26–27; abundance of, 29–30; in mountain country, 36

Burrass (Burrows), Capt. Charles D.: death of, 55

Butler, Gen. William Orlando: 66

Caddoan Indians: 28n.

Calaveras (Calaveros) River: 40

Calhoun, John C., death of: 120

California: Talbot first in, xv; exploration of, xvi; conquest of, xvii–xviii, xix, 33–57; as destination, 14n., 16, 20, 32; Frémont arrives in, 33; war in, 34–35; missions of, 40; new government for, 49; ceded to U.S., 59; gold in, 82, 101, 103; immigrants for diverted to Oregon, 119; Oregon men in, 122; news from, 131–32; land speculation in, 132; Frémont reaches again, 132n.; gold mines of, 126; mail via, 140; celebration for admission of, 151; horses to, 158

California Battalion of the Mounted Rifles: expedition renamed, xvii; officers in, 5n.; Stockton commis-

sions, 43n.; Frémont in command of, 47; surgeon of, 47n.

California Foreigners, Frémont to command: 44

California mountains, Talbot reaches: 37

California War: end of, 49; *see also* California, conquest of

Callao, Peru: expected arrival at, 96; possibility of stop at, 101

Calumet, of peace and friendship: 32

Campbell, J. G., in Oregon: 130

Campbell, Mr. and Mrs., return to Oregon: 155–56

Campbell, Robert: assistance of, 7; as agent and trapper, 7n.; evening with, 13; mail through, 23

Campbell and Smith: as mercantilists in Oregon City, 130n.

Camp followers, in Vera Cruz: 78

Campo Santo, Allen buried at: 67

Canadian River, survey of: 6n.

Cape Disappointment: at mouth of Columbia, 121; named, 121n.; troops to be stationed at, 175

Cape Horn: 98

Cape Virgen: 98

Carmel Mission, letter from: 44

Carpenter, Talbot as: 146–47

Carrillo (Carillo), Jose Antonio, troops under: 45

Carson, Christopher (Kit): and Third Expedition, xvii, 10, 12; as top scout, 6n.; national notice of, 10n.; and knowledge of West, 13n.; to California with Frémont, 32; as lieutenant and scout, 47; to start for U.S., 50; returns to California, 56

Castle of San Juan de Ulúa (d'Ullua): defense of, 59; troops quartered at, 64; Nauman to leave, 68; Talbot's duty at, 76

Castro, Gen. José: orders of, 34, 41;

joins Pico, 43, 48; heads revolt, 44–45; to attack Sonoma, 45; in Los Angeles, 48; flees to Sonora, 49; rebellion led by, 54n.

Catholicism, and Brownson: 166n.

*Catholic Mirror*, comments on: 159

Catholics, and westward move: xii

Cattle, in California: 41

Cerro Gordo, Mexican defeat at: 59

Chain gang, in Hawaii: 110–11

Chalfin, Lt. Samuel F., on return from Vera Cruz: 79

Chapultepec, battle at: 59

Charleston, South Carolina: delay in, 59; transports to, 62; troops bound for, 63

Charleston, West Virginia, Bent partnership formed at: 30 n.

Charleston Harbor: letter from, 62; arrival in, 63

Chase, Mrs. Capt., arrives in Vera Cruz: 66

Chenook Indians: *see* Chinook Indians

Cheyenne (Sheyenne) Indians: smoke with, 27; to make peace with Delawares, 28; enmity of with Pawnees, 28n.; trade with, 30; peace council of, 31; and Kiowas, 31 n.

Cheyenne-Sioux, fight with Delawares: 28n.

Childs, Thomas: in Vera Cruz, 72; death of, 72n.; cared for, 164

Chinook, William: arrives in St. Louis, 5–6, 6n.; as cook, 23; in Talbot mess group, 24

Chinook Indians: charges of, 122; chief of, 141; in Oregon, 141–42; deity of, 168n.

Cholera: rumor of in New York, 100; in U.S., 139

Christmas: in San Joaquin Valley, 37; in Brazil, 81, 87, 94; at Fort Vancouver, 139

Christmas Eve, and visits to Rio churches: 91–94

Churubusco, battle at: 59

*Clermont* (steamer), demonstrated: 81

Clothes, recipe for washing: 174

Coconut (cocoa nut) plantation, visit to: 109–10

Coffee plantations, in Hawaii: 109

*Collingwood* (British ship), off California: 43n.

Collins, Lt. Joseph Benson, wife of: 180–81

Colorado, home of Utes: 36n.

Colorado River: on route of travel, 17; source and tributaries of, 33; mistaken for Rio Grande, 36n.

Colorado of the West: *see* Green River

*Columbia* (Hudson's Bay Company's bark), salute of: 125

Columbia Barracks, Vancouver, Oregon Territory: built, 119; letters from, 157, 160, 161, 165, 168, 171, 174, 176, 179

Columbia (Colombia) River: on Second Expedition, xv; Talbot returns to, xviii; expected arrival at, 101; time for expansion along, 118; arrival at mouth of, 120–21; ship enters, 121; fur trade on, 123n.; crossing of, 120; description of, 124–25; freezing of, 138; Wilkes expedition on, 142n.

Colusa County, California, first treasurer of: 49n.

Comanche Indians: meeting with, 27, 30; Kiowa influence on, 31

Commissary Depot, at Fort Vancouver: 135

Concomly (Concomely), King: grave of, 141; people of, 142

*Congress* (flagship): under Du Pont, 46n.; surgeon of, 47n.; Beale on, 47n.

Conner, Daniel Ellis, and picture of Walker: 13n.
Constellations, in Southern Hemisphere: 87
Continental Divide: crossing of, 33; on route to California, 36n.
Convents, opinion of: xii, 137, 140
Cook's School, in Hawaii: 106, 107
Couillard, Capt., on *Edith*: 163n.
Council Grove, location of: 26n.
*Coureurs de bois*: 19n.
*Courier* (ship), bound for New York: 88
Court-martial: rumors of, 58; of Frémont, 132n.; of Backenstos, 138–39
Courts, in Oregon: 169, 180
Crane, Ichabod Bennett: killed by Indians, 42; orders of, 146; looks out for Childs, 164
Crane's Branch, on route to California: 36n.
Crittenden, Maj. George Bibb, arrest of: 135, 139
Cuba: opinions on, xiv, 82; affair in, 147; annexation of, 161; difficulty in, 181
*Cyane (Cayenne)*: ship off California, 46; surgeon of, 47n.; party sails in, 48; captain of, 57n.; Harrison on, 156n.

Dalles, The: *see* The Dalles, Oregon
Damon, Rev. Samuel C., accompanies ship to Oregon: 120
Davis, Isaac, in Hawaii: 116
Deception Bay, named: 121n.
Deer: in mountain country, 36; supply of in California, 40
Delaware Indians: join Third Expedition, xvii, 25; fight with Cheyenne-Sioux, 28; at Bent's Fort, 28, 31; as scouts, 31n.

Delaware-Cheyenne, peace council of: 28n.
"Delaware Town," stop and dance at: 22–23
Denny, Midshipman: at Fort Vancouver, 136; killed by Indians, 42
Dent, Josiah, in St. Louis: 6, 17
Deserters, at Fort Vancouver: 133
Diamond Point: 104
Dimick (Dimmick), Maj. Justin, at Vera Cruz: 64
Discretion, poem on: 166
Dodge, Col. Henry: dragoon expedition of, 21n., 30n.; employs Delaware scouts, 31n.
Donation Land Law: 153n.
Douglas, James: as governor at Fort Vancouver, 125; leaves for Victoria, 126
Dowry, of furs: 141–42
Drunkenness: in Oregon, 119; of Hatheway, 144–45
Duchesne (Duchene) Fork, on route to California: 36
Du Pont (Dupont), Commander Samuel Francis: commander of ship, 46, 48; message via, 51

Eagle River, on route to California: 36n.
Easy, Mr. Theodore, as nom de plume: 163
*Edith* (steamer): meeting with off South America, 100; row on, 163n.
Eggs, price of in Oregon: 148–49
Elk: in mountain country, 36; supply of in California, 40
Embarkation depot, in New York Harbor: 58
Emerson, Ralph Waldo, on individual history: xx
Emigration, to Oregon: 148, 150
Emory, Capt. William Hemsley:

message via, 50–51; arrives in Vera
Cruz, 65; reminder of, 161
England, interest of in Oregon: 118
Epaulettes, gift of: 172
Episcopalians, and westward move: xii
Equator: weather at, 86; crossing of,
102
Ericsson, Capt. John, and screw pro-
peller: 81, 85
*Eudora* (steamer), arrival of in
Vera Cruz: 71

Fallon, Le Gros, meeting with: 40
Fandango, at Sonoma: 46
*Fanny Forrester* (ship), en route to
California: 87
Fauntleroy, Daingerfield, purser and
commander: 47–48
*Felice* (Portuguese ship): 121n.
"Fighting Joe": *see* Hooker, Joseph
Fillmore, Millard, succeeds Taylor:
147n.
Fitzpatrick, Thomas: joins Kearny,
xvii; with dragoons, 6; as mountain
man and trapper, 6n.; as fur
trapper, 7n.; to act as guide, 28, 30,
32
Fitzwilliam, Earl, son of in Oregon:
180
Fitzwilliam, George Wentworth
(son), arrives in Oregon: 180
Flogging, as punishment: 124n.
Flour, speculation in: 140
Floyd-Jones, Lt. Delancy, death of
wife of: 181
*Flying Fish* (schooner), Knox com-
mands: 142n.
Ford, Henry L.: scouts under, 42;
troops of mounted, 49
Forrest, Edwin, trial of: 169
Forrest, Lt. Richard, in California:
43–44, 47
Fort Brooke, Florida, duty at: xix

Fort Capron, Florida, duty at: xix
Fort Columbus, N.Y. Harbor, letter
from: 83
Fortescue Bay: 98
Fort George: *Frolic* frozen at, 9n.;
Astoria renamed, 122n.
Fort Hall: on route West, xv; Hum-
boldt starts near, 17; commander
of, 129; location of, 130
Fort Jupiter, Florida, duty at: xix
Fort Leavenworth: Talbot ordered to,
21–22; importance of, 21 n.
Fort McHenry, duty at: xix
Fort Monroe, Virginia, duty at: xix
Fort Moultrie, South Carolina: duty
at, xix; disembarkation at, 63;
letters from, 63, 64
Fort Santa Cruz, at entrance to Rio
Harbor: 88
Fort Smith, Arkansas, Reynolds at:
173
Fort Sumter, duty at: xix
Fort Vancouver, Oregon Territory:
fur trade at, 123n.; letters from,
124, 129, 134, 138; expected visit
to, 123; arrival at, 125; Ogden at,
126–27n.; encampment at, 129
Fountain Creek: 30n.
Fowl Cay, Abaco Reefs, Bahamas:
letter from, 60; landing at, 61; embarkation from, 62–63
Franchère, Gabriel, French explorer-
writer: 19n.
Frankfort, Kentucky, home of Isham
Talbot: xiii
Frémont, Jessie Benton (Mrs.): xvi;
at St. Louis, 3; message from, 13;
opinion of, 131–32n.
Frémont, John Charles: as intellectual
frontiersman, xi; Second Expedition
of, xiv–xv, 36n.; Third Expedition
of, xv–xviii, 4–32 *passim*; court-
martial of, xviii, 58; at St. Louis,

3–18 *passim*; titles of, 4n.; pursued by followers, 11–12; meets with prospective travelers, 12; hiring applicants, 14, 15; at Westport, 18; Fourth Expedition of, 32n.; arrives in California, 33; in California, 33–57; tangles with Castro, 34; moves to Los Angeles, 35; route of to California, 35–36n.; promotion of, 47; appointed governor of California, 49, 56; meeting with at Monterey, 55; Campbell with, 130; rumors of death of, 131–32; after court-martial, 132n.; in senate, 151; health and wealth of, 169

French: on exploring expeditions, 19; in Hawaii, 136

French Cathedral, in Honolulu: 109

French Catholic Mission, at Honolulu: 108–109

*Frolic* (steamboat), reaches St. Louis: 9

Frontiersman, stereotypes of: xi

Fruit: tropical of Brazil, 95; in Chile, 101; of Hawaii, 109

Fry, Lt. James Barnet, opinion of: 145

Furs: in Bent's convoy, 25; as dowry, 141–42

Fur trade: men in, 7n.; Sublette in, 17; and Astor, 122n.

Gallapagos Islands: whalers at, 102; piracy at, 103

Gambling: in Vera Cruz, 78; gold mining as, 128

Garfias, Manuel, takes Santa Barbara: 53

"Gate of Mercy," at Vera Cruz: 72

Geology, of White River: 36

"Gibraltar of America": 59, 76

Gibson, Lt. John Bannister: replaced at Castle of San Juan, 76; resignation of, 163–64

Gibson, William, in Oregon: 169

Gilchrist, Dr. Edward, as surgeon in California: 47

Gillespie, Lt. Archibald H.: "messenger of destiny," 42; promotion of, 47; to garrison San Diego, 49; guards Los Angeles, 51; appointed lieutenant governor of California, 49; message from, 52; capitulation of, 53; wounded, 56; to San Pedro, 57

Godare: *see* Godey, Alexis

Godey (Godare), Alexis (Alick): joins Third Expedition, xvii, 13, 32; in St. Louis, 6; as scout, 6n., 47n.; with Frémont, 10; messmate of Frémont, 23, 24; duties of, 25; on buffalo hunt, 26–27

Godfather, Talbot as: 170

Gold: in California, 82, 101; leading to piracy, 103; in Oregon, 122; new discoveries of, 122; starvation among, 124; brought back to Oregon, 126; tragedy of search for, 153; mines on the Umpqua, 159

Golden Gate, named by Frémont: 3

Gold mines: Oregon mail agent at, 128; unhealthy in, 136

Gold mining, cost of: 128

Government Reserve, in Oregon: 153

Governor's Island: awaiting departure at, 58; rendezvous at, 78; letter from, 79; duties at, 80

Grand River, tributaries of: 36n.

Grant, Ulysses Simpson: as soldier, xx; classmate of, 181n.

Grant, Mr. Richard: commands Fort Hall, 129; visit with, 130

Grant, Capt. (British), news of on Frémont: 131–32n.

Great Basin: crossing of, xv, xvii,

33; Walker's knowledge of, 13n.;
on route to California, 36n.
Great Salt Lake: Frémont's description of, 3; route to, 33; camp at,
36; on maps, 37n., 38, 39; discovery of, 126n.
Green River: traced, 33; tributaries of,
36n.
Green River Rendezvous: 13n.
Gunnison, Lt. John W., expedition of:
132n.
Gwin, William McKendree, in
senate: 151

Haines, Thomas Jefferson, returns
home: 145–46
Hamilton, Charles Smith, arrival of in
Oregon: 148, 149
Hammond, Lt. Thomas C., death of:
56
Harrison, Lt. George W., marriage of:
156
Hatheway (Hathaway), Maj. John
Samuel: at Vancouver, 125; at Fort
Vancouver, 129; replaced in Oregon, 135; offers new post to Tal-
bot, 158; attempted suicide of,
144–45; charges of, 163n.; broken
leg of, 170, 172
Hawaii: opinions on, xiv; early
steamer visits, 81; prediction on,
82; visit to, 103–17; population of,
109; horseback riding in, 110;
police system in, 110; departure
from, 114; French in, 136; see also
Honolulu, Oahu, Sandwich Islands
Hawaiians: curiosity of, 105; dress of,
105, 111–12; looks of, 112
Hawkins, Lt. George Washington, in
Oregon: 127
Hays, Lt. Alexander: arrives in Vera
Cruz, 65; resignation and death of,
65n.

Henry, Andrew: fur trade of, 6n.;
trappers for, 7n.
Hickok, Wild Bill, compared with
Talbot: xi
Hill, Lt. Bennett Hoskin: to Nassau,
62; to Nisqually, 126, 129; charges
of, 163n.; sick leave of, 164
Hill, S. S., traveler in Hawaii: 107
Hitchcock, Gen. Ethan Allen: translation for, 160; offended by Talbot,
168
Holden, Dr. Levi R., in Rio with Talbot: 95–96
Honolulu: arrival at, 103; description
of from sea, 104; ashore at, 105;
life in, 107; rides in vicinity of,
109; population of, 109; King
arrives in, 114; departure from,
114; see also Hawaii
Hooker, Joseph ("Fighting Joe"):
with Kearny in Vera Cruz, 77;
arrives at Fort Vancouver, 134
Horace (Quintus Horatius Flaccus):
quote of, 153; maxim of, 155
Horseback riding, popular sport in
Hawaii: 110
Horses: wild, 40; in California, 41;
from Oregon, 158
"Hotel Pharoux," in Rio: 89
Houses: in Vera Cruz, 69–70; of
Honolulu, 104; wooden in Oregon,
125
Howard, Capt. William A., in Oregon: 169
Hudson Bay Express, arrives in Oregon: 180
Hudson's Bay Company: moves headquarters, 118; accusation against,
119; Indians plunder ship of, 121;
and Fort George, 122n.; moves of,
123n.; at Fort Vancouver, 125;
employees of, 126; Ogden with,
126n., 130; Indians as serfs of,

130 n.; link of with natives, 142n.;
army in league with, 154
Hughes, Archbishop, pamphlet of: 159
Humboldt, Alexander von, river
named for: 33
Humboldt River: description of, 17;
route along, 33, 37; on route to
California, 36n.
Hungary, articles on: 165

Ii, John (acting governor of Oahu),
visits ship: 111
Ii, Mary, in Hawaii: 107
Immigrants, in Oregon: 119
Imperial Botanical Garden, in Rio:
95–96
Imperial Church, Christmas mass at:
93–94
Indians: displaced in Oregon, 119;
work for Hudson's Bay Company,
126; as serfs, 130 n.; epidemics of,
141; chastisement of, 158n.; inade-
quate army for, 164; see also indi-
vidual tribes
Ingalls, Capt. Rufus: arrival of at Fort
Vancouver, 129; arrives at Astoria,
152; clerk of, 157
Inspector General, military drill for:
172
Intellectuals, in westward move-
ment: xi
Investment, in Oregon: 153
Iowa (ship), arrives in Rio: 96
Irving, Washington: and journal of
Bonneville, 177; meets Bonneville,
178n.

Jacob, Richard K.: at Louisville, 4,
5n.; in St. Louis, 11; locks Frémont
in, 12
Jacob, Richard T.: 5n.
Jackson, David E., as fur trader: 7n.
Jarauta, Cenobia (Tenobia, Zenobia,

Zenobio): requests permission to
enter Vera Cruz, 66; with Paredes,
77–78; execution of, 77n.
Jefferson, Thomas, schemes of explo-
ration of: xvi n.
Jesuits, in Oregon: 140–41
Jesup, Gen. Thomas Sidney, to com-
mand army: 182
Johnston, Capt. Abraham R., killed:
56
Jordan River, on Warren map: 37n.
Judd, Dr. Gerrit P.: importance of in
Hawaii, 106; influence over
Hawaiian king, 116–17
Jurors, stories about: 170
J. W. Cater (coasting bark), to San
Francisco: 123, 124

Kalama (Hawaiian queen), descrip-
tion of: 115–16
Kamamalu, Victoria, heir apparent to
premiership: 116
Kamehameha, Lot: son of governor
of Oahu, 106; at race course, 110
Kamehameha I (former king of
Hawaii): 109; takes prisoners, 116
Kamehameha III (king of Hawaii):
regal court of, 81; absent from
Oahu, 107; arrives in Honolulu,
114–16, 117; description of, 115
Kansas, Indiana, Frémont party
passes: 26
Kansas River: attempted crossing of,
22; crossing of, 23; route along,
27; on route to California, 29
Kearny (Kearney), Maj. Philip: as
friend of the Talbots, 8n.; in
Oregon, 157–58
Kearny (Karney, Kearney), Gen.
Stephen Watts: scouting expedition
of, xvii; and conquest of California,
xviii; moving west, 4; Fitzpatrick
with, 6n.; as friend of the Talbots,

8n.; expedition of from Fort
Leavenworth, 21–22n.; passed
Bent's Fort, 28, 30, 31; ordered to
California, 35; in Los Angeles, 55;
attacked, 56; with Stockton, 57;
charges Frémont, 58; inspects
troops, 68; in Vera Cruz, 76–77;
Emory with, 161 n.; uncle of
Philip, 158n.

Kekualuohi, death of: 16

Kekuanara (Kekuanaoa), governor
of Oahu: sons of, 106; absent from
island, 111

Kendall, George Wilkins, opinion of
Mexican women: 52

Kentucky River, stop at: 5

Kern (Kerne), Edward Meyer: on
Third Expedition, xvii; value of
letters of, xviii; in St. Louis, 6;
surveying of, 6n.; at Westport, 20;
messmate of Talbot, 23, 24; paints
botanical specimens, 25; on buffalo
hunt, 26–27; river named for,
40 n.; in command at Sutter's Fort,
46

Kern River, naming of: 6n., 40 n.

Kickapoo, Indiana, Frémont party
passes: 26

King, Clarence, Talbot understanding
of: xi

King, Henry, at Louisville: 4, 5n.;
incorrigible, 11; messmate of Talbot, 24; as botanist, 25; assists in
observations, 29; death of, 132n.

King, James of William: 5n.

King, Assistant Surgeon William
Shakespeare: on return from Vera
Cruz, 79; retirement of, 79n.

Kings River, confusion on name of:
40 n.

Kiowa (Kiawah) Indians, influence
of: 31

Klamath (Klamet) Lake, party returns from: 42

Knox, Lt. Samuel R., commands
*Massachusetts*: 142

Kossuth, Lajos, ideas of: 165, 167

La Garita Hills, snows of: 132n.

Lajeunesse, Basil: on Third Expedition, xvii, 10, 13; death of, 10 n.;
on buffalo hunt, 26–27; killed by
Indians, 42

Lambert, Clément: to join Third Expedition, 12–13; returns home, 25

La Motte (Lamotte), Maj. Joseph
Hatch, at Vera Cruz: 67

La Natividad Mountain, camp at: 41

Lancaster, Pennsylvania, Talbot in:
xix

Land: speculation in, 132; Oregon
bill on, 153

Lane, Gen. Joseph: arrives in Vera
Cruz, 65; in Oregon, 65n.; leaves
Vera Cruz, 77; at Fort Vancouver,
125–26; escort of, 127; first governor of Oregon Territory, 123;
delegateship of, 159

Larkin, Thomas, leadership of: 34

La Torré, Capt.: pursuit of, 42;
skirmish with, 45; escape of, 46

Lavender, David, on Thurston: 148n.

Leadbetter, Lt. Danville: in Oregon,
142; report of, 143

Leadville, Colorado, on route to California: 36n.

Lee, Maj. Richard Bland: arrives in
Fort Vancouver, 134; opinion of,
134–35; at Fort Vancouver, 135

Lee, Judge William L., importance of
in Hawaii: 106

Lee, Mrs., poetess in Hawaii: 107

Leese, Jacob P., capture of: 42n.

Leonard, Maj. Hiram, arrives at Fort
Vancouver: 134

Leonard, Zenas: letters of, xviii; and picture of Walker, 13n.; on party of trappers, 178n.

Leonid Shower, as Cheyenne date: 29n.

Lesser Youta Lake, on route to California: 36

*Levant* (ship), off California: 46

Lewis and Clark: achieve goal, xvi n.; and Concomly, 142n.

Lewis, Meriwether, as intellectual frontiersman: xi

Liholiho, Alexander: heir apparent, 106–107; at race course, 110; sister of, 116

Liholiho, King and Queen, death of: 106

Livingston, Robert, Talleyrand prediction to: 3

López, Narciso, and invasion of Cuba: 161n.

Loring, Col. William Wing: commands in Oregon, 135; at Fort Vancouver, 139; orders from, 146; departure of from Oregon, 157

Los Angeles (Angeles, Ciudad de Los Angeles, Pueblo de Las Angeles), California: governor of, 34; insurrection in, 35; letters from, 48, 50, 56; Castro at, 48–49; description of, 49; Gillespie guards, 51; taken by Garfias, 53; retaken, 55; rebellion in, 56

Louisiana Battalion, at Vera Cruz: 68

Louisiana Purchase, bargain of: 3

Louisiana Regiment, leaves Vera Cruz: 76

Louisville, Kentucky, Talbot at: 5, 6

"Luther the Second," Kossuth as: 165

McDowell, Dr. James: at Westport, 18; relatives of, 18n.; at ease in camp, 20; messmate of Talbot, 23,

24; Talbot to assist, 25; leaves party, 29

McKinley, Mrs., at Fort Vancouver: 127n.

McLane, Capt. George, in charge of commissary: 135

McLoughlin, Dr. John, at Fort Vancouver: 127n.

Macomb, Maj. Gen. Alexander, letter to from Bonneville: 178n.

Maddox, William A. T., in California: 47

Maigret, Bishop, at French Mission in Honolulu: 108

Mail: steamers coming to Oregon, 143, 147, 152, 157, 179; accidents to, 171

Man of War, French in Rio Harbor: 88

"Manifest destiny": 161

Marti, Werner: 42n.

Mary's Lake, party reaches: 37

Mary's River: see Humboldt River

*Massachusetts* (steamer): Talbot sails on, 81; embarkation on, 83; letters written on, 84, 97, 102, 103, 114; life on board, 86–87; as object of curiosity, 105; Hawaiians visit, 111; king and queen visit, 114; king leaves, 117; sails from Oregon, 130; leaves for California, 142–43

Mathews, Father, endowing Academy: 182

Maui, Island of; Hawaiian king visits, 107; king leaves, 114

May, Lt. Julian: arrest of, 136

Maxwell, Lucien: joins Third Expedition, xvii; in St. Louis, 6; and land grant, 7n.; as lieutenant, 47; to start for U.S., 50

Maxwell Land Grant: 7n.

Meares, John, names Cape Disappointment: 121 n.
Medford, Oregon, Indian battle near: 158n.
Melrose, plantation of Isham Talbot: xiii
*Memoirs of My Life*, account of Third Expedition in: xviii
Men of War, in Rio Harbor: 97
Merrick, Col., appointment of: 168
Merritt, Ezekial, as California leader: 49
Mervine, Capt. William, defeat of: 57
Meteorological observations: 25, 29
Methodists, and westward move: xii
Mexicans: fights with, xviii; at Bent's Fort, 32; patriotism of, 59
Mexican War: Frémont involved in, xvii; Gen. Smith in, 124n.
Mexico: border difficulties with, xvi; hostilities with in California, 34; declaration of war on, 50; war with, 59–60; weather in, 60, 64, 68, 73–74
Mexico City: 59
Micheltorena, Gen. Manuel: overthrow of, 41 n.; soldier of as pilot, 54; Garfias with army of, 53n.
Midnight mass, in Rio churches: 91–94
Miller, Alfred Jacob, paints Walker: 13n.
Miller, Capt. Morris Smith, in Oregon: 168–69
Missionaries: visit ship in Hawaii, 108; in Oregon, 141
Mission of St. Johns, to the rescue of: 55
Missions, of California: 40
Missouri, mountain men in: 17
*Missouri* (steamboat), in St. Louis: 9
Missouri River: trappers on, 7n.;

travel on, 18; rise of, 21; crossing of, 22; mail via, 23
*Monitor*, designer of: 85n.
Monroe, James, Talleyrand prediction to: 3
Monterey, California: first message from, 33, 35; consul at, 34; retreat to, 35; orders from Castro at, 41; marines in possession of, 43; Frémont ordered to, 46; Spanish ladies in, 46–47; party leaves, 48; meeting with Frémont at, 55; *Relief* bound for, 86
Montgomery, John Berrien, commands *Portsmouth*: 45
Monticello, Oregon, letter missent to: 161–62
Moon, to determine longitude: 32
Moore, Capt. Benjamin D., killed: 56
Morris, Lt. Lewis O.: brother arrives at Vera Cruz, 73; ordered to castle, 76; on return from Vera Cruz, 79; brother of, 79n.; mention of, 84
Moses, Dr. Israel: in Backenstos case, 139; receives books, 155
Mosquitoes, on Arkansas River: 30
Mountain men, Fitzpatrick among respected: 6n.
Muir, John, Talbot understanding of: xi
"Muy Valiente Onze": 73

Napoleon, prediction of: 166–67
Nassau, Hill to engage transports at: 62
Nauman, Capt. George: in charge of Castle, 64; to leave Castle, 68; on return trip, 79
Navajo Indians, kill McLane: 135
Negroes, in Brazil: 81–82, 90, 96
New Jersey Battalion, embarkation of: 58
New Mexico, ceded to U.S.: 59

*New Orleans* (ship), arrives at Vera
Cruz: 65, 66
New Plymouth, Oregon: settlers at,
125; modern name for, 125n.
New Providence, Island of: 62
New Year, welcomed in Brazil: 97
Nisqually, Oregon: soldiers to, 125–
26; Hill stationed at, 129
Northwest Coast, U.S. exploring
expeditions to: 86n.
North West Company: merges with
Hudson's Bay Company, 126n.; *see
also* British North West Company

Oahu, Island of: harbor of, 104; governor of, 106; population of, 109;
extinct craters on, 109; departure
from, 114; chaplain at, 120; *see
also* Hawaii
Ogden, Peter Skene: and Talbot, xiii;
in charge of Fort Vancouver, 126;
exploits of, 126–27n.; visit to,
127n.; at Fort Vancouver, 130–31
Ogden, Maj. Edmund Augustus, in
Oregon: 142
Ohio River, sandbars in: 5, 10
Old Point Comfort, Virginia, duty at:
xix
Oregon: party starts for, 42; mail
directions to, 83; expected arrival
in, 96, 101; disgruntled immigrants
in, 119; Talbot's stay in, 119–82;
gold in, 122; prices in, 122, 126,
132–33, 148, 181; depopulation of,
126; mail for, 128; American
society of, 131; mail arrives in,
139–40; types of people in, 150–51;
feeling toward army in, 154; not
so isolated, 157; population of, 159;
daily life in, 160; weather in, 166,
167; court scenes in, 169–70; military force in, 175; settlement of
accounts in, 178–79

*Oregon* (steamer), in Valparaiso: 100
*Oregon* (Pacific mail steamship): 151,
152
Oregon City, Oregon: Governor Lane
at, 123; expected station at, 124;
Lt. Hawkins at, 127–28; Campbell
resident of, 130; inhabitants of,
131; winter quarters at, 135; trial
in, 138; newspaper item from, 154
Oregon Territory: first governor of,
123n.; *see also* Oregon
Oregon Trail: xiv
Oregon Treaty: 118
Orizaba (Orisaba): proposed expedition against, 64; Bankhead in command at, 67
Owen, Robert: support for, 166n.;
new clothes from, 168
Owens, Richard: 6n., 47

Pacific islands, exploring expedition
to: 86n.
Paki, accompanies Hawaiian king:
117
"Pali," ride to: 109
*Panama* (steamer), mail on: 100
Papists, army in league with: 154
Paredes y Arrillaga, Gen. Mariano:
assumes presidency of Mexico, 59;
squabbles with Santa Anna, 59;
party of gaining strength, 77;
policies of, 77–78
Parkman, Francis, as intellectual
frontiersman: xi
"Paseo," at Vera Cruz: 72
Patagonia, on shore of: 98–99
Patterson, Capt. Carlisle Pollock,
commands *Oregon*: 152
Patterson, Gen. Robert, waits for
transportation: 75
Pauahi, Bernice: in Hawaii, 107–108;
father of, 117
Pawnee Indian, scalp of: 28

Pawnee Fork of Arkansas River: 26, 27, 29
Pawnee Rock: 25n.
"Peace of Mexico Treaty": 72
Peck, Lt. William G.: joins Third Expedition, xvii; in St. Louis, 6; assignment of, 6n.; enthusiasm of for trip, 9; at Westport, 18, 20; messmate of Talbot, 23, 24; description of, 25; on buffalo hunt, 26–27; departure of, 28, 32
Pedro II, Dom: midnight mass with, 81, 93–94; palace of, 89; wife of, 93n.
Penal code, of Hawaii: 106n.
Perry (brig), in Rio Harbor: 88
Pettrich, Ferdinand (Frederick August): in Rio, 97–98; as sculptor, 97n.
Pico, Andrés: 55
Pico, Pio: orders to, 34; Castro move against, 41; Castro joins, 43, 48; appointment of, 44; to give up, 49; rebellion led by, 54n.
Pierce, Pres. Franklin, election of: 181
Pillow, Gen. Gideon Johnson: in Vera Cruz, 71; feuds with Scott, 72n.
Piney Creek, on Warren's map: 36n.
Planters House: stop at, 5–6; letters written at, 8, 11, 14
Platte River: xv
Point Adams: 121
Police system, of Hawaii: 110
Politics: and religion, 166; of Talbot, 173
Polk, Pres. James K.: campaign issue of, xvi; law partner of, 71 n.; Mexican policy of, 72; brother of, 75n.
Polk, Maj. William Hawkins, in Vera Cruz: 75
Port Famine, Chile: 99–100

Portland, Oregon, mail arrives in: 139–40
Port Orford, Oregon: detachment at, 172; troops stationed at, 175; ship to arrive at, 177; ship wrecked at, 179
Portsmouth (ship), guards San Francisco Bay: 45, 46
Portuguese, as language of Brazil: 90–91
Pottawattomie Indians, peace pipe of: 31–32
Powell, John Wesley, as intellectual: xi
Pratt, Judge O. C., politics of: 173
Presbyterianism, and Brownson: 166n.
Presbyterians, and westward move: xii
Preston, Surveyor General, arrives in Oregon: 159
Preuss, Charles, on First and Second expeditions: xvii, 6n.
Prices, in Oregon: 122, 126, 132–33, 143, 148, 181
Princeton, U.S.S., first screw-propelled ship: 85n.
Promotions: of Talbot, 47, 57; question of, 58, 71; slowness of, 159, 169
Proue (Proulx), Raphael: with Frémont, 10, 13; death of, 10n., 132n.
Provisions, for Third Expedition: 7, 8, 11, 15, 18
Provost, Étienne, as fur trapper: 7n.
Prudon, Col. Victor, capture of: 42n.
Pueblo, Colorado: 12
Pueblo de San José, rendezvous at: 40
Puget's Sound, Indians at: 125
Purgatory River, survey of: 6n.
Pursuit (British bark): 85

Quartermasters: Talbot as, 146–47; advice to, 150

"Rag house": 58
Railroad, feasibility of: 132n.
Recipe, for washing: 174
Red River: survey of ordered, xv;
  exploration of, 32
Reed (Read), Lt. William: embarks
  for Charleston, 62, 63n.; arrival of
  at Charleston, 63
Regiment M Rifles, Kearny in charge
  of: 158
*Relief* (store ship), reputation of:
  85–86
*Republic* (ship), arrival of at Vera
  Cruz: 64
Reynolds, Maj. Robert B., letter from:
  173
Reynolds, Stephen, parties of: 112–13
Riley (Reilly), Gen. Bennet: 21 n.,
  87; arrives in Rio, 96
Ringold, Dr., arrives at Vera Cruz: 65
Rio de Janeiro (Rio, Rio Janeiro),
  Brazil: visit to, 81–97; letter to be
  sent from, 83; length of trip to,
  84; expected arrival in, 87; letters
  from, 88, 94; arrival in, 88; sights
  of, 89–91; botanical garden in,
  95–96; departure from, 96, 97;
  harbor of, 97; *see also* Brazil
Río Grande River: crossing of, 36;
  time for expansion along, 118
Río Grande Valley: 132n.
Robbins, Thomas, Talbot housed with:
  52n.
*Robert F. Stockton* (ship), with screw
  propeller: 81
Robidoux Pass, Frémont crosses: 132n.
Rocky Mountains: route through, 35;
  yarns about, 131; Bonneville travels
  in, 177
Roland, Capt. John Frederick, embarks at Vera Cruz: 74
Roman Catholics: *see* Catholics
Romantic, Talbot as: 81, 82

*Rome* (ship), arrives in Rio: 96
Roosevelt, Pres. Theodore, compared
  with Talbot: xi
Rostow, W. W., on army in West:
  xviii
*Rover* (British bark), near South
  America: 98
Royce, Sarah, as intellectual: xi
"Rua d'ouvidor," in Rio: 89–90

Sacramento, California: 34, 43
Sacramento River: Sutter fort at, xv;
  crossing of, 41
Sacramento Valley: route through, 34;
  search for gold in, 82
Sacred arrows, loss of: 28n.
Sagundai (Delaware scout): 31 n.
St. Charles, Missouri: 14–15
St. Johns Mission: 48
St. Louis, Missouri: Talbot returns
  to, xv; Third Expedition stops at,
  xvii; spirit of, 3, 9; letters from,
  4, 8, 11, 14, 15; weather in, 9;
  departure from, 15, 18; Bent's Fort
  trade to, 30 n.
St. Vrain, Céran de Hault de Lassus de:
  welcome by, 30; activities of, 30 n.;
  duties of at Bent's Fort, 30 n.
Salmon Trout River, lake of: on
  route to California, 36n.; party
  reaches, 37
Salt Lake: on route to California, 35;
  *see also* Great Salt Lake
San Benedict (church), description of:
  91–93
San Carmel, Mission of: 43
San Cristobal, royal residence of
  Brazil: 94
San Diego, California: peaceful possession of, 48; departure from,
  48–49; skirmishes in vicinity of, 56;
  naval force takes, 57
Sandwich Islands: possibility of visit

to, 96; Jarves on, 103–104; notes from, 114–17; trip to Oregon from, 120; French in, 136; real estate of, 151; Hill to, 164; *see also* Hawaii
San Francisco, California: Sloat takes possession of, 43; Stockton to, 51; ships deserted at, 101; mail kept at, 128; crew paid to go to, 129; Grand Ball in, 151
San Francisco Bay: crossing of, 41; La Torré crosses, 43; guarded, 45n.; abandoned ships in, 82, 123; time for expansion along, 118
Sangre de Cristos Mountains: 132n.
*San Jacinto* (ship), commanded by Wilkes: 86n.
San Joaquin Valley: arrival in, 33, 36n.; rendezvous in, 37
San José, California: 40
San Juan de Ulúa: *see* Castle of San Juan de Ulúa
San Luis Valley: 132n.
San Luiz Rey, Mission of: 49
San Marco Ranch: 54
San Pablo, Mexico: 43
San Pasqual (Pasadena), California: Garfias at, 53n.; Mexicans at, 55n.
San Patricie (Patricio) Brigade: 77
San Pedro, California, Stockton at: 49
San Rafael, Mission of: La Torré leaves, 43; skirmish at, 45; Talbot to hold, 46
Santa Anna, Antonio López de: age of, 34; political squabbles of, 59; return of to Mexico, 73
Santa Barbara, California: Talbot at, xix; Talbot in charge of, 35, 51–52; women in, 52; attacked, 53–54; retaken, 53n.
Santa Cruz, California: 41
Santa Fe Road, departure from: 29
Santa Fe trade, from Fort Leavenworth: 21n.

Santa Fe traders, at Bent's Fort: 28, 32
Santa Fe Trail: first military escort for, 21n.; Pawnee Rock on, 25n.; Council Grove on, 26n.; traffic on, 26
Santiago, Chile, side trip to: 102
Sausalita, California: boats at, 43; crossing from, 46
*Savannah* (ship): off California, 46, 48n.; captain of, 57n.
Scalp dance: 28
Scott, John, on Third Expedition: 32
Scott, Gen. Winfield: battles of, 59; labels Paredes, 59; Butler succeeds, 66n.; feuds with Pillow, 72n.; death of, 132n.; votes for, 181, 182
Screw propeller: 81, 83, 85
Seminole Indians, Loring fights: 135n.
Serra, Junípero, Talbot understanding of: xi
Sevier Valley, massacre in: 132n.
Seymour, Adm. Sir George F.: 43
Sheyenne Indians: *see* Cheyenne Indians
Shipwreck, on coral reef: 60–62
Shoshonean Indians: Comanches from, 31n.; Utes in, 36n.
Siberia, S. S. Hill visits: 107
Sierra Nevada Mountain: crossing of, xv; on route to California, 33, 36n.
Simonson, Maj. John Smith, arrest of: 135–36, 139
Sioux Indians, and Kiowas: 31n.
Skookum (Skookoms), god of the woods: 168
Sloat, Com. John Drake: replaced, 35, 43n., 46; orders of, 43, 46
Smith, Adam, anti-colonial doctrines of: 118
Smith, Hamilton, visit to: 5
Smith, Jedediah S.: 6n., 7n.

Smith, Col. John Lind: in Oregon, 142; description of, 143

Smith, Gen. Persifor Frazer: recommends increased soldier pay, 124; orders of, 129; arrives at Fort Vancouver, 134; leaves for California, 139

Smoky Hill Fork, of Kansas River: 27, 29

Sonoma, California: Frémont reaches, 34; garrison at, 43; possession of, 45; rush to rescue of, 45; July 4 at, 46

Sonoma Mission, garrison at: 42

Sonora, California: 49

South America, *Massachusetts* sails around: 81–82

Southern Cross: 87

Southern Great Plains: Indians on, 31 n.

Spain, war with: 181

Spanish: Talbot's knowledge of, 73; proverb, 164

Speiden, William O. (P.), on ship off California: 47

Spinoza, translation of: 160–61

Spoilers, in Oregon: 119

Stanley, John M. (artist): 113n.

Starvation, of Frémont's men: 132n.

Steamboats: en route to St. Louis, 5, 10; to West, 81; as curiosity, 105; on river in Oregon, 159

Steam mills, in Oregon: 153

Steilecoom (Steilacoom), Oregon Territory: troops stationed at, 175; new post at, 177

Stewart, Sir William Drummond, Walker meets: 13n.

Stockton, Com. Robert Field: in conquest of California, xviii; rushed to California, 35; moves to Los Angeles, 35; at Monterey, 43; replaces Sloat, 46; lands at San

Pedro, 49; leaves Los Angeles, 51; forces of, 57

Stonestreet, M., appointed to Jesuit post: 176

Stover, Com., flagship of: 88

Straits of Magellan (Magelhaens): expected passage through, 96; description of, 98–99

Strong, William, arrives in Oregon: 148–49

Sublette, William M.: as fur trapper, 7n.; visit to in St. Louis, 17; death of, 17n., 18n.

Sugar plantations, in Hawaii: 109

Suicide, in Oregon: 119

Sullivan's Island: 63

Sulphur Springs, Missouri, Sublette house in: 17n.

Sutter, John: dinner with, xv; and independence, 34

Sutter's Fort: 40, 41; prisoners to, 45

Swanok (Swanick), Jim: 31

Swift, Capt. Granville P., troops of: 49

Tabeau, Antoine: 19n.

Talbot, Adelaide (mother), relations with Theodore, xii–xiii: 8

Talbot, Isham (father): xiii

Talbot, James Theodore: as frontiersman, xi; as Catholic, xii; as bachelor, xii, 149, 156; early life of, xii–xiii; education of, xiii, xv; self-characterization of, xiii–xiv; politics of, xiv, 173; on Second Expedition, xiv–xv; health of, xv; on Third Expedition, xv–xviii, 4–32, 35–36n.; promotions of, xviii, xix, 47, 57, 58, 71; value of letters of, xviii, xix, xx; again to Far West, xviii; death of, xix, xx; journals of, xxi; at St. Louis, 4–17; at Westport, 18–21; messmates of,

23, 24; barometrical and meteorological observations of, 25; at Bent's Fort, 26–32; in California, 33–57; embarks for Vera Cruz, 59; stay in Vera Cruz, 59–78; toward the West by sea, 81–103; in Hawaii, 103–17; in Oregon, 118–82; pessimism of in Oregon, 119–20

Talbot, Margaret Garrard (first wife of Isham): xiii

Tallmadge (Talmodge), Grier, promoted and ordered home: 139

Talleyrand, prediction of: 3

Taos, New Mexico: fur trade base at, 30n.; Frémont to, 132n.

Taplin, Charles Van Linneus: at Westport, 18; with Frémont expeditions, 18n.; leaves California, 41; in Vera Cruz, 71

Taylor, Gen. Zachary: and slaughter of Mexicans, 43; in Mexican War, 124n.; death of, 147

Ten Eyck, Anthony, difficulties of with Hawaiian government: 113, 114–15

Tennessee Pass, on route to California: 36n.

Tenobia, Col.: see Jarauta, Cenobia

Texas: admission of, xvi; companies to from Oregon, 164

Theater of "San Januario": 90–91

The Dalles, Oregon, troops stationed at: 175

Third Expedition: recruiting for, 11–12, 14, 15, 16; numbers on, 12, 15, 18, 24–25; route of, 35–36

Thompson, Bluford K.: 55

Thurston, Samuel R. (congressman): 148n.

Tierra del Fuego: 98; party of people from, 99

Timpanogos (Timpanoga) River: 36; examined, 36n.

Tisdale, John B. (artist): 20, 24

Todd, Edgeley W.: 178n.

Torrey, John, Frémont letter to: xvi

Towson, Gen. Nathan, in Vera Cruz: 71

Transit instrument: 29, 32

Treaty of Cahuenga: 45n.

Tucker, Maj. Stephen S.: marriage of, 156; resignation of, 158

Tulare Lake: 37

Tulare Valley: 54

*Tulma* (Yankee schooner), embarks for Charleston: 63

Turrill (Turrell), Judge Joel, in Honolulu: 105

Twiggs, Gen. David Emanuel: in Vera Cruz, 66; advice of to quartermasters, 150

Uinta River: 36n.

Umpqua (Umqua) River: gold found on, 122, 159; troops stationed at, 175

Union Fur Company, steamer of: 9n.

Unitarianism, and Brownson: 166n.

United States, expansion of: 118

United States Army: problems for, 118; unpopularity of in Oregon, 119, 154; arrangements for in Oregon, 127; inadequacy of, 164, 175–76; new cap for, 168

Universalism, and Brownson: 166n.

Utah, home of the Utes: 36n.

Utah Lake: 36–37n.

Ute Indians: meeting with, 36; massacre of, 132

Utley, Robert M.: xviii

Vallejo (Valejo), Gen. Mariano G., capture of: 42, 45

Vallejo, Salvador, capture of: 42

Valparaiso, Chile: visit to, 81, 82; letter to be sent from, 84;

expected arrival at, 96; arrival at, 100; description of, 101; departure from, 102

Vancouver: Hudson's Bay Co. moves to, 118; expected station at, 124; new post at, 158; departure from, 177; *see also* Fort Vancouver

Vancouver (Vancouver's) Island: fur trade on, 123n.; Hudson's Bay Co. headquarters on, 126

Van Ness, Capt. David: 63, 64

Vera Cruz, Mexico: embarkation for, 58, 59; journey to, 58–80; battalion reaches, 59; evacuation of, 59; description of, 60; arrival of *Republic* at, 64; letters from, 65, 68, 71, 73, 76; elections in, 68; dullness of life in, 68–69; houses in, 69–70; churches in, 70; to declare itself a free city, 75; embarkation of troops from, 76; Gen. Smith at, 124n.

Victoria, Vancouver Island, B. C.: fur trade at, 123n.; founding of, 125n.; Douglas to, 126

Vinté River, exploration of: 36

Vinton, Maj. David Hammond, arrives at Fort Vancouver: 134

Volcano, in Hawaii: 109

Voltigeurs: 77n.

Walker, Joseph Reddeford: sent to California, xvi n.; joins Third Expedition, xvii, 13; on Bonneville expedition, xviii; information on, 13n.; to California with Frémont, 32; hired by Frémont, 33; as guide for Talbot, 36–37n.; lake named for, 36n.; on Second Expedition, 36–37n.; sent ahead, 40; leaves party in California, 41; with party of trappers, 178n.

Walker, Lt. William Stephen, in Vera Cruz: 77

Walker Pass: discovery of, 13n.; Talbot to, 36n.

Walker's Lake: 33, 36n.

Wallen, Capt., in Oregon: 178

Wampum, in peace ceremony: 31

War of 1812, and fur trade: 122n.

Warren, Lt. G. K.: map of, 36n., 37n., 38, 39

Washing, recipe for: 174

Water, distilled on ship: 85

Waugh, Alfred S. (artist): 20, 24

Weather: in St. Louis, 9; at Westport, 19; in Mexico, 60, 64, 68, 73–74; at equator, 86; in Oregon, 166, 167, 169

Weber River, on Warren map: 37n.

Webster, Daniel, death of: 120, 181

West Point Cadets, in exploring party: 15

West Pointers, conspiracy of: 58

Westport, Missouri: on route West, xv; Third Expedition begins at, xvii, 4; men to be engaged at, 12; applicants waiting at, 15; arrival at, 18; letters from, 18, 19, 21; weather at, 19; departure from, 21–22; camp 110 miles from, 24–26

Whalers: and suspected fire, 102–103; in Honolulu Harbor, 104

Wharton, Maj. Clifton: 22

Wheeler, Mr., brings Gibson on board: 163n.

"White Cloud" (boat), on Missouri River: 18

White River: 36

Whiting, Gen. Henry, instructions from: 84

Whiting, Col. Levi, on sick leave: 164

Whitman, Marcus, westward trip of: xv

Wild horses, as food: 40
Wilkes, Capt. Charles: delayed by ship, 86; passage of, 121 n.; expedition of, 142
Willamette (Wilhamet) River: fur trade at, 123n.; visit to mouth of, 123; New Plymouth on, 125; Oregon City on, 127; inhabitants near, 131; Portland on, 139
Williams, Old Bill: and knowledge of West, 13n.; as guide for Frémont, 132n.
Wilson, Col. Henry, relieves Twiggs: 66
Winder, Capt. John Henry: at Vera Cruz, 67; company under Talbot, 79
Winter quarters: at Fort Vancouver, 129, 134; at Oregon City, 135
Women: in Monterey, 46–47; in Santa Barbara, 52; on board *Massachusetts*, 87; Brazilian, 90; at Rio theater, 91; at San Benedict

Church, 92–93; Hawaiian, 112; hold premiership in Hawaii, 116
Wood, Capt.: on *Massachusetts*, 84; crew deserts, 129
Wyllie, Robert Crichton: in Hawaii, 105–107; in king's cabinet, 116

"Year the Stars Fell," Cheyenne date: 28n.
Yellowstone River: fur trappers from, 9
Yellow Wolf, at Bent's Fort: 30 n.
Yerba Buena, California: supplies secured at, 41; taken, 46
Young, Brigham, compared with Talbot: xi
Young, John (premier of Hawaii): 116
Youta Indians: *see* Utes
Youta Lake: *see* Utah Lake

Zenobia, Col.: *see* Jarauta, Cenobia